Praise for

HELL AND GOOD COMPANY

"*Hell and Good Company* is characteristically pacy, vivid and emotive. It reliably conveys the conflict's broad outlines for those who know nothing about the bloody 1936–39 war between the leftist Republican government and the insurgent Nationalist forces of Francisco Franco, while adding enough well-sourced fresh material to interest those more familiar with its horrors. . . . Mr. Rhodes succeeds in re-animating familiar scenarios. His solidly researched account of the initially hesitant, even reluctant gestation of Picasso's 'Guernica,' in particular, makes thrilling reading."

—*The Wall Street Journal*

"[S]ublime . . . The most extraordinary book about the Spanish Civil War I've ever encountered. His subject is not the war itself but the tremors it produced, the feelings it evoked and the terrible horror it begat. He masterfully extracts huge meaning from small shards of conflict."

—*The Washington Post*

"It is through the lives and works of individuals involved in this wasteful conflict [The Spanish Civil War] that Rhodes so graphically allows contemporary readers to appreciate all the nuances of what transpired in Spain in those dark years."

—*Booklist* (starred)

"[A]n interesting collection of observations on good guys lost but which produced important c advances."

"[An] informed and elegant narrative."

—*The Economist*

"[A] vivid look at how the desperate struggle appeared to participants."

—*Publishers Weekly*

"Rhodes, a Pulitzer Prize winner, always has a provocative perspective. His new book proves no exception. He skillfully explores the Spanish Civil War, dropping names such as Picasso and Hemingway along the way. His goal: to make us grasp this terrible conflict. He succeeds."

—*AARP Magazine*

"Readers unfamiliar with the Spanish Civil War will discover the tragicomic experiences and human costs of Europe's first war against fascism."

—*Library Journal*

"A vivid, wrenching view of war, art and love."

—*Shelf Awareness*

"[A]ccessible and memorable."

—*The Washington Times*

RICHARD RHODES

Simon & Schuster Paperbacks

New York   London   Toronto   Sydney   New Delhi

HELL AND GOOD COMPANY

---◆---

THE SPANISH CIVIL WAR
AND THE
WORLD IT MADE

---◆---

Simon & Schuster Paperbacks
An Imprint of Simon & Schuster, Inc.
1230 Avenue of the Americas
New York, NY 10020

First Simon & Schuster trade paperback edition February 2016

SIMON & SCHUSTER PAPERBACKS and colophon are registered trademarks of
Simon & Schuster, Inc.

For information about special discounts for bulk purchases, please contact
Simon & Schuster Special Sales at 1-866-506-1949 or business@simonandschuster.com.

The Simon & Schuster Speakers Bureau can bring authors to your live event.
For more information or to book an event, contact the Simon & Schuster Speakers
Bureau at 1-866-248-3049 or visit our website at www.simonspeakers.com.

Interior design by Akasha Archer

Manufactured in the United States of America

10   9   8   7   6   5   4   3   2   1

Library of Congress Control Number: 2015300015

ISBN 978-1-4516-9621-9
ISBN 978-1-4516-9622-6 (pbk)
ISBN 978-1-4516-9623-3 (ebook)

For Stanley Rhodes, 1936–2013

A grant from the Alfred P. Sloan Foundation
supported the research and writing of this book.

CONTENTS

HELL AND GOOD COMPANY

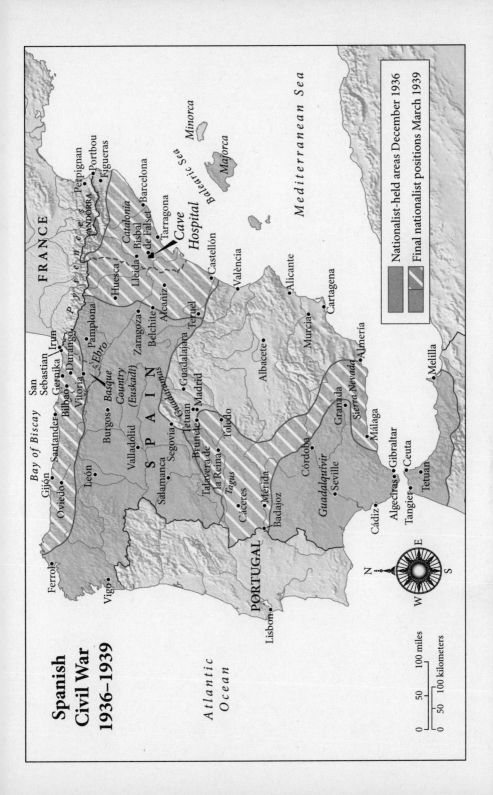

PREFACE

Ernesto Vinas, a tall, ruggedly handsome man in his late thirties, a husband and father, lives on the edge of an old battlefield in the small Spanish town of Brunete, fifteen miles west of Madrid. In 1937, in the heat of Spanish summer, thousands of young men died at Brunete, one side defending the Spanish Republic, the other side fighting for Francisco Franco and the generals he led in rebellion. Ernesto is a dental technician, but he knows more about the battle of Brunete than anyone else in the world.

Ernesto mastered Brunete from the ground up. Curious about a battle fought decades before he was born but only blocks from his door, he started searching the battlefield with a metal detector. Seven decades had embedded the Brunete debris, but the metal detector found some of it: bullet casings, badges, belt buckles, shell fragments, empty grenades. The iron objects were blistered with rust, the brass and copper sulfated gray-green. Ernesto's trowel uncovered more, calcined a chalky gray and dirt-dusted: eyeglass frames, toothbrushes, nests of carpals, shards of femur, shells of skull. Flesh had weathered until only what was hard remained, a flattened and scattered map.

I toured the battlefield with Ernesto one brisk, sunny day in October. Afterward, he led me down into his basement, where his years of collections were arrayed floor-to-ceiling on white shelves—thousands of relics of metal and bone. I photographed the grenades, some of the badges, and particularly the burned-out casings of incendiary bombs. Those bore German markings: in April 1937 the German Luftwaffe's

Condor Legion had rained down similar bombs on the Basque village
of Gernika, to the world's outrage and Picasso's inspiration.

Ernesto's collecting had been a beginning for him. He had paralleled
it with reading, visits to the archives, and discussions with veterans. So
did I. All the veterans are gone now, but many left recollections. At
New York University's Tamiment Library I found folders filled with
them, never published, brown with age. World War II began in Europe
only five months after the Spanish struggle ended, in 1939, and the war
in Spain that had been a laboratory for the larger war and a test bed for
the best and worst of its technologies was all but forgotten.

Spain had convulsed with civil war between 1936 and 1939 when
her generals had revolted against a government determined to retire
them from their positions of well-upholstered privilege. "The ambition
of every Spanish general," writes the Spanish diplomat and historian
Salvador de Madariaga, "is to save his country by becoming her ruler."
Spain had suffered from an excess of generals since the turn of the
twentieth century, when the loss of her colonies in the Philippines and
Cuba in the Spanish-American War had sent them crowding home.

At the beginning of the 1930s the long-suffering Spanish people had
finally laid claim to a share of their country's natural wealth, wealth
that the landed nobility for centuries had colluded with the military and
the Catholic Church to hoard. Turning against a military dictatorship
allied with King Alfonso XIII, popular leaders had proclaimed a republic, deposed the dictator, and forced the king into exile. The Spanish
Republic's new constitution endowed universal suffrage, public educa-
tion, land redistribution, and Church disestablishment. From 1931 to
1936, the Republic struggled to improve its people's lives during the
worst years of the Great Depression even as it fought off first an armed
revolt of the Right and then an armed revolt of the Left. The civil war
that began in July 1936 was another and final armed revolt of the Right,
led by yet another general, Francisco Franco, who then ruled Spain as
its absolute dictator for more than three decades until his death in 1975.

Many books have been written about the Spanish Civil War. Few of them explore the aspects of the war that interest me. This book only incidentally concerns Spanish politics. Spain today is a democracy. Who was a communist, who a fascist, who connived with whom in the Spanish labyrinth are questions for academics to mull. I was drawn, rather, to the human stories that had not yet been told or had been told only incompletely. I was drawn as well to the technical developments of the war. If destructive technology amplifies violence, constructive technology amplifies compassion, and the lessons of technology are universal.

Some of the innovative technologies of the Spanish war still have direct application today. Spanish and foreign volunteer doctors made medical advances in blood collection, preservation, and storage; in field surgery; in the efficient sorting of casualties. Fortuitously, these innovations came just in time to save lives not only in Spain but worldwide, among combatants and civilians alike, in the larger war that followed. The Catalan physician Josep Trueta's method of cleaning, packing, and then protectively casting large wounds in plaster was recently independently rediscovered; in its new incarnation, as vacuum-assisted wound therapy, it is preserving limbs that organisms resistant to antibiotics might otherwise destroy.

Narratives are usually pinned to the lifelines of their participants, but none of the combatants, innovators, and witnesses I write about was on the ground in Spain throughout the entire three years of the conflict. Many were injured or killed. I might have simplified the story by narrowing its frame to the limits of their participation. Doing so, it seemed to me, would distort it and cheat the reader of its realism as well. War is chaotic. People come and go. I decided to pin my narrative not to the people but to the chronology of the war itself, starting at the beginning and marching through to the end.

I found authority for that decision in something one of the war's veterans wrote in an unpublished memoir: "War is psychologically like hell," the volunteer American surgeon Edward Barsky observes, "supernatural like it and also, as we have been taught to expect, full of good company." You'll find an abundance of both—of hell and good company—in the pages that follow, and a narrative strategy that mirrors a further observation by Barsky, this one ironic: "Another analogy is that apparently only the devil knows what will happen next."

Unlike the men and women who experienced it, however, we know what happened next: the firebombs came back to haunt Germany in World War II, the medical inventions continue to save lives, and the art, the literature, and the witness yet endure to move us to pity and to terror.

PART ONE

The Overthrown Past

ONE

News Arrives of the Death of Others

Barcelona, 25 July 1936: In the glare of Spanish summer, the first witnesses to the igniting civil war are leaving to tell the world. Many are American and European athletes enrolled for the anti-fascist People's Olympiad, canceled now, meant to be an alternative to the official Olympics about to open in Nazi Berlin. They crowd the deck of an overburdened Spanish boat hired to evacuate them, pressing at the dockside railing for a last look. Above the harbor the high pedestaled statue of Christopher Columbus, its gilding gone like Spanish power, points them west to the New World, but the promenade of the Ramblas behind it that follows an old streambed up into the heart of the city is strewn with shattered trees, dead horses, burned cars. Bullets have pockmarked the façades of churches; blood dries on barricades of paving stones. The city has been pacified and crowds sing, but fascist snipers still hammer death from rooftops and empty windows.

A young American woman at the railing, Muriel Rukeyser, poet leaving to tell the world, locates her Bavarian lover on the crowded pier—

At the end of July, exile. We watch the gangplank go. . . .

They met on the tourist train coming down from Paris, the tall, voluptuous woman and the tall, lean man, a runner, an exiled anti-Nazi. They wasted no time. Three days and nights of lovemaking with no common language on the hot train halted by the general strike outside the battling city and then he released her, joined the International Column—

> *. . . first of the faces going home into war*
> *the brave man Otto Boch, the German exile . . .*
> *he kept his life straight as a single issue—*
> *left at that dock we left, his gazing Brueghel face,*
> *square forehead and eyes, strong square breast fading,*
> *the narrow runner's hips diminishing dark.*

An English journal had commissioned her to cover the People's Olympiad, a last-minute substitute for an editor who had begged off to attend a wedding. She had departed London for Spain that late July unaware that the shooting had already begun. From mid-June to mid-July more than sixty people had been assassinated in Spain and ten churches set on fire; a spate of bombings had shaken the country. In that season she would remember as the "hot, beautiful summer of 1936" she was twenty-two, with dark, thick hair and gray eyes, intensely intelligent, already a prizewinning poet. It was her first time out of America.

Muriel Rukeyser was an early eyewitness to Spain's civil war. Those germinal days would change her; the war would be a touchstone of her poetry for the rest of her life. The war of Spanish democracy against its fascist generals and landed rich and their North African mercenaries would change the lives of everyone it touched. Enlarging to a "little world war"—*Time* magazine's coinage—it would serve as a test bed for new technologies both of life and of death.

In London the porter at Victoria Station had spoken to Rukeyser of European war. She found Paris bannered with "posters and notices of gas-masks." There she had boarded the metal-green night express to little Cerbère in its Mediterranean cove, the last stop in France, where a fan of rail yard behind the town narrowed to cross the border through a tunnel and fanned out again behind Spain's Port Bou.

The different gauges of the two countries' tracks required a change of trains. While Rukeyser and her fellow passengers transferred on the shuttle train that Sunday, the forty-three-year-old traitor Francisco Franco Bahamonde, once the youngest general in the Spanish army, approached his country from the Atlantic side. Since March Franco had been idling in rustic exile in the Canary Islands, a thousand miles from Madrid, expelled there by the Republic to limit his influence. Now the London correspondent of a Spanish royalist newspaper was spiriting him in a chartered twin-engine Dragon Rapide to Tetuan, in North Africa opposite Gibraltar, where Spain's faithless Army of Africa awaited him. The generals' rebellion on the mainland needed reinforcements for its coup to succeed; the Spanish people, taking up arms, were already putting down rebel uprisings in cities all over Spain.

After Rukeyser passed through customs in Port Bou there was time for a swim. The train on the Spanish side was slow, local, and hot, Olympic teams and Spanish and foreign passengers stifling now on benches in wooden third-class cars. Beyond the train windows the terrain turned mountainous, the earth red-gold.

"The train stops at every little station," Rukeyser notices, "rests, moves as if exhausted when it does move." Two Spanish soldiers pass through the car in black patent-leather hats and "comic-opera uniforms with natty yellow leather straps," smoking English cigarettes and pointing out olive orchards, castles, and churches. "There is time to point out any amount of landscape," Rukeyser notes drily. At the stations the soldiers stick their guns out the windows, saluting the armed workers patrolling the platforms.

Nearer Barcelona the signs of fighting increase, militiamen with rifles guarding road intersections along the way. At one station a *miliciana,* a girl in a simple cotton dress leading a troop of boys with guns, works through the train. The determined girl searches bags and luggage for photographs, *fotografías,* confiscating them, pulling film from cameras. A panicked American woman tells Rukeyser the girl and the armed boys must be communists bent on stealing, but a calmer Spanish passenger says the "fascists"—Franco's nationalists—have been killing any armed civilians they identify from photographs. The young people handle the cameras carefully and return them to their owners intact.

Around midday that Sunday the train halts in Montcada, a small town seven miles above Barcelona: the beleaguered government in Madrid has called a general strike. How long they would be stuck there no one knew. They would not have wanted to continue into the Catalan capital yet; the uprising was still raging. The *New York Times*'s Barcelona correspondent, Lawrence Fernsworth, described hearing "continuous volleys of rifle fire" in the city that bloody Sunday, "clattering hoofs and bugle calls . . . men shouting and others screaming in anguish . . . screeching flocks of swallows flying back and forth in a frenzy as bullets whistle among them." Fernsworth saw "riderless horses [that] galloped over the bodies of the dead and the dying. From windows and rooftops everywhere spat more rifle and machine-gun fire. Motorcars overfilled with armed men raced through the streets. . . . Fieldpieces, now in the hands of the populace, boomed from street intersections. Their shells tore through the length of the streets, slicing off trees, exploding against a building or blowing a stalled streetcar or an automobile to bits."

By Monday evening the republic's militias had gained control and Fernsworth found only "splotches of blood drying on the pavement where the wounded had been taken away" in the Plaza Cataluña, the city center at the head of the long, tree-lined walk of the Ramblas. "Empty cartridges and bandoliers were lying about everywhere." With bloodshed and more broken walls and Dolores Ibárruri, the woman they called La Pasionaria, on the radio crying *"No pasaran!* [They shall not pass!]" Madrid had been secured as well.

The Spanish people were fighting alone. Even the government they had elected, a coalition just six months old, was riven with dissent. In the past decade they had endured a rump monarchy and then a right-wing dictatorship. In 1934 the coal miners in the northern mining district of Asturias had revolted. Franco, hastily appointed army chief of staff, had been called in to put down the revolt and had done so brutally with mercenaries from Spanish Morocco, the people the Spanish called *Moros*. The Moroccans were enthusiastic and inventive killers: castrating the wounded was a favorite sport, robbing the dead a recreation.

When Spain voted for democracy in February 1936 the new leaders had banished Franco to his post in the Canaries. From that exile he had plotted with his fellow generals to stage a coup d'état. Moors had first invaded the Iberian Peninsula in A.D. 711 and it had taken the Spanish seven hundred years to drive them out. Ferdinand and Isabella had completed that *reconquista* and Columbus had sailed in the banner year 1492. Now the rebel generals were rallying the Moors' descendants in the name of Christian Spain to overthrow the legitimate Spanish government and hack their way to power. "Glory to the heroic Army of Africa," Franco radioed the mainland army and navy bases in late July 1936, floridly, when he had secured North Africa at the beginning of the coup. "Spain above everything! Accept the enthusiastic greetings of those garrisons which join you and all other comrades in the Peninsula in these historic moments. Blind faith in victory! Long live Spain with honor!"

It was urgent that Franco move the Moroccan mercenaries and Spanish Foreign Legionaries who supported the rebel generals to the Peninsula—to mainland Spain—or the nationalist coup d'état would fail. But ordinary seamen in the Spanish navy rejected the rebellion. When their nationalist officers resisted, the seamen killed them. In those first days of conflict the chemist José Giral, for a few brief weeks the prime minister of republican Spain—it was he who had dissolved the army and ordered the people armed when the coup began on 19 July—sent the navy to blockade Morocco and quarantine the colonial rebellion in North Africa.

The rebels' few gunboats were no match for the Spanish navy—no match, for that matter, for even the antiquated Spanish air force, which could strafe and bomb the nationalist transports. To move his forces to the Peninsula, Franco realized, he needed aircraft. A mission he sent to Italian prime minister and fascist Duce Benito Mussolini in Rome collided with one sent there from Navarre by Franco's fellow rebel general Emilio Mola, confusing Mussolini about who was in charge. The nationalists' leader at the outset had been sixty-four-year-old senior general José Sanjurjo, styled "the Lion of the Rif" for his victories in the coastal Rif region of northern Morocco, but with a trunkful of uniforms he had overloaded the little Puss Moth biplane sent to fetch him from Lisbon and it had crashed on takeoff and burned. Mola now commanded in the north, operating independently, and Franco in the south. Mussolini hesitated.

Franco had better luck in Germany. His first message went out through diplomatic channels on 22 July, asking for ten transport aircraft, payment to be deferred. The German foreign ministry saw no benefit in supporting the rebellion and denied the request within twenty-four hours. Fortunately for Franco, Adolf Hitler's Germany had a dual-track government. Franco's second appeal passed through Nazi Party channels directly to Hitler's deputy Rudolf Hess, who alerted the Führer. The two expatriate German businessmen who carried Franco's appeal from Morocco to Berlin in a commandeered Lufthansa Junkers-52 traveled on with Hess to Bayreuth, where Hitler was attending the annual Wagner festival.

Fresh from a performance of *Die Walküre,* "The Ride of the Valkyries" slow-rolling in his head, Hitler met Franco's delegates in the Wagner villa at ten thirty on the evening of 25 July 1936. They had not had their dinner. The Führer asked a few skeptical questions. The rebels had no money? "You cannot begin a war like that." Without help, Franco would lose? "He is lost." But he warmed to the challenge and lectured Franco's delegates undined for the next three hours. He called in his war and air ministers, Werner von Blomberg and Hermann Goering. Goering misread the Führer's mood and objected to supporting the rebels—the Luftwaffe itself, he complained, only recently emerged from its Lufthansa camouflage, was short of planes—until he realized that Hitler had made up his mind. Then Goering discovered his enthusiasm for the Spanish project. At his Nuremberg trial the air marshal claimed he urged Hitler "to give support under all circumstances, firstly, in order to prevent the further spread of communism in that theater and, secondly, to test my young Luftwaffe at this opportunity in this or that technical respect."

Hitler had different motives. He paid lip service to keeping the Strait of Gibraltar free of communist control—to the Nazis, Spain's Popular Front coalition was communist—but in fact he wanted to distract England and France from German rearmament with a challenge to France's rear and Britain's access to the Suez Canal. To fuel rearmament he wanted Spanish iron ore, mercury, and especially pyrites, the cubic crystals of fool's gold—iron and copper sulfide—that yielded iron, copper, lead, zinc, and sulfuric acid for industrial processing. Spain, a country rich in metals, had mountains of pyrites to trade. Franco had asked for ten transports. Grandly, Hitler decided to send him twenty trimotor Junkers-52s that could be converted into bombers, with crews and maintenance personnel and six fighter escorts. With a nod to Wagner, he christened the operation *Feuerzauber*—Magic Fire—and went to bed contented; for the Führer, wizarding the fate of whole populations was all in a night's work.

The Spanish republican forces needed aircraft as well. Giral had telegraphed Léon Blum, the socialist French prime minister, on 20 July, asking for bombs and bombers, but the French right wing howled. Blum in London on 23 July heard, he said later, "counsels of prudence . . . dispensed and sharp fears expressed." English prime minister Stanley Baldwin put it bluntly enough. "We hate Fascism," he is supposed to have said. "But we hate Bolshevism just as much. If, therefore, there is a country where Fascists and Bolsheviks kill each other, it is a boon for mankind." Under pressure from the English, who favored Franco, Blum decided that nonintervention was the better part of valor.

The French were not opposed to private sales, however. The air ministry dispatched thirty-four-year-old André Malraux, the novelist and cultural buccaneer, to Madrid on 23 July to assess republican requirements. Briefed about the vicissitudes of the Spanish air force, most of whose officers however had remained loyal, Malraux toured the Madrid area and met with the Spanish president, Manuel Azaña. In an optimistic dispatch to the Paris newspaper *L'Humanité* he reported, "Madrid has been completely cleared as far south as Andalucía, to the east as far as the sea, to the west as far as Portugal. It is only in the north that the rebel army has sent out small advance guards, which have been beaten and pushed back beyond the hillsides of the Sierra de Guadarrama"—the mountain range that barricaded Madrid to the northwest. Back in Paris Malraux began buying planes and recruiting pilots. Both were dear, the planes antiquated, most of the pilots mercenaries prepared to engage the fascists in aerial dogfights for a monthly 25,000 francs in combat pay (about $35,000 today).

Mussolini, having sorted out who among the rebels was in charge, wanted cash for his aircraft. A fascist Spanish financier, Juan March, put up almost $5 million for the first twelve Italian planes, a mix of fighters and transports. Later March would buy the factory and recoup his investment several times over. The Italian aircraft began arriving in Morocco at the end of July, as did the German Feuerzauber flight.

In the harbor in Barcelona on 25 July, while Hitler in Bayreuth was tumefying over Wagner, Muriel Rukeyser spoke to her lover for the last time:

When I left you, you stood on the pier and held
your face up and never smiled, saying what we had found
was a gift of the revolution—and the boat sailed. . . .

At a mass meeting that afternoon the head of the games had celebrated "the beautiful and great victory of the people" in driving the rebels out of Barcelona. Instead of the games, he said, the athletes and visitors would carry to their home countries—it would be their duty—the story of what they had seen in Spain. Rukeyser did her duty on the crossing to France, drafting her great poem "Mediterranean." The *New Masses* published it in mid-September. "If we had not seen fighting," it urges,

> *if we had not looked there*
> *the plane flew low*
> *the plaster ripped by shots*
> *the peasant's house*
> *if we had stayed in our world*
> *between the table and the desk*
> *between the town and the suburb . . .*
> *If we had lived in our city*
> *sixty years might not prove*
> *the power this week*
> *the overthrown past. . . .*

Franco had not waited until the German Feuerzauber transports arrived to initiate his airlift. He used the few planes he had on hand and supplemented his fleet with Italian Savoia bombers as he received them. By 1 August he had moved eight hundred legionaries across to Spain. Frustrated at the slow pace, he began shipping legionaries and Moroccans by sea as well, using his available fighter aircraft to fly cover. The Feuerzauber flights began a week into August. Thus bootstrapping, by the end of September Franco had thirteen thousand men on the Peninsula and some four hundred tons of equipment. Another thousand men and another hundred tons of gear would follow in October. It was the world's first large-scale military airlift, and it kept the rebellion alive.

"Barcelona's black July 19 passed into history," the *New York Times*'s Fernsworth reports, but rebellion was spreading through Spain like an underground fire, "burst[ing] out again in new places." The Republic had secured most of the major cities—Madrid, Valencia, Málaga, Alicante, Almería, Bilbao. There was still fighting in the cities of Old Castile, the region of central Spain north of Madrid beyond the Gua-

darrama Mountains that extends up to the Bay of Biscay; in Extremadura touching Portugal to the west; in Galicia, the far northwestern
Spanish province that was Franco's birthplace; in Asturias along the
Bay of Biscay east of Galicia; in Catholic Navarre in the northeastern
corner of the country, from the Ebro River up into the Pyrenees. "In
these regions," says Fernsworth, "the rebels held Burgos and Valladolid;
Granada, Seville and Cadiz; Badajoz, La Coruna, Oviedo, Santander
and Pamplona. And across the Straits of Gibraltar the Moroccans had
come under the standard of revolt and were being poured into Spain."

Staging inland from Gibraltar, which the British continued to control, Franco intended to drive northeast toward Madrid, the Spanish
capital. Taking it while the republican government scrambled to train
and organize an army that had lost its officer corps might have short-
ened the war. But partly because his experience had been limited to field
command in Africa, partly because he was fighting a civil war, Franco
determined to advance only as rapidly as he could pacify the territory
behind him. Otherwise, he feared, any opposition could reemerge to
attack him from the rear.

For all his nationalistic rhetoric, Franco was politically credulous.
One of his first acts as commander of the nationalist army was to outlaw
Freemasonry; he believed that the Masons, of all people, were the dark
force behind the socialists and liberals of the Popular Front. Short on
imagination, he was physically short as well: five feet four, with small,
girlish hands, a high-pitched voice, and a paunch he had acquired early
in adulthood. In the Academy for Infantry Cadets in the Alcázar fortress in Toledo, which he entered at fourteen in 1907 and from which
he graduated as a second lieutenant at seventeen in 1910, his classmates
had nicknamed him Franquito, little Frankie, "Frankie-boy." The
school disciplined with physical punishment. Fastidious and sexually
inhibited, Franco was bullied as well. He learned to hold a grudge.

His school experiences compounded a childhood under an abusive
father who regularly beat his children while his unresisting wife, the
pious mother Franco idealized, stood by. Both home and school expe-

riences preconditioned the boy for the violent socialization required of military men. Franco's father, Don Nicolás, was everything his fragile son came to despise, one of Franco's biographers writes, a womanizer, garrulous, explosive, "a political free-thinker with a marked sympathy for the freemasons and profound distaste for religion." Childhood is always the first arena of personality, but few childhoods map more directly onto adult identity than Franco's. In pursuing a latter-day, reverse *reconquista* he was less a fascist than an aggrandized martinet.

Pacification as the rebels conceived it meant torture, rape, and slaughter. General Mola, Franco's northern counterpart, proclaiming martial law in Pamplona on 19 July, made his intentions explicit: "It is necessary to spread terror. . . . Anyone who helps or hides a communist or a supporter of the Popular Front will be shot."

The colonial forces that Mola and Franco commanded were conditioned to violent repression; they repatriated to Spain the extreme violence that Spanish officers had encouraged them to use to dominate the Moroccan countryside. *Chicago Tribune* correspondent Edmond Taylor met them socially and observed them in action. "The Moors," he writes, "many of whom were irregulars recruited in the mountains for the occasion, were simply savage mercenaries fighting for infidels against infidels, and the Sacred Heart scapulars they wore pinned to the burnooses of Islam were the badges of their tragic Berber blood that was always ready to spill itself for alien faiths."

The legionaries were something more, Taylor goes on: nearly all Spanish, the creation of a bitter, one-armed general named José Millán-Astray, not just mercenaries but also "exalted pessimists," fearless fighters who made a cult of duty, killing, and death, "the kind of soldiers who would shoot their officers if they tried to turn back."

The record of nationalist atrocities is sickening, extending to gang rape, castration, and mutilation in the name of restoring the glory of Christian Spain. In the towns the nationalists occupied they routinely set up markets to sell their thievings from the houses and bodies of the dead.

Crossing the strait in increasing numbers in August 1936, Franco's forces had begun methodically conquering the southwestern Spanish region of Andalusia. The booty of that conquest included the valuable Rio Tinto district, where gold, silver, and copper had been mined since the Bronze Age. In the towns and villages behind the line of advance, reprisals extended not only to men but sometimes also to women and children.

A particularly brutal atrocity followed the mid-August battle of Badajoz, a city on the Portuguese border 250 miles northwest of Gibraltar. *Chicago Tribune* reporter Jay Allen heard the story from eyewitnesses, nine days after the city fell, and went in to see for himself. "This was the upshot," he writes—"thousands of Republican, Socialist, and Communist militias and militiawomen were butchered after the fall of Badajoz for the crime of defending their Republic against the onslaught of the Generals and the landowners."

Allen describes driving out along the city walls to the bullring, where he remembers having seen the bullfighter Juan Belmonte once "on the eve of the fight, on a night like this, when he came down to watch the bulls brought in." The massacre was continuing before Allen's eyes, "files of men, arms in the air," herded into the bullring as the bulls had been herded for Belmonte. "They were young, mostly peasants in blue blouses, mechanics in jumpers. 'The Reds.' They are still being rounded up. At four o'clock in the morning they are turned out into the ring through the gate by which the initial parade of the bullfight enters. There machine guns await them." After the first night, Allen adds, "the blood was supposed to be palm deep on the far side of the lane. I don't doubt it. Eighteen hundred men—there were women, too—were mowed down there in some twelve hours. There is more blood than you would think in eighteen hundred bodies."

If the republican people's militias were less brutal, their violence more often defensive, they were only somewhat less homicidal. But the nationalists' repression was deliberate, planned in advance and based on their colonial experience of dominating with violence a native population they believed to be savage and inferior—and for the *Africanista* rebels, the proletarian population of Spain was savage and inferior or worse.

From a distance, wars and revolutions can seem uniform in their moil of blood and death. Close up, they sometimes reveal strange singularities. One oddity of the Spanish Civil War was the fascist dosing of women prisoners with volumes of castor oil sufficient to cause uncontrollable and humiliating diarrhea; the practice emigrated from Italy, where Mussolini's Blackshirts similarly used castor oil, a well-known folk laxative, for intimidation.

The Spanish filmmaker Luis Buñuel, who participated in the defense of Madrid in the first days of the rebellion, recalls another and larger oddity, one that opens a window into the depths of the conflict. "Certain exploits," Buñuel writes of that time, "seemed to me both absurd and glorious—like the workers who climbed into a truck one day and drove out to the monument to the Sacred Heart of Jesus about twenty kilometers south of the city, formed a firing squad, and executed the statue of Christ." The London *Daily Mail* published a photograph of that exuberant "execution" on 7 August 1936, claiming it illustrated "the Spanish Reds' war on religion." Within a month, workers with chisels and explosives had destroyed the ninety-two-foot statue at the geographic center of the country in Getafe as they were destroying similar religious monuments throughout republican Spain.

The demolitions had more to do with fighting oppression than with warring against religion. The Getafe monument had been unveiled by Alfonso XIII in May 1919, at the end of the Great War, when he reconsecrated Spain to the Sacred Heart of Jesus, a long-standing Roman Catholic cult associated with royalty since before the French Revolution. With the king's endorsement, Sacred Heart statues and plaques had proliferated all over Spain. Many of Spain's urban and rural poor lived from season to season in abject poverty, on the raw edge of starvation. The Spanish school system in the 1930s was 17,500 schools short. More than 30 percent of Spanish men and an even higher percentage of

Spanish women were illiterate. To that exploited population, the prolif-
eration of monuments meant no escape from the presence of a corrupt
church that flaunted its wealth and power.

When the people voted for a republic in 1931, the new government
went to work reclaiming public spaces; removing religious symbols
from schools, streets, and cemeteries; and opening secular equivalents.
A new constitution decreed the separation of church and state and the
dissolution of some religious orders and prohibited religious orders from
engaging in commerce, industry, and teaching. The Church fought its
increasing disenfranchisement with new lay organizations, political action, and lawsuits. Processions, festivals, and retreats became demon-
strations, which leftist groups in turn found ways to interrupt. In those
years, the historian Hugh Thomas writes, the Getafe monument "became the spiritual and physical centre of Catholic mobilization." Whatever else they were doing, the young militiamen who executed Christ at
Getafe were expressing a commitment to social transformation.

With the challenge of the generals' rebellion to the existence of the
secular Spanish state, a challenge that Franco elevated to the status of
a religious crusade, churches were burned, icons destroyed, religious
vestments cut up and resewn into militia uniforms. More radical anticlericals went beyond slapping idols. They exhumed the desiccated
bodies of priests and nuns from church crypts and put them on public display to expose their fetid mortality. In a period seemingly free
of legal constraints, with bullets flying in both directions and artillery
shattering buildings, the anarchist militias began killing priests, the
living idols of a church that had conspired with their class enemies
to oppress them. Four thousand, one hundred eighty-four priests,
283 nuns, and 2,365 other religious would be murdered in republican
territory in the course of the war—significantly, half during the first
six weeks. Lluís Companys, the president of Catalonia, told a French
journalist that the killings represented "the explosion of an immense
store of wrath, an immense need for vengeance, which had been gathering force from very early times."

Long afterward, an anthropologist asked a Spaniard why they burned images of the Virgin Mary, the least of the anticlerical offenses of the civil war. He responded:

> You don't understand why the images of the Virgin were burned? . . . I will tell you. Because the Virgin was a shameless whore and God had no sense of justice. . . . A mother who sees her children go hungry and turns away is a whore. . . . What a little mother she is. . . . Tell me, has she ever answered [your prayers]? Does she speak to you? Has she helped you? No? Well, now you understand [why the images were burned]. It's all lies. Those images were lies and lies have to be destroyed for the truth to live.

Of the twelve Italian Savoias that Mussolini had sent Franco at the end of July, only nine had reached him in Tetuan. Their navigators failing to account for headwinds, the other three had run short of fuel. Two had crashed, killing their crews. The third had landed in French Morocco, where the French impounded it. News that Italy was supplying Franco with aircraft forced the French prime minister's hand. Léon Blum hoped the revelation would justify his support for what was, after all, a legitimate Spanish government resisting a rebellion, but his cabinet demurred. As an alternative, the French government proposed an embargo on arms sales to either side. While waiting for an agreement from the other governments of Europe, France announced, it would supply the Spanish government if asked.

Through this brief window, on 13 August, André Malraux and the twenty pilots he had recruited delivered fourteen worn bi-wing Dewoitine D.372 fighters and six lumbering Potez 540 bombers to Barajas airport, outside Madrid. The French authorities had insisted that the aircraft be stripped of their armaments, which the Spanish now had to laboriously reinstall. Malraux was not himself a pilot, but his Foreign Legion of the Air would fight the rebel air assault that intensified throughout the rest of 1936 as Franco added German and Italian aircraft to his stock.

What had been a purely Spanish conflict was widening to take in alliances on both sides. The American oil company Texaco, betting that the nationalists would win, had begun supplying Franco with oil on credit in July; Shell, Standard Oil of New Jersey, and Atlantic Refining would supply the nationalist rebels as well. The first International Brigade volunteers, all Europeans like Otto Boch, had arrived in Spain the day before Malraux and his planes. A week later, on 23 August 1936, the first British medical unit left London for Spain, volunteer doctors and nurses assembled in record time to aid the government forces. On 27 August, the first Russians arrived—Marcel Rosenberg, the new Soviet ambassador, and his large staff, billeted at Gaylord's Hotel behind the Prado Museum in Madrid. Soviet aircraft and tanks would follow, and the pilots and crews to operate them.

War had been Ernest Hemingway's best subject; the hazard of violent death enlivened him. That summer and fall he was busy writing *To Have and Have Not,* but he chafed to cover his third war. "When finish this book hope to go to Spain if all not over there," he telegraphed his editor, Max Perkins, from Wyoming at the end of September. ". . . I hate to have missed this Spanish thing worse than anything in the world but have to have this book finished first."

Franco had promised Hitler and Mussolini a short war; Malraux had rushed in aircraft because he also believed the war would be brief and any delay fatal. How long the war would last was not yet clear, with Mola's Column of Death grinding up from Andalusia toward Madrid. But when the nationalist forces turned aside on 22 September just forty-six miles from Madrid to relieve the republican siege of the Alcázar fortress in Toledo, the massive sixteenth-century compound that still housed Franquito's cadet academy, it was obvious to all that Franco meant to fight a ground war: the conflict had only begun.

TWO

Today the Burning City Lights Itself

Though they cooperated cynically to advance their common goals, Hitler and Mussolini were rivals. Both had strategic and commercial interests in Spain. Hitler wanted Spanish ore, Mussolini Spanish gold. Both men wanted a fascist ally at France's back and on the Mediterranean, which Mussolini notoriously had proclaimed a "Roman sea." Both wanted pressure on Gibraltar (ceded to the British in perpetuity in 1713) and an ally dominating the strait. In September and October 1936, as Franco's forces butchered their way toward Madrid, the two fascist dictators vied with each other to supply the rebels with military equipment and men. Less enthusiastically, and also for Spanish gold, Joseph Stalin began to supply the Republic.

Evidently Franco had not even considered asking for tanks. In early September, when his German liaison, Colonel Walter Warlimont, proposed supplying him, Franco seemed surprised by the offer. Berlin shipped out forty-one tanks and armored cars as well as several types of artillery. The tanks were light Mark I panzers armed with only a single machine gun. When Franco learned that the Soviet Union was delivering tanks armed with 37- and 50-mm cannons, he called in Warlimont, who found him "very upset. . . . I could only advise Franco that not even Germany had any heavy tanks." Warlimont offered him antitank guns instead. The antitank gun Franco eventually got, the 88 Flak-18, was designed as an antiaircraft weapon, with a semiautomatic breech that could load fifteen to twenty high-velocity rounds per minute. It proved efficient and deadly against republican tanks as well as troop concentrations, with an effective range of nine miles.

Besides tanks and guns, the Germans shipped Franco an impressive array of other war matériel in September. Operation Otto, the support mission that followed Feuerzauber, comprised thirty-six biplane fighters, 80 million rounds of rifle and machine-gun ammunition, 20,000 rifle grenades, 100 tons of bombs of various sizes from 20 to 1,000 pounds, radios, telephones, 300 miles of wire for field communications, and 45 trucks. Four hundred German officers and men accompanied this equipment to teach Franco's forces how to use it.

The Spanish Republic's forces had nothing like Franco's supplies at first. Soviet intelligence estimated in late August that only one out of three republican soldiers even had a rifle, and there was only a single machine gun per company of 150 to 200 men. They were arming themselves by the desperate expedient of picking up the rifles of their dead and wounded comrades as they moved forward to replace them.

Toledo is an old walled town that descends the back slope of a high bluff above the Tagus River, forty-five miles southwest of Madrid. Except for its arms factory, located outside the city walls, it had no military value in 1936. The Alcázar, its massive Renaissance fortress built on the height of the bluff, was Spain's West Point, where Franco had trained as a cadet. Republican forces began besieging the Alcázar on 21 July, at the beginning of the generals' revolt, when renegade civil guards, army officers, fascist civilians and their families, and a few cadets took shelter there after raiding and burning the local arms factory. In mid-September, republican miners dug tunnels beneath the fortress, set dynamite charges, and largely destroyed one large section, but the 1,670 men, women, and children sheltered deep inside held out, living on horse and mule meat, until Franco and his Moroccans drove the republican forces out of Toledo and relieved the fortress on 27 September. Anarchist militiamen had executed some 222 local fascists during the siege; Franco's legionaries now perpetrated a two-day bloodbath that counted more than eight hundred dead, including a ward full of pregnant women who were driven outside and shot. The hundred or more hostages held in the Alcázar during the siege disappeared. The American journalist John T. Whitaker reports the Moroccans "killing the wounded in the Republican hospital in Toledo" by lobbing grenades into the wards. "They blew up more than 200 screaming and panicked men with hand grenades and they boasted about it."

Whitaker, a friend of a German captain who was Hitler's key agent in Spain, saw Franco's Moroccans in action in the early months of the war. "It is uncanny how both sides know when a battle is won," he writes:

> For a few minutes an awesome quiet would fall on that sector of the front. And then suddenly the noises of hell would be raised as the Moors smashed in doorways and began the looting. They were like children with their spoils. One would have a side of meat under one arm and a Singer sewing machine under the other, while his hands would clasp a bottle of brandy and a picture off the wall of some home. One Moor found a saxophone and carried it for two days before wearying of it.

After Toledo, the cabal of traitor generals crowned Franco as their supreme leader. Sanjurjo's death in the Puss Moth crash had narrowed the field of candidates, but Hitler's decision to work only through Franco and Franco's command of Moroccan mercenaries ensured his election. On 30 September the little general flew to Burgos, the old capital of Castile 140 miles north of Madrid, where his fellow conspirators elected him commander in chief of the nationalist military forces and head of government, El Caudillo. "You can be justly proud," Franco told the generals grandiosely. "You took over a broken Spain. You hand over to me a Spain united in a single great ideal. Victory is on our side. . . . I shall not fail. I shall take the Motherland to her summit, or die in the attempt." From Burgos the newly anointed Caudillo moved into the bishop's palace in Salamanca, 135 miles northwest of Madrid, his headquarters during the first year of the war.

With sanguinary bathos, the right-wing journalist Ernesto Giménez Caballero imagined the Caudillo slicing and dicing in his Salamanca war room:

> We have seen Franco in the early hours of the morning, in the midst of heat or of snow, his soul and his nerves stretched to breaking point, leaning over the battle plan or the map of Spain, operating on the living body of Spain with the urgency and tragedy of a surgeon who operates on his own daughter, on his own mother, on his own beloved wife. We have seen Franco's tears fall on the body of this mother, of this wife, of this daughter, while over his hands runs the blood and the pain of the sacred body in spasms.

The Soviet Union responded urgently to the fall of Toledo and the republican arms shortage, offering its best weapons to counter the Italian and German buildup. The first shipment of Soviet arms arrived in Spain on 4 October 1936: 20,000 rifles with 7 million rounds of ammunition, 100,000 grenades with launchers, and six howitzers—short-barreled, mortarlike cannon—with a thousand shells each. Fifty ten-ton T-26 tanks, each armed with a 45-mm cannon and two machine guns, arrived in mid-October, with another 50 to follow as well as 45 advanced fighters and bombers with crews.

British and American businessmen allowed Franco to order on credit; Germany and Italy supplied him in exchange for shipments of Spanish minerals. The Soviet Union required the Spanish Republic to pay in gold, however, for its strictly commercial transactions. Spain shipped $518 million in gold to the USSR in late 1936, primarily to move it beyond the reach of Franco's forces. The transfer became the basis for fascist propaganda claiming the Russians had stolen Spain's gold reserves. They hadn't, but they expected payment for the equipment they sold. In any case, more than $340 million of the gold Spain sent to the USSR was moved to the Banque Commerciale pour l'Europe du Nord of Paris to be spent gradually across the next two years on the beleaguered Republic's war needs.

From Toledo, the Army of Africa—Moroccans and legionaries twenty thousand strong—had a straight drive up the broad plain of the Tagus River valley to Madrid. Pushing back the Spanish capital's untrained militias, which often panicked under attack in open terrain, the nationalists made twelve miles a day until heavy rain and the necessity of waiting for deliveries of German and Italian tanks and artillery slowed them. Mola had predicted he would take his morning coffee in the cobbled square of the Puerta del Sol by 12 October; Madrileños set out a coffee for him at an empty table from that morning forward, marked "Reserved for General Mola." The Cuban-born general was killed before he could collect it.

By late October, writes the historian and participant Robert Colodny, "The sound of gunfire could now be heard clearly in Madrid, and the aspect of the city began to change. A commission for the defense of the city took over the regulation of municipal life. An eleven-p.m. curfew was clamped down. Milk, water and food were rationed. With the loss of heavily populated towns within a thirty-kilometer radius west and southwest came the floods of refugees [and] hunger, aggravated by the cold autumnal rains." The first bombing, by Junkers-52s with German pilots, peppered Madrid's Northern Station railroad terminal (Príncipe Pío today) on 23 October. A second bombing followed the next day against the rail yards, the Madrid gas works, and the main republican fighter air base in the southern suburb of Getafe. Nationalist ground forces overran the base on 4 November.

Madrid appeared doomed. A city of nearly a million people on a plateau 2,100 feet above sea level, thirty miles southeast of the Guadarrama Mountains, it lacked natural defenses. An approach from the west, through the great park of the Casa de Campo, six square miles that had once been the king's hunting grounds, across the Manzanares River and through the unfinished new University City campus of ancient Complutense University, would allow the rebel forces to penetrate directly into the heart of the city. The Manzanares was the only serious obstacle, less than one hundred yards wide but flowing canalized between masonry walls on the eastern edge of the park, with only four bridges to defend.

Bombing meant to soften Madrid's defenses toughened the population. "Although about 1,000 people appear to have been killed," the British scientist J. B. S. Haldane reports, "and a good many more wounded, these raids were defeated by a new phenomenon—mass heroism." Showing fear was socially unacceptable in wartime Madrid, Haldane found. One Spaniard told him, "We old chaps can't fight, and if we started running we would be setting a bad example to the boys in the trenches."

While the people of Madrid watched the first bombings from their open windows, the Republic's panicked leadership prepared to abandon the city and move the government elsewhere. Francisco Largo Caballero, the prime minister, made the decision on the gray, cold, rainy Friday afternoon of 6 November, when he learned that the government's supply of artillery shells and even bullets was perilously low. Russian fighter aircraft had taken to the air against the slow German Junkers-52s for the first time the day before, and reinforcements were on their way, but Largo Caballero and his cabinet abandoned the defense of the city to a skeleton defense junta that night and fled to Valencia, eastward on the Mediterranean 220 miles in the republican rear. The anarchist militiamen blocking the Valencia road allowed them to pass only grudgingly. Some of the international correspondents covering the war saved themselves time and trouble that night, before they skedaddled out of town with the government, by reporting the rebels marching triumphantly into the city the next day. Chief Hearst correspondent H. R. Knickerbocker even invented a little dog that barked along beside the cheering crowds.

But Largo Caballero had delegated Madrid's defense to doughty general José Miaja, and once Miaja understood that he must either save the city or preside over its fall, he mustered a team of loyal officers and began organizing its defense. He sent his chief of staff, Lieutenant Colonel Vicente Rojo, to search for munitions while he assembled and challenged his sixteen sector commanders. "The Government has gone," he charged them bluntly that Friday night. "Madrid is at the mercy of the enemy. The moment has come when you must act as men! Do you understand me? As men! Machos!" They did.

By midnight Rojo had his inventory: artillery rounds enough for two hours of shelling and enough bullets to give each of the remaining twenty thousand militiamen six each. Rojo knew there was more, but the government had cleared out so hastily that Largo Caballero's officers had forgotten to report its location. Rojo telegraphed Albacete and Valencia to ship rifle and machine-gun bullets immediately by air.

It wasn't much to defend a city, but the people of Madrid had their backs to the wall. The unions, the cooperatives, and a full regiment of Spanish communists deployed under Miaja's command. He told them to take up the arms of the fallen and never retreat. If they held the city for forty-eight hours, he promised them, relief would come.

In the retreat from Getafe, women fought as well as men, New Zealand journalist Geoffrey Cox reports:

> Some looked even more soldierly than the men, with determined faces and rifles carried as if they meant business. But others, in neat blue overalls, with oiled, dark hair, penciled eyebrows, vivid lips, added one more touch of unreality to the scene. Yet they, too, had been under fire all morning, and had been amongst the last to leave, I learnt later. It was like a waiting crowd of extras for a bandit film rather than an army fighting a war notorious for its complete lack of mercy.

Early on the morning of 7 November, Franco's forces under general José Enrique Varela advanced eastward into Madrid under cover of artillery fire. But the republican militias that had withered in the open country knew how to fight in the city, firing from windows and from behind street barricades. Though they took large losses, they held off the advancing rebel forces and sometimes turned them back. They scattered Varela's cavalry by throwing sticks of dynamite from homemade armored cars; they recaptured lost ground in near-suicidal counterattacks. "They knew every corner of the city," writes a veteran, "whereas Madrid to the bulk of Varela's army was a foreign city, a maze of unknown and hostile streets." Loudspeakers in cafés, radios blaring from open windows called the people to defense. Wives carried meals by streetcar or subway to their husbands fighting at the barricades.

On Sunday, 8 November, Miaja's promise of relief was fulfilled. Cox, drinking coffee in a bar on the Gran Vía, heard shouting and clapping and went outside to see. "Up the street from the direction of the Ministry of War came a long column of marching men," he writes. "They wore a kind of khaki corduroy uniform, and loose brown Glengarry caps like those of the British tank corps. They were marching in excellent formation. . . . Over their shoulders were slung rifles of obviously modern design. Many had scarred tin helmets hanging from their belts. Some were young; others carried themselves like trained, experienced soldiers." Their appearance was a mystery: who were they? The crowd thought they must be Russians. "The *Rusos* have come," the barman told Cox, relief in his voice. "The *Rusos* have come." Cox heard a sergeant shouting an order in Prussian-accented German, heard others shouting in Italian and French, and knew they weren't Russians. They were, he quickly learned, the first brigade of the International Column of Anti-Fascists, "the most truly international army the world has seen since the Crusades."

The Internationals added about three thousand men to the city's defense. In the course of the war more than forty thousand would leave their homes in Europe, Britain, and North America to fight with the Spanish republicans against the fascism they believed Franco and his forces to represent. Many, but not all of them, were communists, an

affiliation in the Great Depression that reflected a strong social con-
science more than it did any rigid ideological commitment. Some of
them joined for adventure, others because they had been too long out of
work, but most believed that defeating fascism in Spain might prevent a
second and more devastating world war. For that great cause they were
prepared to sacrifice their lives.

At this stage of the Spanish war they were almost all Europeans,
volunteers whom the Communist International, the Comintern, had
recruited to stand in for the Soviet ground forces that Stalin did not
intend to provide. The Soviet Union would, however, send military
specialists in the months to come, a historian writes, "including advisors, instructors, pilots, tankers, artillerymen, wireless operators, and
code-breakers, as well as a large support staff of translators, medics, engineers, maintenance workers, and sailors." For now, volunteers made
up the relief columns.

They were raw. Some had trained for all of ten days, some for
only twenty-four hours. A battalion normally consists of between 500
and 1,000 men; the Garibaldi Battalion of volunteers, the only one yet
formed out of the mob of recruits, had twenty-five rifles, one machine
gun, and no personal kit. They marched anyway, under the command
of André Marty, a large, blustering man in country suiting and a black
beret, a French naval engineer and a longtime communist member of
the French Assembly. General Pavol Lukács, better known as the Hungarian novelist Máté Zalka (Béla Frankl), commanded the full brigade.

Several detachments of Internationals headed to the hilly, wooded
Casa de Campo to support the Madrid militiamen engaging the nationalist forces there. The nationalists fought their way forward to the
Manzanares at the eastern edge of the park, but the Internationals and
the militiamen drove them back, at great cost. By Monday, 9 November,
the fighting had concentrated within the unfinished campus of University City. "In the early morning," Cox reports, "the rebels bombarded
the University buildings, and pressed forward towards the golf course.
Here the Manzanares was no longer a small canal between built-up

banks, but a stream with low sandy edges, easily crossed. It was the rebels' most open road to the heart of Madrid."

The two sides fought from building to building, viciously, for forty-eight hours, knocking holes in floors and walls, shoving through a machine gun, and sweeping the rooms and stairways beyond. "Republican soldiers put grenades in the service elevator of the Clinical Hospital," writes Colodny, "pulled the pins and sent the lift up to a floor occupied by the Moroccans. Spanish soldiers became experts at attaching grenades to strings and throwing them out of windows so that the explosion would take place in front of the machine guns of the enemy below them." In the philosophy building, the English writer John Sommerfield recalls, "we built barricades with volumes of Indian metaphysics and early nineteenth century German philosophy; they were quite bullet-proof."

The Internationals lost a third of their men killed in that first battle, but they and the republican militias pushed Varela's forces back into the middle of the Casa de Campo, where the two sides stalled. There was further fighting in the University City throughout November, brutal and bloody fighting. In the park, Colodny summarizes, "exhausted, short of ammunition, tactically stalemated, the two armies began the process of throwing up entrenchments and preparing on this sector for siege warfare." Garabitas Hill, in the center of the park, commanded the city from its 2,220-foot height; Varela held it tenaciously and positioned his artillery there.

Franco had failed to seize Madrid. His basic error, the International Brigade leader and military historian Tom Wintringham would argue, was believing that twenty-five thousand troops could capture a city of one million people determined not to give it up.

It could still be besieged. "I will destroy Madrid rather than leave it to the Marxists," Franco had sworn. Now that Germany and Italy had staked their prestige on the outcome of the Spanish conflict, they were stuck with Franco and his war. Both countries officially recognized the Franco government on 18 November 1936. "This moment," the Caudillo proclaimed to the crowd of Salamanca celebrants, "marks the peak of the life of the world!"

Hitler was stuck with Mussolini as well, and worried about the Duce's designs on the Peninsula. So far, Italy had shipped more arms to Spain than had Germany. A German general who participated in the planning said later that Hitler, "despite his firmly-emphasized friendship for Mussolini and his sympathies for Fascist Italy, was not really interested in permitting Italy to become too strong in the Mediterranean." The German military—the Wehrmacht—had organized Feuerzauber and Otto on the assumption that the war in Spain would be short. When the latest-model Soviet guns, tanks, and planes had begun arriving in mid-October, strengthening the Republic's defenses, they had pushed the war toward stalemate. Hitler responded at the end of October by authorizing the creation of an air arm, the Condor Legion, ostensibly a volunteer unit, to support the nationalist armies. According to Warlimont, "General Franco had not asked for it and indeed did not want it." He got it anyway, and under German command.

The Condor Legion deployed to Spain by ship between 6 and 18 November. It consisted initially of thirty-seven officers, 3,786 men, and ninety-two factory-new aircraft, including three squadrons of Junkers-52 bombers, three squadrons of Heinkel 51 biplane fighters, two squadrons of Heinkel 45 and Heinkel 70 reconnaissance bombers, and a seaplane squadron. Its strength grew to about six thousand men in the course of the war, but rotations for training and combat experience meant that the total of German airmen who served in Spain between 1936 and 1939 was several multiples of that number. Hitler also sent tank companies, antitank platoons, signals units, and submarines to bolster Franco's forces. Mussolini contributed not only planes, tanks, and submarines but also tens of thousands of infantry.

Before the first Soviet aircraft began arriving in Spain in November, the *New York Times*'s Herbert Matthews reports, "the Government had virtually nothing but death traps—Breguets, Potez, Dewoitines, Lockheed Vegas, all old models, purchased clandestinely from none too scrupulous agents." Most of the Spanish air force had remained loyal, unlike the officers of the Spanish army, but its planes had been outclassed. "Of that first batch of seventy-five odd pilots," Matthews writes, "I should think not more than a half-dozen remain alive. Some foreigners helped a little, particularly Malraux's French squadron, but they, too, had completely unsatisfactory planes."

Matthews in Madrid saw the first fighters of the new Republican air force on 13 November—Polikarpov I-16s, "little black monoplanes shooting across the skies. Spaniards hailed them with joy, and because of their smallness and speed, dubbed them 'Moscas' (flies). They came in ever-growing numbers." With enclosed cockpits and retractable landing gear, the I-16s were optimized for speed; not surprisingly, the rebels called them Ratas—rats. One afternoon in late November a flight of Moscas ambushed Franco's fighters flying cover for a bomber assault; they shot down no fewer than thirteen in one great air battle watched eagerly by the Madrileños below. The little Soviet fighters were effective, but the Condor Legion and Franco's fleets of German and Italian aircraft controlled the air from October forward.

Air raids had battered Madrid since Franco's forces had begun moving up the Tagus from Toledo. Deliberately designed to terrorize and kill civilians, they had been concentrated in the city's working-class districts where military targets were few. Then, to prepare for the 7 November attack on the city through the Casa de Campo, Franco's bombers had shifted to targeting antiaircraft batteries and barricades and strafing the republican lines. In mid-November, when the fighting on the ground stuttered into stalemate and the Condor Legion became available for missions, the nationalist bombing strategy changed again. Franco moved to fulfill his promise to destroy the city.

The fascist bombing had already drawn Pablo Picasso into the war. The president of the Spanish Republic, Manuel Azaña, seeking international support, had written the celebrated Spanish artist in Paris on 19 September 1936 inviting him to become honorary director of the Prado Museum. The Prado was Madrid's great storehouse of masterpieces, holding works ranging from Hieronymus Bosch's *Garden of Earthly Delights* to Raphael's *Holy Family* to Rubens's *Judgment of Paris,* El Greco's *Holy Trinity,* Velázquez's *Las Meninas,* and Goya's *Saturn Devouring His Son.* The honorary post carried no duties, and Picasso even joked about it, telling friends they would have to call him "Director." But though he was distinctly apolitical, he had "immediately accepted" the offer, he said later, because his "whole life as an artist has been nothing more than a continuous struggle against reaction and the death of art."

When the Prado was hit by artillery fire in November and then heavily bombed, so that part of its roof and upper floors collapsed, Picasso supported removing the museum's great treasures to safety away from Madrid. "An army regiment," writes Claude Bowers, "was busy packing, boxing, and moving the works of art. Money was spent for that purpose without stint. Some of the less priceless treasures were buried in the basement under layer after layer of bags of sand; some were transferred to Valencia; some were placed in vaults in the Bank of Spain until it was found too damp, when they were taken elsewhere." Elsewhere was Las Torres de Serranos, the Serrano Gates—crenellated medieval towers built into the Valencia city wall, massive enough to withstand bombing.

Franco's bomber forces had first attacked Madrid on 27 August, but the bombings that began on 10 November and continued throughout November and December were homicidal, targeting plazas and busy streets, train stations, and hospitals. The nationalists bombed Madrid twenty-three times in November alone. Between 15 and 20 November the Condor Legion began experimenting as well with starting mass fires. Three waves of bombing organized the conflagration: 2,000-pound bombs in the first wave knocked the buildings down; 220-pound bombs next made rubble; then incendiaries started fires while 22-pound shrapnel bombs kept the firemen at bay.

A journalist for a conservative Paris newspaper, Louis Delaprée, a handsome Frenchman with a pencil mustache, reported the attacks in furious prose:

[The bombs] explode, thunder, shatter, slaughter. Ambulances endlessly scour the streets in all directions, renewing their cargo of wounds and suffering once they have unloaded the previous haul at a hospital. But night falls. And then the butchery begins, the horror of the Apocalypse: the assassins wheel endlessly around the sky, releasing explosives, incendiary bombs and shrapnel.

A bomb falls into the subway entrance in the Puerta del Sol, near Alcalá, tearing up the road and sinking a crater fifteen meters deep. In San Jerónimo, a chasm opens up across the full width of the street. From 20 different places, the fire starts to consume the city.

During a brief lull, we dash to the Telephone Exchange.

The Telephone Exchange on the Gran Vía—the Telefónica—housed the foreign press office, where dispatches were censored and cables sent. At fourteen stories it was the tallest building in Spain—"a solidly built skyscraper standing on the highest spot in the center of Madrid," as Herbert Matthews describes it. "From miles around it stands out like the Eiffel Tower over Paris. It makes such a beautiful mark, in fact, that I can well imagine any conscientious artillery officer just itching to take a crack at it." It gave Delaprée a view of the entire city:

> From this extraordinary vantage point, the sight is one of unthinkable horror. A circle of flames converges on [the] Gran Vía with majestic slowness. We observe how rooftops catch fire, and houses burn downwards before crashing heavily amidst a splendor of sparks and flames. Some burnt-out buildings remain upright, like tall sinister figures, licked by reflections from the fire that continues its work further away.

"The image of future war has become clear," *Pravda* correspondent Mikhail Koltsov writes of those first days of terror bombing in Madrid. "On the threshold of 1937, fascist murderers before the eyes of the whole world are destroying an enormous European capital city. The

200 kilo. bombs can destroy five-story buildings. There were dozens of such hits. Three hundred and 500 kilo. bombs are also being used. The fragile structures in the working-class section of the city do not require much. Incendiary bombs will do the job. Yesterday," Koltsov concludes ominously, "the fascists needed flares. Today the burning city lights itself."

THREE

The Hero's Red Rag Is Laid Across His Eyes

Against the bloodshed and destruction Franco and his German and Italian collaborators were visiting upon Spain, Socorro Rojo Internacional—International Red Aid—offered humanitarian relief. The Communist International had founded SRI in 1922 as an "international political Red Cross" to aid political prisoners. In late July 1936 a telegram from SRI in Spain alerted its British counterpart, the London-based Relief Committee for the Victims of Fascism, to the opening of the Spanish conflict. The Relief Committee in turn alerted a Labor Party affiliate, the Socialist Medical Association, and within days that association had organized a Spanish Medical Aid Committee with a distinguished political, scientific, and titled membership.

"The initial work of arranging meetings and raising funds was easy," committee member and former Labor MP Leah Manning recalls. "It was quite common to raise £1,000 at a meeting, besides plates full of rings, bracelets, brooches, watches and jewelry of all kinds." At rallies on 8 and 14 August, the British public responded to the Spanish republican cause, donating more than £2,000 (about $161,000 today) to support a first British Medical Unit and equip it with surgical instruments and supplies, drugs, camping equipment, trucks, ambulances, and uniforms.

The unit's four surgeons; six nurses; four medical students; and nine drivers, cooks, secretaries, and translators—all volunteers—departed from Victoria Station on Sunday, 23 August 1936. Daimler limousines borrowed from a sympathetic London funeral service carried them past a cheering crowd of at least ten thousand Londoners, including the mayors of six London boroughs in full regalia. A month later a second group, the Scottish Ambulance, organized and funded by the wealthy coal exporter and former Glasgow University lord provost Daniel Stevenson, left for Spain with six ambulances and a van.

Modern wars depend on blood as well as bullets; controlling shock and bleeding and replacing lost blood are the first lines of defense against wounds from bullets, explosives, and shrapnel. Blood differs by type, however, and transfusion with the wrong type of blood can be fatal. Blood comes from living donors, but donors can hardly be trucked to the front lines en masse to transfuse the wounded arm to arm. Each of these problems had to be solved before blood could be used effectively on the battlefield. Doctors in the Great War solved some of them. The rest remained to challenge doctors during the war in Spain.

Blood transfusions before the twentieth century were improvised and often dangerous. Blood typing was unknown; blood was assumed to be interchangeable between humans and even between humans and animals. Not surprisingly, many patients died from blood incompatibilities, so many that by the 1870s, blood transfusion had fallen into disrepute. For the next thirty years saltwater transfusions substituted for blood, inadequately. This so-called normal saline, which is a sterile solution of salt and water with the same degree of saltiness as blood, could replace lost liquid volume, but without red blood cells it could only temporarily sustain recovery. Milk transfusions even enjoyed a brief vogue.

The discovery early in the twentieth century that blood differs by type and the development of methods for rapid blood typing made safe transfusion possible. But because blood clots when exposed to air, transfusion was still limited to various methods of immediate transfer between donor and recipient. Blood storage became possible in 1914 with the introduction of anticoagulants, most notably sodium citrate, an innovation introduced more or less simultaneously by researchers in the United States, Belgium, and Brazil.

British technique lagged behind, however. Not until April 1917, with the United States's declaration of war on Germany and the reinforcement of the British Army Medical Corps in France with U.S. Army doctors, did blood transfusion begin to be practiced widely in the field. An American of English parentage introduced the use of citrated blood. Oswald Robertson grew up in California's San Joaquin valley at the turn of the century, when the region was still a semi-wilderness. He graduated with distinction from Harvard Medical School and planned to study at the Rockefeller Institute for Medical Research in New York under pathologist Peyton Rous, who in 1915 had reported successfully transfusing citrate-treated blood after two weeks of refrigerated storage. Robertson had hardly begun research at Rockefeller when the U.S. entry into the war drew him to France with the noted surgeon Harvey Cushing's Harvard medical team.

Working out of U.S. Army Base Hospital No. 5, a twelve-thousand-bed hospital on the Channel coast at Dannes-Camiers in northern France about thirty miles below Calais, Robertson is credited with establishing the first blood bank. In fact, he had little time or need to store the blood he collected for transfusion, as a grisly but typical 30 November 1917 entry in his wartime diary reveals:

> By noon, the wounded began to arrive, then more and more till there was a solid string of ambulances extending down the road as far as you could see. We were simply deluged. We couldn't operate [on] more than a small fraction of the cases; we couldn't get rid of them as the ambulance trains were hung up several miles away—couldn't get thru because ammunition trains had the right of way. They piled up and piled up. The resuscitation ward was a veritable chamber of horrors— worse than anything before. Men were horribly mutilated—many

were dying when brought in, an occasional one had already died by the time he reached the ward. The beds were filled and we began putting stretchers on the floor. Hemorrhage, hemorrhage, hemorrhage—blood everywhere—clothes soaked in the blood, pools of blood in the stretchers, streams of blood dropping from the stretchers to the floor. I was blood up to my elbows and my rubber apron was one solid red smear. All we could do was to stop the bleeding and get the patients as comfortable as possible.

In that disaster Robertson operated nonstop until three or four in the morning before he stumbled away for a bare two hours of sleep. He learned later that the hospital had taken in 1,800 patients across twenty-four hours, trying to staunch the slaughter at Passchendaele. The cause was hopeless: more than a half million men died in that three-month series of battles, and the battle lines moved hardly five miles.

With the fundamental scientific challenges of blood transfusion met, hospitals and medical organizations in the 1920s began assembling panels of volunteer blood donors, tested for syphilis and their blood type recorded. Minnesota's Mayo Clinic maintained a list of a thousand donors; a privately organized service in London listed four hundred donors, including private citizens, police officers, and Rover Scouts, who were called seven hundred times in one typical year. The British Red Cross began managing that service in 1926. Since whole blood is perishable and demand for it in peacetime is irregular, donors were alerted day or night as needed to travel to hospitals and give blood arm to arm.

If it was easy enough in Britain to find donors willing to visit local hospitals to give blood, it was far more difficult in the Soviet Union, a vast country sprawled across eleven time zones. The Soviet surgeon Sergei S. Yudin observed the effectiveness of blood transfusion in surgery during an extended visit to the United States in 1927, when he was thirty-five years old. He admired American medical innovations, particularly those of the Mayo brothers, in whose Minnesota clinic he spent two months observing. But when a leading surgeon at the Cleveland

Clinic, George W. Crile, encouraged him to introduce an American-style blood system at home, he had to explain "that, due to poverty in Russia . . . the opportunity for blood transfusion is very limited. We operate for free, but nobody would give blood for free!"

After his return, Yudin was appointed chief surgeon at Moscow's Sklifosovsky Institute—the Sklif—a vast emergency hospital off Kolkhoz Square that served some ten thousand patients annually. There, in 1930, needing a larger blood supply than walk-in donors could provide, he began collecting blood from fresh cadavers and transfusing it, a strategy he had learned from a Soviet researcher in Kharkov who had experimented transfusing dogs with cadaver blood and concluded such blood could be used safely within ten hours of death. It even had the virtue in cases of sudden death of releasing enzymes that caused it to reliquefy after its initial clotting. Yudin published a book about cadaver blood transfusion in 1933 and reported the results of his first thousand such transfusions in the British medical journal *The Lancet* in 1937, but physicians in Western Europe, Britain, and the United States generally rejected the practice as culturally unacceptable.

Yudin also collected placental blood at the Sklif and, increasingly, blood from living donors. To make it available across the Soviet vastness he and his colleagues began treating it with sodium citrate and holding it in cold storage for weeks at a time. They set up sixty major and more than five hundred regional blood centers throughout the country to facilitate distribution.

In 1934, Frederic Duran Jordà, an innovative young Catalan physician, heard Yudin lecture in Barcelona on preserved-blood transfusion. A handsome man with a strong chin and dark, curly hair, Duran Jordà had working-class roots. His father was a self-educated carpenter who had moved his family to Barcelona and opened a wineshop when Frederic, the youngest of four boys, was ten. Frederic's teachers encouraged Amadeu Duran-Coll to send his brilliant youngest son to university. Frederic would have preferred to study chemistry; his father convinced him to study medicine instead—it paid better, his father argued, and was socially more prestigious. Duran Jordà graduated from medical school in 1928 at twenty-three.

A progressive like his father, Duran Jordà established an internal-medicine practice in Barcelona near his parents' wineshop in the working-class district of El Raval, near the harbor and crowded with brothels and bars. At Barcelona's Clinic Hospital he investigated intestinal parasites, pollen allergies, and liver function, reporting his results in the *Barcelona Medical Journal*. He learned Esperanto, an artificial language created in the late nineteenth century to foster international communication toward world peace. In a series of articles published in 1933 he proposed that Spain introduce compulsory medical insurance with physicians paid salaries rather than collecting fees. In 1935 he gave a course of public lectures on human sexuality, part of a program to educate the working class at a time when discussion of sexuality was taboo in Spain. In December 1936, with civil war threatening, he and four other physicians delivered a course of public lectures on first aid and emergency care.

In the first days of the rebellion, two of Duran Jordà's colleagues at the Clinic Hospital volunteered to serve on the Aragon front, where the nationalists held Zaragoza, the capital of Aragon on the Ebro River, two hundred miles west of Barcelona. Letters from the two volunteers to their Barcelona medical school classmate Serafina Cordoba-Palma appealed for blood services to help treat the wounded. Cordoba-Palma in turn appealed to Duran Jordà.

Duran Jordà faced the same problem at home. Fighting among Barcelona's contentious political factions was crowding the city's emergency rooms. In the rush of wounded there wasn't time or room for the tedious process of direct transfusion arm to arm. "The only solution," Duran Jordà concluded, "is a stock of well prepared and preserved blood."

The service the innovative young physician and his colleagues proceeded to set up would be the most advanced in the world at the time. It was supported by the Republican Army Health Services and the Generalitat de Catalunya—the regional government of Catalonia. An effective blood service needed "a large town," Duran Jordà says, "where the altruistic spirit of the citizens can be aroused and organized so that they volunteer as donors." Nightly radio broadcasts solicited donors, as did posters displayed throughout the city; they were solicited in their workplaces, unions, cooperatives, clubs, city districts, and small-town and village administrations on the city's outskirts. With increasing food shortages, a powerful draw to volunteering was a reward of ration certificates for extra meat, eggs, milk, and vegetables, or, later, when the blood center moved to central Barcelona, a meal in the center's dining room, which the military supplied. During the course of the war, Duran Jordà's Barcelona Blood Transfusion Service accumulated a donor pool of some 28,900 Barcelonans, the majority of them women, who contributed a pint of blood once a month.

Potential donors gave blood and urine samples and a medical history and had their reflexes checked and their chests X-rayed. Duran Jordà's team tested their blood for syphilis and malaria, typed it, and did a red-blood-cell count to exclude the anemic. Almost 90 percent of these Catalan donors had either type A or type O blood, O being the especially valuable universal type that can be transfused into any patient. Only type O was sent to the front, to eliminate the need for typing the wounded under battlefield conditions (blood-type identification on dog tags had not yet been introduced); blood of the other types was used in Barcelona and elsewhere in the rear.

Duran Jordà devised a unique blood-processing system, a flask-shaped blood bottle with a ported cap for suction. Suctioning out the donor's blood accelerated collection, although the suction had to be closely adjusted to avoid vein collapse. The Barcelona team regularly processed thirty to forty donors per hour and sometimes as many as seventy-five. After typing the blood, they filtered it through a fine-mesh silk bag to strain out any clots. They added citrate and glucose as preservatives and then, another innovation, mixed together the blood of six different donors of the same type. The mixed blood was then ported into individual tubes for refrigeration and delivery. From collection to delivery, the blood was protected from the open air to reduce the risk of clotting.

Mixing together blood of the same type from different donors had important advantages, Duran Jordà writes: "A very homogeneous blood (biologically speaking) is obtained, with a normal quantity of cells, hemoglobin, glucose, urea, and other constituents, and the product of the mixture of several bloods tends to approximate more nearly to ideal blood." Mixing the blood also reduced the risk of immune reactions, which had plagued blood transfusion before typing was understood. Duran Jordà gives as an example a surgeon who hesitates to operate on a wounded man who is near death from blood loss; with mixed universal type O blood it was possible to give 3,500 cc in one transfusion— that is, about seven pints, more than two-thirds of the entire volume of blood in the adult human body.

J. B. S. Haldane, the British biologist, would describe the effect of one such large transfusion that he observed several months later on his first mission to Spain:

> A successful transfusion is a wonderful sight. A Spanish comrade was brought in with his left arm shattered. He was as pale as a corpse. He could not move or speak. We looked for a vein in his arm, but his veins were empty. [The doctor] cut through the skin inside his right elbow, found a vein, and placed a hollow needle in it. He did not move. For some twenty minutes I held a reservoir of blood, connected to the needle by a rubber tube, at the right height to give a steady flow. As the new blood entered his vessels his color gradually returned, and with it consciousness. When we sewed up the hole in the arm he winced. He was still too weak to speak but as we left him he bent his right arm and gave us the Red Front salute.

The blood storage units Duran Jordà used were patented 300-ml (half-pint) glass tubes, closed on one end, part of a system invented by a Madrid engineer for storing saline, glucose, or other solutions and infusing them into the body. The system was called *autoinyectable rapide*—"fast autoinjectible"—and as adapted by Duran Jordà it stored the donated blood under low pressure, pushing it into the patient being transfused just as the donor's blood had been suctioned out. Once a *rapide* tube was filled and pressurized, melting its open end closed with an electric arc sealed it. Fitted with rubber tubing, a sterile filter, various clamps, and a sterile needle protected in a glass tube, the *rapide* units were then boxed and refrigerated to just above freezing. Under those conditions, Duran Jordà found, the blood would remain usable for eighteen days or more—in that way, at least, it was much like milk, which is similar to blood serum.

The pioneering blood service acquired a sturdy, four-ton Diamond T truck manufactured in Chicago and outfitted with a refrigerated van body that had been used to transport fish. Duran Jordà delivered the world's first battlefield shipment of preserved blood, seven liters, to the Aragon front in late September 1936. A second truck and a railroad car would expand delivery capability in the months to come. Blood was hauled in insulated cases to off-road posts that lacked refrigeration. Once the *rapide* tubes had stood in warm water for twenty minutes, a first-aid technician could begin transfusing a wounded soldier in a matter of seconds—the time it took to roll up a sleeve, swab the injection site, and insert the needle, conveniently hanging the *rapide* tube from a tunic buttonhole.

Commercial air service was still operating in republican Spain despite the war, and in late October 1936 André Malraux had flown to Paris to round up spare parts and ammunition for his ailing *escuadrilla España*. With the arrival of modern Soviet fighters and bombers, many of them built from licensed American designs, Malraux's decrepit squadron of Great War–era aircraft had been relegated to secondary fronts; it flew first out of Albacete and then from a base near Valencia, on the Mediterranean 220 miles southeast of Madrid. "The only rebel plane which has showed any superiority over the Russian-American models," Herbert Matthews reports, "is the German Junkers bomber. The Italian Savoia-Marchetti and Caproni bombers, the German Heinkels, and the Italian Fiat and Romeo combat planes have all proved inferior to the Russian machines." The *escuadrilla España* lost its independence as well, absorbed into the republican air force when the experienced new Red Army advisers who arrived with Soviet aid began organizing the Republic's ad hoc fighting elements into an effective military. Malraux soldiered on.

Traveling from Paris to Madrid on 3 November on the same commercial flight as Malraux was the doctor whom J. B. S. Haldane would observe transfusing a wounded soldier early in the new year. Norman Bethune, a forty-six-year-old firebrand Canadian thoracic surgeon and an ardent communist, was flying to Spain to contribute his services to the republican cause. He was aware that Malraux would be returning on the same flight; the record is silent on whether they talked.

Bethune was lean, strong, and prematurely bald, with high cheekbones and chiseled features. He was arrogant and explosive when challenged but caring and attentive with his patients and with children. He had shipped for Spain after two years of campaigning unsuccessfully at home for a national health service. Officially, Bethune represented the Canadian Committee to Aid Spanish Democracy (CASD), an entity sponsored by the Canadian League Against War and Fascism, a political coalition of several hundred labor and educational organizations with a combined membership of some 300,000 Canadians. And though he is usually said to have discovered a need for a frontline blood transfusion service after he arrived in Spain—and indeed is often credited with having developed the first such service in the world, despite the Duran Jordà team's clear priority—he had decided at least a month before he left Canada that a mobile transfusion service would be the best use of the CASD's resources. Word had come from President Manuel Azaña himself through Canadian Communist Party leaders who visited Spain in the second month of the war that medical services and supplies were the Republic's greatest need. And Bethune wanted his contribution to be visible, not submerged in routine military medicine. Publicity about an independent Canadian service would encourage further Canadian donations to the Spanish cause.

Bethune spoke no Spanish. After he had found a room at the Gran Vía Hotel, opposite the Telefónica building, he met up with the man assigned by the CASD to guide him. A Canadian-resident, Spanish-speaking Dane and fellow communist named Henning Sorensen was his translator and liaison with the republican government. Bethune had arrived just in time for the nationalist attack on Madrid through the Casa de Campo and the battle of University City. He and Sorensen toured several of the fifty-seven hospitals extant or improvised in hotels throughout the city with the battle raging around them. They walked out to the front lines in University City and reviewed the casualty stations there. "They passed through streets where buildings were aflame or had been reduced to smoldering rubble," write Bethune's biographers Roderick and Sharon Stewart. "In the Avenida Castellana they had to throw themselves to the ground, narrowly escaping injury as a bomb exploded nearby." Bethune saw shortages everywhere of medicine and staff. "Privately," another of his biographers, David Lethbridge, reports, "he noted the totally inadequate facilities for blood transfusion, and he knew that the people of Madrid were dying because of blood shortage."

Riding down to Albacete with Carlos Contreras, the political commander of the tough communist Fifth Regiment, which was leading the fight to save Madrid, Bethune found "notable optimism" about eventual victory and encouragement for his plans. Contreras reviewed Bethune's alternatives: he could work as a surgeon in one of the hospitals or with the International Brigades, or he could set up a Canadian Medical Unit to serve in the cities or at the front. Anything he decided would be helpful, and Contreras would support him in whatever he chose to do.

In muddy Albacete Bethune met the chief of the International Brigades' Foreign Health Service, "a little Frenchman who suggested I work with him. It was something to consider, and we left Albacete with him the following day (November 8) to 'inspect the front lines.' We never got anywhere near a front line and we lost our way four times. That was enough for me. We wasted two days with him for nothing. I told him politely as I could that I had other plans, and we returned to Madrid, luckily getting transportation on a truck." Bethune had served as a stretcher bearer in the Canadian army during the Great War and had been wounded at the Second Battle of Ypres, where the casualties exceeded 100,000; he knew war well enough. "I couldn't work with the bastard," he told Sorensen. "He doesn't know what he's doing."

"Unless we were able to offer the Government some definite proposal and concrete scheme our efforts would peter out," Bethune reported to the CASD. He intended to fly the Canadian flag, not merely join the line. "It seems better to emulate England and Scotland and establish ourselves as a definite entity. England has the 'English Hospital,' Scotland has the 'Scottish Ambulance.'" In Valencia, to which the Spanish government had just retreated from Madrid, the "definite proposal" Bethune offered the Socorro Rojo was his plan for a Canadian Blood Transfusion Service, based in Madrid, which would collect blood there from the civilian population, citrate and refrigerate it, and deliver it to the battlefield.

The SRI doctors were skeptical at first. In the confusion of multiple authorities in the early months of the war, not even they were aware of Duran Jordà's fully operational blood service in Barcelona. Bethune marshaled facts and passionate argument and won their support, with the proviso that the money for such a service would come from Canada. Bethune assured them it would. Sorensen was horrified, knowing Bethune had no authority to commit the CASD financially. Afterward the surgeon dismissed Sorensen's foreboding: how could the committee refuse?

The Madrid to which Bethune and Sorensen returned that third week in November 1936 was suffering under intense Condor Legion bombardment. Mikhail Koltsov described it in *Pravda* in a dispatch datelined 19 November:

> The last two days were the most horrible that the city has experienced. Madrid is burning. On the streets it is hot and light on a November night. Enormous fires light my way. The German aviation has fired the city. Public buildings, hospitals, hotels, houses are burning. The residential areas are in flames. The firemen cannot cope with the inferno. They lack the equipment to control the flames. . . . The firemen are trying to prevent explosions and casualties. They are cutting gas mains, removing gasoline and evacuating threatened areas.
>
> There have been many nervous breakdowns. This is just the beginning. The fascists are reacting in a blind rage, hoping to force the city to surrender. They have concentrated all their aviation here. During the day twenty Junkers and thirty fighters were over Madrid. Republican aviation is much weaker. Courage cannot compensate for the numbers of the foe. Two Nazi fighters and two Nazi bombers were knocked down. The bombardment was renewed every three hours. Crowds prayed in the streets. Most of Madrid's windows were blown out.

Bethune cabled the CASD describing his plan and the financial commitment it required. He needed a vehicle for transporting blood to the front lines, but none was for sale in Spain. He directed the CASD to Paris for money transfer. On Saturday, 21 November, he and Sorensen flew there, to find an American Express money order awaiting them for $3,000 (about $51,000 today). As Bethune had predicted, the CASD had supported his plan. "A really snappy service can be set up," he wrote the CASD chairman, Benjamin Spence, giddily, "with special badges for donors, stars for each donation . . . it's a beautiful idea . . . and Canadian!"

There were no cars for sale in Paris, either, at least none of the kind Bethune wanted, a station wagon capable of carrying up to one and a half tons of equipment and supplies to serve as an ambulance but comfortably load four passengers. Ever impatient, Bethune decided to leave Sorensen in Paris searching out medical supplies while he ran up to London. There he found the station wagon he wanted, a Ford with light-colored wood exterior trim, of the type Americans called a woody; the Spanish would call the Bethune blood wagon *la rubia,* the blonde. He paid £175 for it and had a rooftop luggage rack added and storage boxes built in.

Through the informal network of Montrealers living in London— in this case, the brother of one of Bethune's former lovers—he picked up another acolyte, a wealthy young Canadian architect named Hazen Sise. As soon as they met, Sise recalls, Bethune "immediately started launching into a description of what Madrid was like under the siege, what the incredible emotion was of a people's army in resistance, the whole citizenry of Madrid manning the barricades, and the emotion of the first of the International Brigades marching into the line at University City." A galvanized Sise responded, "My gosh, I would like to go with you." Later, after dinner and a public rally in Albert Hall, he urged Bethune, "I'm quite serious about this. I would like to go back with you. I've been so immensely concerned for months about what is going on there." Bethune could use a driver and general assistant. When the CASD cabled its approval, he added Sise to his team.

Telegraphing Sorensen to join him in London, Bethune proceeded to stock *la rubia* with the equipment and supplies he would need to sustain his blood transfusion unit. Everything had to be mobile. His refrigerator ran on kerosene, his autoclave—for sterilizing solutions, bottles, instruments, and dressings—on gasoline. The autoclave alone weighed 450 pounds; with the other apparatus, including a kerosene-powered water still, the total weight came to nearly a ton. "They take up the major part of the interior," Bethune reported.

He found room for more: 175 pieces of glassware including vacuum bottles, blood flasks, drip bottles, and containers; three complete direct transfusion sets; a complete set of instruments for Bethune's specialty, thoracic surgery; hurricane lamps; gas masks; chemicals to make up solutions for intravenous injections; a three-month supply of glucose and sodium citrate, all the chemicals packaged in watertight tins in measured weights, ready for mixing.

Despite the urgency of his mission, the Canadian surgeon took time to have a batch of silk shirts made for himself—using CASD funds—and custom uniforms for all three men, one-piece jumpsuits like the *monos* of the republican militias but cloth-belted and light blue, with a red cross and the word "Canada" embroidered on the chest pocket. Nattily outfitted, they ferried the loaded Ford across the Channel and drove down to Paris, hung a canvas sign on the door identifying themselves as the Service Canadien de Transfusion, and followed the Rhône valley south to Port Bou, where they passed through customs. For five hours they continued down the Spanish coast to Barcelona, where they stopped overnight for repairs—the garage manager refused to charge them—then drove twelve more hours to Valencia, arriving late Wednesday, 9 December 1936. The French had demanded they pay customs duties on their vehicle and all their medical gear despite its humanitarian purpose, another burden the nonintervention nonsense imposed.

The Socorro Rojo had just the place for them, Bethune learned in Valencia: the luxurious fifteen-room Madrid apartment of the German Embassy's Spanish legal counsel—"Fascist," Bethune says, "now in Berlin"—on the second floor of a seven-story building in the prosperous Salamanca district, where many embassies were located and which Franco's forces had excluded from their shelling and bombing campaigns. The Socorro Rojo itself occupied the floor above. The district was no haven, however. Louis Delaprée, the French journalist, had sketched its miseries in a late-November dispatch:

This district, with its elegant houses, has been spared by the shells and bombs. It has been rumored that several days ago Franco's planes dropped leaflets ordering the civilians to take refuge in these bourgeois streets. Nobody has seen these "butterflies," but all believe in the immunity of the Salamanca district. So they are going there, by families, by entire blocks, as crowds of emigrants. The heads of households walk in front, carrying mattresses on their heads. Behind, the children splash through the dirty streets, without laughing, without smiling, with their somnambulant eyes, with their faces pinched and drawn like little old people. Women bring up the rear, their arms laden with household effects. Donkeys, loaded to the breaking point, trot along in the midst of these moving throngs.

When these tribes of emigrants reach the Salamanca district, they stop, and despair drops like a mask of ashes on all faces. The place is taken. Thousands of people are camping in the open, exposed to wind and rain.

The households are reconstituted, with chairs around tables, cooking utensils, mattresses, beds. Only around these abstract dwellings, there are no walls; above there are no roofs.

Twenty thousand people are living like this in the rain and cold.

Arriving there from Valencia, Bethune's team chose the apartment's former library for its operations center, "the walls entirely lined by 8,000 books," Bethune noted with delight, "gold brocade curtains and Aubusson carpets!" The apartment foyer would serve as a waiting room; the central room off the foyer would hold two operating tables for blood donors, worktables, a refrigerator, and an autoclave. Bethune claimed the best bedroom, off the library, but there were bedrooms down the long hall to the kitchen for Sorensen and Sise, service staff, and guests passing through.

In mid-December, Bethune & Company began soliciting blood donations from the people of Madrid. Back in Key West, Florida, Ernest Hemingway was still dithering. "I've got to go to Spain," he wrote Max Perkins on 15 December. "But there's no great hurry. They'll be fighting for a long time and it's cold as hell around Madrid now!"

FOUR

Bombs Falling Like Black Pears

Ernest Hemingway's mid-December 1936 assessment of the civil war in Spain, "They'll be fighting for a long time," reflected Franco's failure to take Madrid. A final brutal clash had begun at Pozuelo, west of the Casa de Campo, on 29 November between the nationalists' Moroccan and German forces and the Republic's less numerous Spanish fighters and international volunteers. German and Italian tank companies, German signal units, and American gasoline and oil supported Franco's battalions. The republicans marshaled inadequate supplies, but they still dominated the battle with their superior Soviet tanks and aircraft.

Nationalist general José Enrique Varela launched a surprise attack against Pozuelo that November Sunday morning with infantry and cavalry, followed by tank units. Condor Legion Junkers bombers softened up the lines for Franco's Moroccans; Stuka dive-bombers, the first to see combat in Europe, joined the attack as well. But the machine guns of the German tanks were no match for Soviet tanks armed with cannon, and swarms of Moscas harassed the German aircraft. The nationalist line advanced no farther than the Pozuelo cemetery.

Both sides had sustained major losses in the weeks of fighting for Madrid, each counting some fifteen thousand casualties. A thousand men among the three thousand International Brigaders who had marched through Madrid to join the republican defense were killed. At that awful cost the Spanish capital was saved. The victory filled Madrileños with hope. The *No pasaran* banners came down and new banners proclaiming *Nosotros pasaramos*—"We shall pass"—went up. The Madrid defense junta put a stop as well to most of the killing of priests and the summary executions of imprisoned fascist army officers.

(The worst single republican barbarism, the November massacre of prisoners held in the Cárcel Modelo—the Model Prison—in Madrid, saw some two to three thousand men and women bused to Paracuellos del Jarama and nearby Torrejón de Ardoz, northeast of Madrid near the Barajas airfield, beginning on 7 November 1936, when Franco's forces had just launched their main ground attack on Madrid. In three days of bloody work between 7 and 10 November, the prisoners were shot into mass graves. Communists in the republican government ordered and carried out the massacre. La Pasionaria had branded the prisoners and their like with General Mola's notorious "fifth column" label, and the Comintern's delegate in Spain, Boris Stepanov, would report to Stalin that the communists "in a couple of days carried out the operations necessary to cleansing Madrid of fifth columnists." Certainly it was an atrocity. But Franco's mass killings were both more numerous and more vicious, perpetrated even against communities that had surrendered without resistance.)

With Red Army generals now advising a professional general staff, the Republic's military was transforming an ad hoc defense into a professional operation. "From the exaltation of the first weeks of November," Colodny says, "the city passed to the grim monotony of siege, complicated by cold and hunger and the familiar spectacle of air-borne death and desolation." At least the bombings decreased. One late November afternoon, Herbert Matthews reports, "Russian planes laid a trap for the rebel air force over Madrid and shot down no less than thirteen Italian and German chasers. . . . Franco had already been stopped on the ground; now he was stopped in the air." Only over Madrid, however. Nationalist aircraft bombed the rest of Spain with near impunity.

Weakened by these defeats, Franco turned to Italy and Germany for reinforcements. The Duce was willing to send ground forces; Hitler was not. Some six thousand Italian troops landed at Cadiz on 22 December 1936, another four thousand in early January 1937, the first of many thousands yet to come.

Editors put celebrity news ahead of war reports in the 1930s just as they do today. By December 1936 the Spanish war had slowed to a grinding near stalemate that editors no longer considered newsworthy, while Edward VIII, the king of England, had abdicated his throne for a Baltimore divorcée, telling the British people on 11 December, "I have found it impossible to carry the heavy burden of responsibility, and to discharge my duties as King as I would wish to do, without the help and support of the woman I love." For the French journalist Louis Delaprée, who had been covering the war in Spain since its first days in late July, Wallis Simpson and Edward VIII's invasion of the front page was the last straw. His newspaper, *Paris-soir,* had increasingly cut, censored, and buried the stories he filed as they had expressed his increasing outrage at the savagery of Franco's bombing attacks on Madrid. Geoffrey Cox saw Delaprée in Madrid's Miami Bar on the evening of 4 December defending his newspaper to a suspicious civilian, a Spaniard convinced that anyone writing for *Paris-soir* must be a fascist. "But how can I be?" Cox quotes Delaprée as saying in defense. "I was sent away from Burgos by Franco's people because they did not like what I wrote. Do you call that Fascist?"

Cox thought Delaprée was "one of the finest people I have met— intelligent, human, cheerful, courageous, good-looking." He was "that rare type who is liked by both men and women" and "a journalist of the first rank." That same night, at the Telefónica, Delaprée had dictated a final bitter message to his editor at *Paris-soir:*

You have not published half my articles. That is your right. But I would have thought your friendship would have spared me useless work. For three weeks I have been getting up at 5 a.m. in order to give you the news for your first editions. You have made me work for the wastepaper basket. Thanks. I am taking a plane on Sunday unless I meet the fate of Guy de Traversay [a reporter for another newspaper, killed in Majorca], which would be a good thing, wouldn't it, for thus you should have your martyr also. In the meantime, I am sending nothing more. It is not worth the trouble. The massacre of a hundred Spanish children is less interesting than a sigh from Mrs. Simpson, the royal whore.

Delaprée's prediction came true, though not in the way he expected. He flew out not on Sunday but on the following Tuesday, 8 December, on an Air France plane chartered to the French government; the converted Potez 54 bomber, which carried embassy mail and personnel and sometimes non-embassy passengers between Madrid and Paris, had to be repaired twice between Sunday and Tuesday for mechanical problems.

One of the other non-embassy passengers was a Swiss, Dr. Georges Henny, who represented the International Committee of the Red Cross in Madrid. Henny had learned of the Paracuellos and Torrejón de Ardoz massacres, and had even toured the killing sites and seen the arms and legs of half-buried corpses sticking out of the ground. He carried with him a report he intended to present to the League of Nations security council, due to meet in Geneva. Besides Henny, Delaprée, and French journalist André Château of the Havas news agency, there were two children aboard the plane, "two little daughters of the Brazilian Ambassador," according to the British journalist Sefton Delmer.

Delmer believed the Soviet NKVD *rezident* in Spain, Alexander Orlov, acted that December Tuesday to prevent Henny and his report from reaching the League. Orlov could have stopped the Air France flight from departing, Delmer writes, but he had a more effective strategy in mind: "So the diplomatic courtesies were observed and the embassy aircraft with Dr. Henny, Delaprée and the [other passengers] safely aboard was allowed to take off." Delmer's account at this point is garbled, but the pilot testified later that an unknown plane buzzed the French charter not long after takeoff. "Some time later," writes the historian Martin Minchom, "when the Potez 54 had reached the Guadalajara region, it was attacked by a second aircraft, a biplane, at an altitude of about 10,000 feet." The Potez 54 crash-landed in a field, flipping over as it did so. Delmer picks up the story: "Two passengers were killed outright, Dr. Henny was slightly wounded, and Delaprée was hit by a bullet which came up through the seat of his chair and bedded itself in his abdomen."

An abdominal wound was usually fatal in that era before antibiotics. Delaprée was unaware of his terminal condition when Delmer visited him at the convent clinic in Guadalajara where he had been taken for treatment, but a priest had asked Delmer to encourage the French journalist to accept extreme unction. Delmer suggested it but didn't press Delaprée; urging him to accept the sacrament would have signaled to him that he was dying.

Instead, they discussed the identity of the plane that had attacked the French charter—a Soviet air force plane, Delmer says, "clearly identified by its republican markings." Evidently Delaprée also believed a Soviet pilot had attacked the Air France plane, which was in transition from military service to civilian use and not clearly marked, but believed the attack had been a mistake. "I cannot think why they did it," the dying man told Delmer. "It must have been some stupid misunderstanding." It may have been. A Red Army pilot, Georgi Zakharov, who arrived in Spain in October 1936 to fly Moscas under the alias "Enrique Lores," has been identified in Russian sources as the pilot. The Republic never reprimanded Zakharov, however, while the Soviet Union awarded him the Order of the Red Banner and promoted him to captain for his multiple kills in aerial combat over Spain.

Delaprée died on Friday, 11 December 1936. As he had bitterly predicted, Delmer writes, he got "the full treatment by his newspaper . . . a kind of Viking's funeral." But the Delaprée affair wasn't over. Someone—probably the French journalist Georges Soria, Minchom speculates—acquired the copies of Delaprée's dispatches to *Paris-soir* filed with the censor's office in the Telefónica, uncut copies with all their outrage intact, and leaked them to a rival newspaper, the Communist *L'Humanité*. During the Christmas season, *L'Humanité* prepared to report the scandal of their suppression. And unlike *Paris-soir*, *L'Humanité* was a newspaper Picasso read.

At the beginning of December 1936, Geoffrey Cox reports, "for one moment it looked as if Franco would use gas. Ten men of the International Column were taken to hospital suffering from the fumes from exploded rebel shells. The doctors declared their symptoms were exactly similar to those produced by a gas of the Green Cross type." The Green Cross designation came from a standard marking on the base of German gas shells used in the Great War that designated lung agents, typically a mixture of chloropicrin and phosgene. Gas had been outlawed under the League of Nations Geneva Protocol of 1925, but Spain's King Alfonso XIII had authorized its use in Morocco against the forces of Abd El-Krim, and Mussolini had used it against Haile Selassie's Ethiopians in 1935–36.

The Spanish government shipped truckloads of French gas masks to the front lines and sought an expert in poison gases to advise it on anti-gas precautions for civilians. J. B. S. Haldane, the British biologist, had been waiting for this opportunity.

John Burdon Sanderson Haldane, known as Jack, was a big man, tall, burly, and abrupt, forty-four years old in 1936. The journalist Charlotte Franken, whom he later married, first encountered him at Cambridge in 1924 when she sought his advice about a book she was writing. If she had hoped for a conversation, she got a lecture instead. "When he talked," she recalls, "it was like listening to a living encyclopedia."

Haldane tended to bark to disguise his shyness. He could be brusque to the point of rudeness. A warm, compassionate man, committed to social justice, he was also a gifted biologist. The blunders and slaughter of the Great War had made him a socialist. After taking a first-class degree in mathematics and classics at Oxford University in 1912, he fought in that war as an artillery officer, in France and Mesopotamia, and was twice seriously wounded.

Haldane's father was an Oxford physiologist who studied respiration. John Scott Haldane had discovered the function of hemoglobin, the metalloprotein in red blood cells that transports oxygen, as well as the action of carbon monoxide in blocking that transport. He was an expert on noxious gases in mines. The British government had turned to him in April 1915 when Germany initiated the first use of poison gas—chlorine—against French troops at Ypres. J. S. Haldane had pulled his twenty-two-year-old son from the front lines to help develop a gas mask that could protect Allied soldiers. Jack Haldane went to work with other volunteers under his father's supervision testing gas masks in a hospital in St. Omer, ten miles inland from Calais. "There was a small glass-fronted room," young Haldane recalls, "like a miniature greenhouse, into which known volumes of chlorine were liberated. We had to compare the effects on ourselves of various quantities with and without respirators. It stung the eyes and produced a tendency to gasp and cough when breathed." The volunteers also worked a heavy wheel in the constricting masks and ran fifty-yard sprints outdoors. "None of us was much the worse for the gas," Haldane writes nonchalantly, "or in any real danger, as we knew when to stop, but some had to go to bed for a few days, and I was very short of breath and incapable of running for a month or so."

Haldane's nonchalance about danger was typical, and rooted in a careful estimation of risk; he was legendary among soldiers for the nerveless pleasure he took in frontline fighting—"this truly enviable life," he called it, though few of his compatriots agreed. He knew enough to throw himself into the nearest ditch when enemy planes came by, a reflex that, once acquired, stayed with him for weeks afterward even in safety well behind the lines.

Haldane had published a small book about poison gas in 1925, *Callinicus: A Defence of Chemical Warfare*. In the book he argues that gas is more humane than high explosives, since in the case of gas "those who did not die almost all recovered completely." He cites his own near-death experiences in comparison:

> I regard the type of wound produced by the average [high-explosive] shells as, on the whole, more distressing than the pneumonia caused by chlorine or phosgene. Besides being wounded, I have been buried alive, and on several occasions in peacetime I have been asphyxiated to the point of unconsciousness. The pain and discomfort arising from the other experiences were utterly negligible compared with those produced by a good septic shell-wound.

Not many agreed with him about gas warfare, either.

In the 1930s, besides teaching at University College London, conducting research in genetics, and writing bestselling books and articles about science for the general public, Haldane had begun working to help the victims of European fascism. With the outbreak of the Spanish Civil War he turned to speaking at public rallies to raise money to support the International Brigades then organizing.

Whether Haldane went looking for the war or the war came to him isn't clear from the record. Charlotte Haldane—the Haldanes were married in 1926—reports him eager to go to Madrid. As she tells the story, she opened the way. Her son by an earlier marriage, Ronnie, was sixteen years old and wanted to go to Spain to fight. She tried to persuade the boy otherwise, but since she herself was speaking at rallies and raising funds to send volunteers, she didn't feel she could deny her son his choice. She raised the question with her husband. "J.B.S. said it was not for him to decide," she writes, "and rightly. But that if Ronnie went he insisted on only one thing: he must have a gas-mask."

To acquire a gas mask for her son, Mrs. Haldane went to see Harry Pollitt, the general secretary of the Communist Party of Great Britain, in his office up a stairway behind the Party's propaganda bookshop in Covent Garden. "Pollitt was a short, square, virile individual," she recalls, "hardly taller than myself, [with] a mischievous grin. 'Well,' he said, in a dour north-country accent, but a pleasant baritone voice, 'Ah suppose ye've coom to tell me 'e can't go?'"

No, she told him, she had not, but J.B.S. insisted Ronnie had to have a gas mask. Pollitt was just then in the process of tracking down a supply of gas masks to equip the international volunteers. Charlotte Haldane brought the two men together, and Haldane's connection with Pollitt began his direct involvement in the war. He saw Pollitt and discussed gas masks. He saw the Spanish ambassador and discussed deep bomb shelters. He wanted to go to Madrid, his wife writes. "So he got himself a most curious outfit, a motor-cyclist's cap with a visor, and black leather jacket and breeches, and went." In the meantime, according to Cox, "lorry loads of gas masks of French design were hurried forward to the troops."

An Irish International Brigade volunteer, Joe Monks, saw Haldane in Albacete on 17 December—in the Casa Salamanca, where they were being fed. It seems Haldane spoke to them. Monks reports him "spending his Christmas vacation as an adviser to the defenders of Madrid on matters to do with the enemy's suspected use of gas bombs and shells." Monks's company was the first to be assigned to the new Fifteenth International Brigade—the IB—which included Americans, Canadians, and Europeans and was English-speaking. After Haldane's Casa Salamanca speech the company marched out to the town bullring and listened to André Marty, the excitable French communist who was commander of the Albacete training camp.

The Red Volunteers from the Dublin Brigade, as they called themselves, had to train without weapons. Lacking rifles, Monks writes—none was available—"our training concentrated on the relationship that exists between the infantryman, under fire, and the kindly earth to which he must cling for most of the time if he is to go on living. It was up, plunge forward and down faster than one got up. Nothing . . . was beneath notice. The low scrub or the wisp of dry grass, nodding in the breeze. These were the things that might save one's life; that might cause a foe to send a bullet on a path which lay an all-important one eighth of an inch away from one's skull." Rifles arrived two days before Christmas. Haldane arrived in Madrid the same day, stiff from a night ride up from Albacete in an open truck.

The British scientist found quarters in the comfortable apartments Norman Bethune had commandeered, and Bethune assigned Hazen Sise to assist him. In a photograph that survived the war, Haldane and Sise pose before the rubble of a bombed-out building, Sise standing easy wearing a gas mask, Haldane beside him with his left hand on the younger man's shoulder and what appears to be the gas-mask case under his right arm. Haldane, who is explaining how to adjust the mask, has ditched his leathers for dark fatigue pants and a fatigue blouse worn over a sweater, a matching fatigue cap warming his balding head.

After several weeks of careful inspections, Haldane concluded that the nationalist and republican trenches in the Casa de Campo were too close together and too meandering for effective gas warfare. Gas blows around, making blowback a serious threat. Nor were the lines of men sufficiently concentrated. "Gas is effective if you have a great deal of it," he writes, "but the amount needed is enormous." Gas was not used against Spanish towns for the same reason. It also only slowly leaks into houses, especially unheated houses with no fires to draw in outside air, "and there is very little fuel in loyal Spain." He estimates it would take at least ten times as much gas to poison people in their houses as to poison them outdoors. Overall, Haldane concludes, you can kill a lot more people with high explosives than with gas bombs: "Franco's friends in England say that he does not use gas for humanitarian reasons. Anyone who has seen even a few children killed by high explosive bombs will dismiss this statement as nonsense."

Haldane had expected to find Madrid's population panicked by the

German and Italian bombings. "A few people camped in one of the Madrid Metro stations," he discovered to the contrary, "but I never heard of anyone sleeping in a cellar. It simply 'wasn't done' to be frightened, though of course there were isolated cases. But on the whole everyone carried on." In the first air raid Haldane experienced after arriving in Madrid he found the Madrileños more than carrying on: they leaned out of windows, he says, to watch the fun.

Such bravura might cause extra casualties, Haldane agrees, but the people of Madrid were determined to set an example for the men in the front lines. It worked. "The militia rallied. They felt that they could not let such people down. If there had been a panic evacuation of civilians I think it is quite likely that the army would have run too."

All sorts of activities continue in wartime under regular bombing and shelling, from banking to research in genetics, Haldane's specialty. Busy as he was in Madrid, the British scientist found time to look up his fellow biologists and inquire about their research. In a letter to the British journal *Nature* that winter, he reported that a professor I. de Zulueta, when not busy hiding the exhibits of the Museum of Science in the museum's bombproof cellar, was continuing his research on beetles (recalling Haldane's famous quip about that most varied of all insects, "God has an inordinate fondness for beetles"). Another professor Haldane found "very appropriately" breeding the explosive cucumber *Ecballium elaterium,* which blasts open to disperse its seeds when the spikes on its case are triggered, like an old-fashioned harbor mine, as they would be when the fruit fell ripened to the ground. An air raid interrupted their discussions, Haldane concludes drily, but no bombs fell near them that day, and when he left the Museum of Science it was still intact.

Haldane's disgust with Franco's bombing of civilians matched his admiration for the people of Madrid who were experiencing it. Franco's propagandists in Britain had painted the loyalist Spanish people as communist scum, Reds no more worthy of military restraint than the Rif peoples of North Africa had been when Franco and his fellow

Africanistas had fought them in the 1920s with unrestrained violence and poison gas. To counter that propaganda, Haldane delivered several radio talks during and after his visit. One in particular recalled his experience of Madrid on Christmas Day 1936.

Courage, Haldane testified, was not the only virtue he found among Madrileños. They were short of fuel and it was cold—the coal lines were longer than the bread lines—yet even those who had been billeted in commandeered houses didn't burn the furniture or strip the woodwork. Nor had they cut down many trees; rather than mutilate their elegant capital, they suffered the cold instead. Madrid was "extremely orderly" despite the absence of policemen. The Madrileños had "put themselves under a voluntary discipline," Haldane thought. "They believe that their efforts and sacrifices will mean the death of Fascism, and the birth of a new social order. They are determined that their fight shall be noble, not only in its main plan, but in its tiniest details." He concluded his broadcast enthusiastically: "And that is why, if I lived for a thousand years, it might still be my proudest boast that on Christmas day, 1936, I was a citizen of Madrid."

The *New York Times*'s Herbert Matthews was in Madrid that Christmas as well, having finally arranged credentials and made his way into republican Spain on 2 December. He'd been working in the Telefónica the previous day when it was shelled as usual at teatime—the sturdy, reinforced-concrete building, an easy target for the nationalist artillery on Garabitas Hill, lost an occasional cornice but otherwise held up well. "While the rest of the world celebrated Christmas Eve," he writes, "Madrileños returned sadly to homes whose menfolk were dead, wounded, or fighting, and to dinners that except in rare cases consisted of barely enough to keep them alive."

They fared better at the American Embassy, Matthews notes; the ambassador "had scraped together a fabulous meal." At midnight at the embassy they ate the traditional twelve grapes that Madrileños usually ate in the Puerta del Sol to mark the arrival of the holiday. Franco had something uglier in mind: "At the same time the rebels sent twelve high explosives into the vicinity of the square, thus ushering in the holiday with a characteristic display of vicious levity."

Franco's forces delivered a brutal shelling on Christmas afternoon in the vicinity of the Telefónica. "The street cleared as if by magic," Matthews reports, "but not before a shell had struck at the corner of Calle Chincilla, literally tearing three men and a woman apart. Ironically enough, that was on the supposedly safe side of the street. The pavement was literally running with blood when we got up there. I had read in books about 'streets running blood' but never thought to see it."

Shells hit the Telefónica eleven times that afternoon. "Of all the damage I contemplated," Matthews concludes, "nothing impressed me so much as the splinters of glass which had been driven in one room from the street windows across the room and a corridor, embedding themselves deeply in the wall just like darts."

Hitler had a Christmas gift for Spain as well. He delivered it privately at a conference in the Reich Chancellery on 22 December. Goering attended, as did the commanders of the other military services and Germany's ambassador to Spain, General Wilhelm von Faupel. Faupel recommended sending a large body of ground forces to Spain to ensure Franco's early victory. No one else in the room agreed. Hitler explained his cynical reasoning for continuing limited support to Franco: "German policy would be advanced if the Spanish question continued for a time to occupy Europe's attention and therefore diverted it from Germany." Or in plain English: dragging out the war in Spain would keep France and Britain busy while Germany prepared its moves and rearmed. Franco would get the Condor Legion and little more.

"We were heavily bombed from the air today about 12 noon," Norman Bethune reminded his fellow Canadians of Christmas season conditions in Spain in a shortwave radio broadcast home. The surgeon spoke of "twelve huge Italian tri-motored bombers" that passed over the city that day to bomb women, children, and old people in the poor neighborhood of Cuatro Caminos. "People hurried to 'refugios,'" Bethune continued, referring to the Madrid air raid shelters; "a hush fell over the city—it was a hunted animal crouched down in the grass, quiet and apprehensive. . . . Then in the dead silence of the streets the songs of birds came startlingly clear in the bright winter air."

The bombers that Bethune calls "huge" were smaller than a modern airliner. They appeared huge because they flew low; they flew low and slowly, bombing where they chose, because Madrid lacked antiaircraft weapons. The Western democracies' policy of nonintervention denied the Spanish Republic such weapons; it bought the few it had from the Soviet Union.

Continuing his broadcast, Bethune sounds as if he's been discussing the effects of bombing with Haldane. "It is practically useless to go into a building" for protection, he says—"even a ten-storey building. The bombs tear through the roof, through every floor in the building and explode in the basement, bringing down concrete buildings as if they were made of matchwood." At this point in history, hardly any civilians had yet been bombed in this way except in the colonies of the Great Powers; bombing civilians simply to spread terror was a new excrescence of airpower theory in that 1936 holiday season:

> It is not much safer to be in the basement or the lower floors, than in the upper stories. One takes shelter in doorways to be out of the way of falling masonry, huge pieces of facade and stone work. If the building you happen to be in is hit, you will be killed or wounded. If it is not hit, you will not be killed or wounded. One place is really as good as another.
>
> After the bombs fall—and you can see them falling like great black pears—there is a thunderous roar. Clouds of dust and explosive fumes fill the air, whole sides of houses fall into the street. From heaps of huddled clothes on the cobblestones blood begins to flow—these were once live women and children.

Bombs falling like great black pears—such was the bitter fruit that year of Spanish Christmas. More help was arriving, but not much— Soviet food ships and foreign volunteers. The Spanish people welcomed it. "They look at each other sorrowfully," Bethune radioed his countrymen from blacked-out Madrid, "and when they talk of the fascist assassins, their faces express fortitude, dignity and contempt."

PART TWO

Dream and Lie of Franco

FIVE

Fandangos of Shivering Owls

At the beginning of the year 1937, more than a half million men, divided more or less equally between republican and nationalist, fought for control of Spain. The republicans still held the Mediterranean coast, although the nationalists occupied the island of Mallorca, east of Valencia about two hundred miles, from which German and Italian aircraft bombed republican ports and shipping. Inland from the coast, republican forces controlled the eastern half of the country—Catalonia, Valencia, Castile–La Mancha, Madrid, Murcia, and part of Andalusia. Franco's nationalists held the western half—Andalusia, Extremadura, Castile and León, Galicia, La Roija, and Navarre—except for the Basque region along the Bay of Biscay to the north.

Fighting still centered on Madrid. Nationalist general Luis Orgaz began a renewed offensive against the capital in fog and piercing cold on 3 January 1937, determined to cut its connection with republican forces in the Sierra de Guadarrama to the north. The republicans, with general José Miaja continuing in command, resisted until their ammunition ran out. Miaja, in desperation, sent up blanks to keep them firing until reinforcements could be rushed out from Madrid and up from Córdoba.

Mussolini had decided on 10 December 1936 to bolster Franco's nationalist forces with Italian reserves, intending to shorten the war, and 20,000 Italian regulars and 27,000 black-shirted fascist militiamen began arriving at Cádiz in January. The Blackshirts were motorized, the first time infantry units had been supported with motor transport in a European war. Franco wanted them in the battle for Madrid, but the Italians meant to operate independently and proposed attacking Málaga, far from the capital on the southern Spanish coast eighty miles above Gibraltar. The battle north of Madrid, below the Guadarramas, ground to a halt on 15 January. Orgaz achieved little gain; each side lost about fifteen thousand men—in Orgaz's case, more than he had led across four hundred miles of fighting from Gibraltar to Madrid. The historian Hugh Thomas reviews the resulting stalemate:

> The character of the winter of 1936 in Spain was . . . best expressed by the long convoy of [trucks], laden with food brought by the national-ists to feed Madrid once it had fallen. Their contents slowly rotted in the snow and rain. A mile away, behind the republican lines, the peo-ple of Madrid stoically put up with rice, bread, and increasing hunger, the consequence of the killing of herds and immediate consumption during the first days of revolution, and of general economic disloca-tion, as well as the presence, in the republican zone, of a million refu-gees who had fled during the course of the autumn from one province after another.

Food was short in the republican zone in part because Spain's animal- and grain-rich provinces, including Galicia, Rioja, Asturias, and Navarre, were in nationalist hands. Under strict production con-trols and price supports, sheep, pig, cattle, and goat numbers actually increased in the nationalist zone in the course of the war. Mules as well, as important to the war as jeeps and artillery tractors would be to later conflicts, were bred in greater numbers in the largely agricultural terri-tories the nationalists occupied.

The first organized contingent of ninety-six American International Brigade volunteers sailed from New York on the *Normandie* on the day after Christmas 1936. Determined to stop fascism before it engulfed the world in war, they had converged on New York via Greyhound bus from as far away as San Francisco, bunked at the Twenty-Third Street YMCA, and cleaned out Manhattan's army-navy stores buying military gear. More would follow in the months to come until the Abraham Lincoln Battalion, as they named themselves, totaled three thousand men. A third were Jewish, two-thirds were communists; their average age was twenty-three. They were miners, steelworkers, longshoremen, students, and teachers. One was a writer, another a dressmaker, another a retired U.S. Navy sailor, another a lawyer, another the only Japanese-American to fight in the Spanish war. They arrived at Le Havre on New Year's Eve and passed through Paris on 2 January 1937. On the train to Perpignan they joined other eager volunteers from Britain, France, Germany, Italy, Yugoslavia, Poland, Austria, and Hungary. From Perpignan, a few miles above Port Bou, they crossed into Spain by bus to Albacete and then rode thirty-eight miles farther north to the village of Villanueva de la Jara, where they would train.

Their trainer was another American, twenty-nine-year-old Robert Hale Merriman, a tall, vigorous lumberjack's son, scholar, and athlete from Eureka, California. Merriman's own training consisted of two years commanding an ROTC unit at the University of Nevada, his alma mater, and upon graduation a second lieutenancy in the U.S. Army Reserve. From teaching economics at the University of California, Berkeley, Merriman had traveled to the Soviet Union in 1934 on a research fellowship to study collective farming. He arrived in Spain in early January 1937 from the USSR, leaving behind in Moscow his wife, Marion, who found work there in the *New York Times*'s bureau under the *Times*'s Moscow correspondent Walter Duranty.

The lack of rifles and ammunition limited training. When Merriman sent the men forward in practice advances, he ran a stick across a slatted board to simulate machine-gun fire. Only when they were preparing to go into battle, in mid-February, did they receive rifles and 150 rounds each of ammunition. Merriman, by then the battalion commander, had to stop the trucks along the way to the front so the men could practice firing five rounds each, "428 men tumbling out of the camions," writes one of them, the poet Edwin Rolfe, "spreading across the fields on both sides of the road, hastily wiping the grease from guns which had never been used, shooting their few rounds against the flanks of the hills." And then back into the trucks, greasy-shirted, rolling on to the valley of the Jarama River twenty miles south of Madrid, where Franco hoped to sever the city's road and rail connections with the republican government in Valencia, on the Mediterranean coast.

Picasso had followed the war since its beginning in the summer of 1936. When he accepted appointment as honorary director of the Prado that September he chose his side. He had been singularly reluctant to talk about it. Margaret Barr, the wife of Alfred H. Barr Jr., the first director of New York's Museum of Modern Art, recalls social gatherings in Paris that season when the painter's well-meaning friends burdened him with the latest war news. "He had a little court," she says; "in one way or another these people tried to see him every day. . . . The Spanish Civil War was going full swing . . . and we were in Paris a great deal that long summer. One knew that Picasso was very excited by it, very upset. These friends would feed him every item of news of the war that they could gather. He responded with his eyes, or maybe with some small remark, but he never contributed. . . . He just listened, although he was very much there and obviously intensely interested."

His silence about the war matched his silenced art. He had stopped painting early in 1935, he who painted hundreds of works a year, though he continued drawing and engraving. Art historians attribute his hiatus to a dead-ending of the entire line of conceptual exploration that had begun with cubism. It may have been, in part, but the proximate cause was the breakup of Picasso's marriage to Olga Khokhlova, his wife since 1918. The Ukrainian former ballerina had tolerated his relationship with a young French mistress, Marie-Thérèse Walter, since she had learned of it in 1932. On Christmas Eve 1934, however, Walter had presented Picasso with the news that she was pregnant. The artist had responded grandly that he would divorce Olga the next day. He decided otherwise: presented with his ultimatum, Olga had moved out, hired lawyers, and educated her wayward husband in the French community-property laws. An officer of the court arrived to inventory and seal their common assets—including, writes Picasso biographer John Richardson, "his paints and brushes and sketchbooks as well as his vast holdings of his own work." Picasso was not prepared to give up half a lifetime of paintings, whatever he had promised Marie-Thérèse. He pursued a de facto separation instead, in exchange for which Olga received an opulent settlement. In the meantime, perhaps from depression—he said later this period was "the lowest moment in my life"—or perhaps to produce nothing more of value that Olga might lay claim to, he stopped painting. He might as well have stopped breathing: expression in some form was a daily necessity, if not a compulsion.

In a way Picasso liked it, Gertrude Stein said of those two years of painterly fallow: "It was one responsibility the less, it is nice not having responsibilities, it is like the soldiers during a war, a war is terrible, they said, but during a war one has no responsibility, either for death, nor for life. So these two years were like that for Picasso, he did not work, it was not for him to decide every moment what he saw, no, poetry for him was something to be made during rather bitter meditations, but agreeably enough, in a cafe."

Initially the mayhem and scatology in Picasso's poetry cloaked his frustration with Olga, with lawyers, with a world that for once he couldn't bend to his will, but with the bursting open of the war they masked his anger and horror as well. Then the fear beneath the anger doubled the disguise, including fear for the safety of his mother in Barcelona. She sent him news at the end of July 1936, writes Picasso biographer Roland Penrose, "of the burning of a convent within a few yards of the apartment in which she lived with her widowed daughter and five grandchildren." Anarchist mobs burned convents in those early weeks of the war: more than fire threatened Picasso's family.

He had begun painting again, tentatively, in the spring of 1936: not much, a small painting or two. When Spain convulsed he followed the war in the Paris newspapers, several of which he read every day. He would have read of Louis Delaprée's death in one or more of those newspapers, perhaps *L'Intransigeant*—which had the headline LOUIS DELAPRÉE EST MORT on 12 December. More significantly, as Richardson has identified, Picasso alludes to Delaprée in a painting, *Still Life with a Lamp,* made at the end of December. Allegorically, in a tomblike, marble-walled room, it depicts a sturdy water pitcher—Picasso's usual symbol for himself—on a table next to a bowl of fruit—his disguised representation of curvaceous Marie-Thérèse in many previous paintings. Although a window in the background opens to a clear blue sky, the table arrangement is illuminated further by a single lightbulb hanging under a conical shade, which projects a broad cone of dark shadow upward to the ceiling. There are few scenes more domestic than a water pitcher and a bowl of fruit on a table. A shocking anomaly profaned this one, however, as Madrid was being profaned by Franco's bombing: on the forward edge of the table lies a severed hand.

Beyond the table to the viewer's right, on an otherwise blank wall poster, appears the date "29 Decembre." Picasso painted *Still Life with a Lamp* that day; more significantly, it was also the date of a public rally celebrating Louis Delaprée's life that Picasso's friend Louis Aragon, the French poet and novelist, had organized. Delaprée's impassioned reports from Madrid were then published in a pamphlet, *Bombs over Madrid*, on 8 January 1937, and reprinted in *L'Humanité* the next day. Besides reading *Bombs over Madrid,* Picasso also would have heard by then that Italian forces were marching toward Málaga, his birthplace.

Disgusted with Franco's cold-blooded murder of civilians in the name of Christianity and the glory of Spain, Picasso responded to reading Delaprée's reports with an acrid series of panels engraved on 8 and 9 January. The panels are postcard-sized, discontinuous but related, worked on two larger plates, nine images on the first plate, five on the other, both plates dated 8 January. The artist would title the panels *Sueño y Mentira de Franco—Dream and Lie of Franco*. They evoke the satiric, bawdy little cartoon pamphlets the Spanish call *alleluias*. On 9 January, with the panels finished but his disgust still regurgitant, Picasso wrote out one of his automatic poems, a full page in a fair cursive unpunctuated except for dashes. "Fandango of shivering owls," it begins, "souse of swords of evil-omened polyps scouring brush of hairs from priests' tonsures standing naked in the middle of the frying pan. . . ."

The sword-bearing, thin-mustached, evil-omened polyp of the drawings is Franco, with a multi-lobed head and hemispherical torso ringed like an armadillo. Legs covered to the hip in high-buttoned, high-heeled Spanish riding boots extend below the fat armadillo half-shell of the body, and buttocks warted with coarse hair protrude behind. Franco's head, with its tubular eyestalks, is curiously similar to a page of studies for a woman's head that Picasso had sketched the previous April, except that the woman's head isn't ringed and is attached not to a hemisphere but to a sphere. The woman in these earlier sketches is Marie-Thérèse, polyped and evil-omened. The visual association may be a comment on Franco's manhood; it's at least a Spanish insult, though why Picasso associated Franco with Marie-Thérèse is obscure.

In the first of the panels the Franco polyp sits astride a grinning, high-stepping caricature horse—the Spanish people or Spain in Picasso's iconography. This horse is wounded, however, its guts hanging out like a picador's gored horse in a bullfight. Indifferent to his mount's wounds, the Caudillo wears a bishop's miter and carries in one hand a banner depicting the Holy Virgin, in the other hand a sword, signifying the Church and the Spanish state for which Franco claimed he fought. The sun shines on the scene. In the second panel a bare-assed Franco with an erection nearly as long as he is tall walks a circus low wire, his sword raised in his right hand for striking or for balance, his phallus

holding up the Virgin's banner, his left arm like a second phallus ejacu-
lating a cloud. In the third panel Franco with a pickax attacks a serene,
unperturbed Sphinx—Marie-Thérèse again in classical guise. In the
fourth panel he parades in Spanish-noblewoman drag with a fan in one
hand and a rose in the other; in the fifth he's tossed ass over elbow by a
Spanish fighting bull; and so on to the fourteenth and final panel, where
the Franco polyp has become the picador's horse down on its back and
dying, its spilled guts trampled by a realistic bull that surely represents
the force of the Spanish people in defense.

Sueño y Mentira de Franco alludes to the late engravings of Goya,
particularly the twenty-two plates of *Los Disparates (The Follies),* which
are also known as *Sueños (Dreams),* and to *La Tauromaquia,* a series
of thirty-three prints of bullfighting scenes. The nineteenth-century
Spanish artist executed *Los Disparates* and *La Tauromaquia* between
1815 and 1823, when a revolution in Spain against King Ferdinand VII
resulted in 1820 in a liberal government, the Trienio Liberal, which
survived for three years before succumbing to an invasion by a French
army that restored the king. The parallels, which Picasso surely meant
to invoke, are striking.

Early in January 1937 an official Spanish government deputation
called on Picasso in Paris: the Catalan architect Josep Lluís Sert; the
Spanish novelist and playwright Max Aub, who was a cultural attaché
at the Spanish Embassy; and Picasso's friend Louis Aragon. In December, Sert, with his colleague Luís Lacasa, had completed the design for
a Spanish Pavilion to be built for the 1937 Paris International Exposition, which would open in mid-July. "We went to see [Picasso]," Sert
recalled, "to ask him to paint a mural for the Spanish Pavilion." The
painter had something else for them to see—his fourteen new satiric
etchings. They heard a passionate reading of his poem as well.

Prints of the *Sueño y Mentira* etchings would eventually be sold at
the Paris exposition to benefit the Spanish republican government, and
Picasso would seem to have planned them for such a purpose when he
sized each panel to the dimensions of a French postcard. But accord-

ing to Sert, the deputation that called on him in early January was not previously aware of the etchings. Nor could it have been when Picasso himself had conceived and executed them only a day or two previously. He had done so in response to the publication on 8 January of Delaprée's reports from Madrid. Perhaps he engraved the postcards in response to Sert's request for an appointment as well.

If so, it may be that Picasso intended to offer the etchings to Sert and his colleagues as his contribution to the exposition. He had not been painting much for two years. He had sized the etchings for postcards and presumably for sale, and, most crucially, he had no idea in early January of the subject matter for a large mural, nor would he find a subject for nearly four more months. The question can't be answered, since all the participants in the midwinter gathering at Picasso's rue la Boétie studio in Paris are dead. But it does arise.

"This was a moment in which things looked pretty grim for the cause of Republican Spain," Sert said, explaining the visitors' intention. "And certainly many Spanish intellectuals in Paris were very concerned about what they could do and what kind of reaction would be appropriate. . . . So the idea of approaching Picasso to contribute to this project seemed like a very reasonable one."

Picasso hated commissions and deadlines. Did he knock out the *Sueño y Mentira* etchings to avoid having to commit himself to a large commissioned work? Given his black state of mind that autumn and winter, given the ongoing battle with Olga and his native country's war with Franco, he may well have.

If he did, Sert, Aub, and Aragon convinced him otherwise—or he at least allowed them to think so. Perhaps they told him his Catalan colleague Joan Miró had agreed to paint a large mural for the pavilion as well and activated his ferocious competitive drive. He committed to a mural. They went on their way, and he was stuck with a commitment he had no idea of how to fulfill. The closest he had come so far to painting the war was that uncanny severed hand abandoned on the table before Marie-Thérèse's marbleized bowl of fruit. Time to return to serious painting. "So in 1937 he commenced to be himself again," Gertrude Stein sums up. But what he painted, for months to come, were not war scenes but portraits of his two mistresses, blond Marie-Thérèse and his new conquest, the brunette surrealist painter and photographer Dora Maar.

Canadian surgeon Norman Bethune's Servicio Canadiense de Transfusión de Sangre was getting down to business in Madrid as the new year began, working toward typing and cataloging a thousand Madrileños on call for monthly blood donations. J.B.S. Haldane, who had been bunking in the luxurious commandeered Socorro Rojo apartments with Bethune and his crew since his arrival before Christmas, had uncovered a problem with the service and had helped Bethune resolve it. In the press of the early months of the war, the service had accepted any healthy-looking donors who volunteered. Some of them, despite swearing otherwise, had been infected with malaria or syphilis, potentially infecting the wounded who received transfusions. "Doubtless a few wounded soldiers had been affected with one or other of these diseases," Haldane says. "This could not be helped. If the transfusion unit had refused to accept blood until proper tests had been made, a lot of men would have died. It was better for them to run the risk of infection with two curable diseases."

Following up on Haldane's alert, Bethune had located a private laboratory in Madrid to run Wasserman tests for syphilis. He became suspicious of the service, and canceled it, when it reported a percentage of positives well below the national average. A subsequent police investigation identified the doctor who ran the laboratory as a fascist sympathizer, bent on sabotage.

Compared with Frederic Duran Jordà's sophisticated storage technologies, Bethune's Canadian system was crude. A photograph survives of a table loaded with bottles of blood ready for delivery to the front: they are not Duran Jordà's custom-made, pressurized ampules but an improvised assortment of sterilized wine and milk bottles. They were no less effective for being improvised. Bethune made the most of them, he wrote his Canadian sponsors on 11 January:

> Our night work is very eerie! We get a phone call for blood. Snatch up our packed bag, take 2 bottles (each 500 c.c.)—one of group IV [type O] and one of group II [type A] blood—out of the refrigerator and with our armed guard off we go through the absolutely pitch dark streets and the guns and machine guns and rifle shots sound like as if they were in the next block, although they are really half a mile away. Without lights we drive, stop at the hospital and with a [flashlight] in our hands find our way into the cellar principally. All the operating rooms in the hospitals have been moved into the basement to avoid falling shrapnel, bricks and stones coming through the operating room ceiling.

They had done three transfusions the previous day, their daily average, besides delivering blood for hospital use. "Well, this is a grand country and great people," Bethune concludes expansively. "The wounded are wonderful. . . . Madrid is the center of gravity of the world and I wouldn't be anywhere else."

Bethune first visited Frederic Duran Jordà's parallel blood supply service in Barcelona in January 1937. He had learned of it earlier, but he and Duran Jordà had not coordinated their work. On 12 January, when Bethune met with the head of the Sanidad Militar (military medical corps) in Valencia to discuss organizing a unified system to deliver blood to all the fronts, he was asked to do so. He and Henning Sorensen made the twelve-hour drive from Valencia to Barcelona the next day. They met Duran Jordà at Hospital No. 18 the following morning, toured his operation, and then discussed a coordinated program.

Barcelona would be a collecting center, they agreed, because Duran Jordà's system involved what Bethune called "a patented and complicated process of putting up the blood" that couldn't be duplicated in

Madrid. Manufacturing the ampules and collecting equipment for an expanded operation would cost about three thousand pesetas a month, an expense Bethune guaranteed with Canadian funds; he left the first month's payment with Duran Jordà in cash. Duran Jordà now had not only his refrigerated truck, Bethune noted, but also "a [railroad] refrigerator car for the Aragon Front."

"We propose to start a 'shuttle' service from Barcelona to Valencia, Madrid and Cordoba," the Canadian surgeon wrote Sise later that day, "with distributing centres at these other points." They would need staffing, refrigerators, and other equipment at their new centers: Bethune and Henning would continue to work out of Madrid.

Before returning there, Bethune wanted to buy and outfit a larger truck for blood deliveries. Nothing was for sale in Barcelona. He and Sorensen left that same afternoon, 16 January, for Paris and then Marseilles. They bought a two-and-a-half-ton Renault truck and drove it back to Barcelona, where Bethune reports converting it to a refrigerator truck by outfitting it with "2 electro box refrigerators running on 125 volts each (D.C.); 20 batteries; dynamo and gas engine to charge batteries." Installing bunk beds made the new truck a traveling dormitory as well.

By the beginning of February the Spanish-Canadian merger seemed to be complete, although the Spanish government had not yet approved it. "We have succeeded in unifying all remaining Spanish transfusion units under us," Bethune cabled the CASD in triumph. They were serving one hundred hospitals and casualty-clearing stations in and around Madrid, with a twenty-five-person staff including doctors, nurses, lab scientists and technicians, and chauffeurs. They had collected and administered ten gallons of blood in January and expected to increase their collections to twenty-five gallons in February. Reflecting its joint operation, the unit had a new name, the Instituto Hispano-Canadiense de Transfusión de Sangre. Sise and Sorenson had been appointed captains in the republican army; Bethune himself was now a *comandante*. "This is the first unified blood transfusion service in army and medical history," Bethune concludes proudly. "Plans are well under way to supply the entire Spanish anti-fascist army [with] preserved blood. Your institute is now operating on a 1,000 kilometre front."

As he often did, Bethune had jumped the gun. Rather than the Canadians heading the Spanish Republic's national blood distribution program, the Sanidad Militar was preparing to take over the Canadian service at the beginning of March 1937 and appoint a three-man committee to administer it that would include Duran Jordà as well as Bethune. The Spanish government intended to bring the volunteer services operating in Spain under unified command; Duran Jordà was also unwilling to work under a surgeon who lacked his specialized training and experience in hematology—and who spoke no Spanish. Eventually the Spanish physician would lead the entire program.

In the meantime, Bethune found a new focus for his fervor. In mid-January 1937 a twenty-mile-wide strip of Mediterranean coast surrounding the city of Málaga, a republican naval base and stronghold eighty miles above Gibraltar, had come under attack by the combined Italian, German, and nationalist forces of Queipo de Llano's Army of the South. This assault was the diversion of Blackshirts landing at Cádiz that the Italian leadership had demanded. The republican coastal strip was guarded by the Sierra Nevada behind it inland, but a second front of nationalist attack was pushing in as well from the northeast and advancing toward the sea. "The first sentence that we shall pronounce in Málaga is the death sentence," Queipo de Llano had threatened one evening on his regular radio broadcast from Seville. Despite that warning, the republican military leadership somehow missed the strategic aim of the attack, which was securing the southern front, realizing its mistake only when a full-scale invasion of Málaga began on 3 February.

(Among other losses, Italian fighter aircraft finished off most of what was left of André Malraux's *escuadrilla España*. The few remaining Potez 54 bombers in Malraux's squadron were integrated into the republican air force. Malraux himself returned to Paris to write his

Spanish Civil War novel *L'Espoir* (*Man's Hope*), based on his experiences fighting in Spain in the first months of the war.)

Bethune's blood deliveries intersected the Málaga disaster. The Canadian surgeon wanted to test the Renault and its new refrigeration equipment with a long drive, and identified the 533-mile stretch between Barcelona and Granada as the longest available road. Málaga was eighty-two miles farther southwest. Bethune envisioned creating a blood transfusion network between Madrid, Barcelona, Valencia, and Córdoba. He hoped as well to assess the medical needs of the southern front, which, he had learned from a *Daily Worker* correspondent in Valencia, was weakening. He sent Sise and a new volunteer driver, the young English writer and teacher Thomas Worsley, to Barcelona in the Renault to load a stock of blood from Duran Jordà's supply. They returned to Valencia on Sunday, 7 February. At nine o'clock that evening the three men set out driving southwest.

Though Bethune didn't know it at the time, Málaga had fallen. Almost the entire civilian population of the city, some 200,000 people, was fleeing. The evacuation had started that day after a week of continued shelling from nationalist ships in the harbor and offshore. Arthur Koestler, the Hungarian-born novelist and journalist, was there, reporting for a London newspaper and soon to be arrested and imprisoned by the nationalist authorities; the road to Valencia that Sunday afternoon, he says, was "flooded with a stream of lorries, cars, mules, carriages [and] frightened, quarreling people" and had become "a road for one-way traffic." The confused and demoralized militiamen who had been defending Málaga were escaping with the populace, a mass of terrified civilians stumbling toward Almería, 126 miles eastward along the coastal road that ran between the Sierra Nevada and the sea, changing elevation from sea level to more than five hundred feet, with long stretches cut into the mountainsides.

Coming from the other direction, Bethune, Sise, and Worsley arrived in Almería on 10 February. The town was filling with haggard militiamen. The local hotelier had nothing to offer except boiled beans.

They started out again for Málaga at six that Wednesday evening, following the jagged line of the coast. A few refugees on the road, then more. "They flowed past our truck without expression," writes Bethune: "a young girl, hardly sixteen, straddling a donkey, her head drooping over an infant at her breast; a grandmother, her old face half-hidden in her dark shawl, dragging along between two men; a patriarch, shrivelled down to skin and bones, his bare feet dripping blood on the road." A young man hauling a pile of bedding; a woman holding her stomach: "A silent, haggard, tortured flood of men and animals, the animals bellowing in complaint like humans, the humans as uncomplaining as animals."

Where were they coming from? They were coming from Málaga. *"Nada más!"* they told Bethune. "Nothing left!"

We drove more quickly now and as the road banked steeply the line of refugees grew wider. Then there was a sharp turn away from the sea, a slow climb, and suddenly we breasted a hill falling away to a long, level plain. Sise rammed his foot on the brake with a surprised grunt. The truck jolted to a stop against a shuddering wall of refugees and animals. . . .

The plain stretched into the distance as far as the eye could see, and across the plain, where the road should have been, there wriggled twenty miles of human beings, like a giant caterpillar, its many limbs raising a cloud of dust, moving slowly, ponderously; stretching from beyond the horizon, across the arid, flat country and up into the foothills.

Thousands upon thousands of refugees crowded the road, "pressed together, falling against each other . . . filling the plain with the hum of voices, cries, wailings, the grotesque noise of animals." Sise was blowing the horn, Bethune on the running board shouting, trying to clear the way. The refugees flowed around the truck as it descended the hill. How long had they been on the road, living on what? Living on sugarcane from the fields the road ran through. And looking ahead, across the plain, Bethune realized that thousands of them were children, dirty, half naked, many of them barefoot, crying, or, worse, silent and dazed. "They were slung over their mother's shoulders or clung to her hands. Here a father staggered along with two children of one and two years of age on his back in addition to carrying pots and pans or some treasured possession."

No point in going farther toward Málaga. They couldn't have moved had they tried. As night fell on the narrow road, they turned the truck around, unloaded its equipment, abandoned their bottles of blood to make room for passengers. Bethune estimated how many people the truck would hold, and threw open the back door. *"Solamente niños!"* he announced—"Children only!" The crowd surged forward. Bethune tried to block the way and Sise came around to help.

It seemed gruesome, Bethune writes, to have to decide the refugees' fate, worse than being a helpless bystander. But that was what he began to do, pushing into the crowd, pointing to mothers with children, taking their children away, passing the children through the crowd to the truck, where Sise passed them in to Worsley. The truck slowly filled. Mothers hovered nearby, encouraging their children to be calm. Men wandered off into the fields, calling for families lost in the darkness.

Two more spaces left. Bethune pulled a little girl from her mother's arms. The mother screamed in loss even as she gave the child up. He carried the girl to the truck only to find a woman pulling herself up into the back, blocking the way. *Get out,* Bethune ordered. *It's you or the child, do you understand?*

The woman was young. Her long black hair fell about her pale face. She looked at me with hunted eyes, then flung open her cloak and raised her cotton shift high. She was distended with child.

For a moment we looked at each other, I with the child in my arms, she with the child in her womb. She pressed herself down on the tiny space of flooring at her feet, her great stomach between her knees, smiled at me and held out her arms. With her eyes and arms and her smile she seemed to be saying, "See, I will take the child, and it will be as if I am not here, as if I am taking nobody's place." She placed the girl on her knees, pillowing the little head on her shoulders.

So it was done, forty children and two women out of thousands. "I banged the door shut and ordered Sise to take them directly to the hospital in Almería and to stop for nothing and nobody." Pick up some militiamen if he could, Bethune added, to hang on the running boards and keep people off.

For the next four days and nights they shuttled between the crowd of refugees and Almería. On the second day Bethune gave up transporting only children—"the sight of parents separated from their children became too ghastly to bear," he says—and they began moving whole families. They ran out of food and hungered as so many of the refugees were hungering. A man appeared with a cartload of oranges. "In the midst of war, flight, death," Bethune exclaims in wonder, "an ordinary, prosaic street-hawker!" He bought the whole cartload, kept one orange for himself, and distributed the rest.

Coughing in clouds of dust by day, shaking in winter cold by night, the Málagans stumbled toward Almería. As if that suffering weren't enough, Franco's planes attacked them—Italian Fiats, German Heinkels. "They dived toward the road," Bethune saw, "as casually as target-practice, their machine guns weaving intricate geometric patterns about the fleeing refugees."

Almería was a vast encampment. The streets were filled, the main square, the beaches, the hills all the way back to the mountains behind. The Socorro Rojo directed Bethune to the old building where the children had been hospitalized. He found a cot and collapsed. He'd hardly fallen asleep when a siren screamed him awake. Franco wasn't finished. "I scrambled to my feet, and fell on my knees again as the first bomb went off. The explosion was like a giant mailed fist smashing deep into the earth. . . . I could hear the terrible, frightened screams of the children."

Bethune ran outside, heading for the heart of the bombing, where there might be wounded who needed his skills. "Here the streets were no longer dark. Great sheets of flame shot up from the skeletons of buildings, hit by incendiaries. In the glare of the burning buildings, as far as the eye can see, vast crowds of people surged about wildly, running into bombpits, clutching and screaming as they vanished."

The city was nearly defenseless. The planes were free to bomb and strafe at will: "I caught a glimpse of one bomber banking gracefully in the moonlight, disdaining the protection of height or darkness. The devils could afford to take their time! The occasional burst of antiaircraft fire merely prettied up the sky like roman candles." Glaring up from the street, filling with hate, Norman Bethune glared into the future of the new warfare of machines that distanced their crews from the killing.

SIX

A Valley in Spain Called Jarama

Fistfights and clubbings on the New York docks launched the American medical response to the Spanish Civil War. Union organizer Big Joe Curran's 1936 campaign to clear the waterfront of the shipowner-dominated International Seamen's Union and reform the hiring of merchant seamen produced an epidemic of busted heads. Sympathetic doctors and nurses treating the wounded at Beth Israel Hospital on New York's Lower East Side decided to take the treatment to the docks. The group they formed, American Medical Aid, and the clinic they opened was thus preadapted to battlefield service when the war began in Spain.

Edward Barsky, M.D., was a leader of the American Medical Aid clinic group. Barsky was forty-one years old in 1936 and an associate surgeon at Beth Israel, where his physician father was listed among the founders. Tall, gangly, broad-shouldered, he combed his dark hair straight back above a long jaw and sported a mustache. He had graduated from Columbia University's College of Physicians and Surgeons in 1919 and studied abroad in Vienna, Berlin, and Paris before working his way up at Beth Israel through the 1920s and early 1930s.

Barsky remembered the autumn 1936 meeting that had alerted

him to conditions in Spain: confounding stereotypes, a Spanish woman lawyer—a rarity even in republican Spain—and a Basque priest had spoken against the nationalist rebellion. After that meeting, more than one hundred unsolicited requests had poured in from medical professionals asking to be sent to Spain. No organization existed to support such a venture, but American Medical Aid might serve as a nucleus. At an October meeting at the home of a prominent heart specialist, Louis Miller, the participating physicians formed an allied group, the American Medical Bureau to Aid Spanish Democracy (AMB). "We set as our immediate objective the complete equipment of a seventy-five bed mobile hospital," Barsky recalls.

Recruiting personnel was harder than raising money. Barsky worked at Beth Israel by day and at organizing and fund-raising half the night or more through November and December. As head of the AMB purchasing committee, he was responsible for outfitting the mobile hospital, "everything from a safety pin to a special operating room light running on dry batteries (afterward to be known as 'The Light That Failed'), Lister bags for carrying water . . . besides all sorts of special medications, serums, antitoxins." As head at the same time of the AMB personnel committee, Barsky worked to recruit people with exceptional medical and nursing skills who were not what he calls "sentimentalists" yet were prepared to die for their convictions. Such people weren't hard to find, but they tended to be busy. "In the end, just these people came, motivated by the idea of service."

Barsky himself was one of them. Afflicted with inflammatory bowel disease, he had not intended to go to Spain. The chief of the AMB field hospital in Spain was supposed to be the wealthy, progressive fifty-five-year-old Stanford University thoracic surgeon Leo Eloesser, but Eloesser had just become president of the American Association for Thoracic Surgery and wanted to chair that burgeoning organization's annual meeting first; he would join the AMB in Spain later in 1937.

Eloesser's delay was a crisis for the AMB but an unexpected opportunity for Barsky:

Who was to head the outfit? When late one night someone suggested that it might be myself, the idea at first seemed ridiculous. How could I even think about it?

"How can any of us?" they asked. Then somehow all at once I realized that I had been eager to go from the start; perhaps in some deep part of my mind I had known that I would go all along. Yet for days I could not get over my surprise.

In December, short a final $3,000 ($50,000 today) to finance the mission, the AMB held a gala benefit dinner at New York's Hotel Pennsylvania, with one of the ambulances to be sent with the medical team parked in the banquet hall for the guests to examine. The deputy speaker of the British House of Lords, in attendance that evening, wrote a check for $50 ($850 today), others pitched in, and the funds were raised. The total of national contributions collected since October bought them four ambulances and twelve tons of supplies worth $30,000 ($497,000 today), enough to stock their hospital.

With a band playing dockside on 16 January 1937, a crowd cheered when Barsky and his colleagues—three other doctors, six nurses, five drivers, and two secretaries—prepared to board the *Paris,* the art-nouveau ocean liner that would carry them to France. Barsky was unnerved when a physician friend slipped a small box into his hand just as the boarding whistle blew. It held six grains of morphine sulfate, about half a gram, dangerous contraband even for a doctor. If he was caught with it he'd be in trouble. He didn't throw the morphine away, but he worried about it.

"We were so romantic when we started out," head nurse Fredericka Martin said later of their entrance from France into Spain in convoy, ambulances and trucks flying American flags. "We looked like such an important force, so elegant. The people in the fields stopped working—they couldn't believe their eyes." Martin herself was a commanding presence, five feet nine and comfortable with authority. The Carabineros—the Spanish customs officials—had taken good care of them, opening up a hotel in Port Bou for them while their equipment was transferred across the border and checked through customs.

Everyone wanted their services. They in turn were looking for the best place to serve. In Barcelona, writes Mildred Rackley, a striking, multilingual New Mexican artist who had signed on as Barsky's secretary and interpreter, "there had been receptions, press interviews and conferences with Lluis Companys, President of Catalonia." In Valencia they met with General Miaja, now army commander in chief; in Madrid they toured the frontline trenches in University City. Miaja and others gave them the same advice, Martin writes: "For linguistic and logistic reasons, join the International Brigades, which had been set up to cope with a babel of languages and to try to satisfy the stubborn tastes and cultural variances of so many nationalities—some say fifty-two, some fifty-four."

The Carabineros, who had been salted through the republican battalions to bolster the green recruits, operated a hospital at Villarrobledo, a town about halfway between Albacete and Madrid, and hoped to install the Americans there. They were disappointed. "It was with great reluctance," Rackley recalls, "that they handed us over to the Sanitary Service of the International Brigades."

The road down to Albacete was jammed with troops, trucks, ambulances, and refugees. The romance dissipated quickly when Condor Legion planes strafed them in a Ferris wheel formation that laid down a continuous barrage. "In my innocence," Barsky writes, "I had supposed that the red cross"—painted on the roofs of their ambulances—"would be respected." In Franco's war of attrition, to the contrary, ambulances and hospitals were prime targets. "Cover your wagon with mud, comrade," someone told Barsky, "and drive seventy-five yards from the next fellow." That way, the physician adds, "some of us might hope to get to the end of our road." When they stopped to help the wounded, a Spanish officer advised them to move on—their equipment was too valuable to be lost, he told them. They were shocked that equipment, however scarce, took precedence over men's lives.

They arrived in Albacete in early February 1937 prepared to work together as a unit, only to discover that the International Brigade leadership expected them to integrate into the IB battalions. By then they had realized how challenging the language barrier would be. The "seventeen weary but like-minded Americans," as Martin calls them, resisted being separated—stubbornly, it seemed to the Spanish authorities. "They could not understand the need these pioneers felt to stick together and take stock of the situation before sending a young nurse, or one of the young, trained but barely-experienced surgeons who spoke no Spanish to a hospital where no one spoke English. They could not even begin, then, to understand the need to have an American hospital to be the magnetic pole to arouse American pride, to attract generous assistance, to rally other young professionals to follow them."

The IB leaders "considered the American request naïve and ridiculous," Martin says. "The pet phrase condemning these plutocratic Americans was, 'They don't know there's a war on.'" They knew enough: they agreed to work with the IB only if they could operate their own hospitals and control their own personnel and supplies—those already on hand and those they hoped would be coming. "The stunned officers capitulated," Martin concludes, "at least for the time being, and invited the newcomers to supper."

The next morning, Barsky and Martin left early with a Polish IB guide who spoke Spanish and a French driver to find a site for a field hospital near the Jarama front southeast of Madrid, now fully engaged. Their colleagues were supposed to wait in Albacete until they called.

"We interviewed all sorts of officials," Barsky writes, "[and] went from town to town. After thirty hours' continuous search and, it seemed to me, almost continuous conversation, we had still no location." Lillo, thirty miles south of the front toward Albacete, had a building, but its ground floor was a stable and its second floor, up a narrow, ladderlike stairway, was inaccessible to stretchers. Barsky rejected it, to their escort's disgust. They ate lunch in a culvert, safe from marauding aircraft, and managed to drive a few miles out of town before their transmission failed. They were stranded in Lillo for three days: no gas, no car, no working local telephone.

On the morning of the third day, Martin recalls, a Friday, they woke to find their Polish escort missing. Barsky headed for the local barbershop for the consolation of a shave. When he returned Martin thought he seemed cheered. He was: the barber had pointed him to a relatively new school building ten miles away in the town of El Romeral, adaptable for a hospital, with a well in the school yard. They decided to hike there after lunch. While they waited and planned, the rest of their hospital crew rolled up, four ambulances and nine trucks.

Their Polish escort had slipped away and called Albacete. The Americans didn't know there was a war on, he told his superiors. The building in Lillo was adequate. The fountain in the central plaza had water. Send the others on, he'd advised—that would force them to set up in Lillo.

Barsky was furious. "Why in hell have you come here?" he challenged Rackley. After the invective subsided, she handed him their first official orders:

SET UP ONE-HUNDRED-BED EMERGENCY HOSPITAL AND BE READY TO RECEIVE PATIENTS IN FORTY-EIGHT HOURS.

Not in Lillo, an angry Barsky decided; not in a stable. While the Lillo town officials organized a mutton barbecue in the central plaza for the new arrivals, he and Martin took the group's small Ford ambulance and drove off to inspect Romeral.

The two-story school building, when they found it, looked promising from the outside. Its interior was more challenging. The windows were large, offering light and air, but there was no interior stairway connecting the floors. Exterior access would have to serve even though patients would have to be carried outside and around. The bright, airy classrooms opened onto a large central hall. Those on the lower floor could accommodate an admitting ward, operating rooms, a laboratory, and a kitchen with an adjoining storeroom. The five large classrooms on the second floor would serve as wards, with smaller rooms there housing a pharmacy and a linen room

The Romeral *alcalde*—the mayor—was eager to add a hospital to the assets of his village. There were refugees living in the cottage-like row houses across the street from the school building, most of them women and children from Madrid who had abandoned the city to escape the bombing and shelling. The *alcalde* asked them to move: the hospital staff would need the housing. "With alacrity they bundled up their few belongings," Martin writes, "and cheerfully faced the necessity to crowd into already-crowded village homes." Before they moved out they joined village volunteers in cleaning the school building. The rest of Barsky's travel-worn team arrived and pitched in. By dark the building was clean. "The Spaniards packed up their buckets and with affectionate wishes for a good night's sleep, faded away. The village inn contrived a meal of eggs, potatoes and tomatoes." In the houses across the street from the hospital, "weary Americans fell asleep on couches and unmade beds, huddling together for warmth. Unwashed, teeth unbrushed, without removing their clothes they fell asleep, satisfied that, at last, they had their own hospital."

The setting was less romantic by morning light: the building was bare of plumbing. No sinks, no baths, no toilets. No electricity. "Then came a second shock," Martin writes. "The well water, thick with lime, was only—and that with difficulty—useful for cleaning and laundry. Drinking water would be brought from a distant well for storage in large earthenware jars." The village was up to the challenge. "This first morning it looked as if the whole adult population had responded to the alcalde's call for help. Masons and carpenters tackled repairs. Electricians wired the building. Two telephones were installed. Men unloaded and helped unpack the great cases."

The cases held twenty tons of hospital equipment: operating tables, a hundred beds, ten bales of cotton, hundreds of sheets, ice caps, blankets, rubber sheeting, bedpans, urinals, electric heaters, flashlights, rubber gloves by the trunkful, sheepskin coats, suture material, cases of scalpels, anesthesia apparatus, a complete pharmacy, equipment for a laboratory, dozens of tires, ambulance and truck tools, parts and supplies, canned milk, powdered coffee, and cheeses, as well as their own trunks and suitcases—unloaded in no particular order.

Another shock: twelve cases of supplies were missing. They knew two of them had disappeared before Port Bou; Rackley had filed a claim for those. The other ten had disappeared somewhere along the way inside Spain—"organized," Martin says mournfully, using the current slang for stolen.

The worst loss was the large autoclave they had shipped. Boiling water isn't hot enough to kill every disease organism. An autoclave, also called a sterilizer, is a specialized medical pressure cooker that sterilizes objects and materials such as surgical gloves and instruments, bandages, and liquids. Fifteen minutes in an autoclave under 250° Fahrenheit steam pressurized to 15 psi is sufficient to denature the proteins in bacteria and viruses—to cook them. "The loss was a catastrophe," Martin writes. "The autoclave was the main defense against the peril inevitable in hospitals, infection of wounds." Sterile procedure, introduced at the turn of the twentieth century, had revolutionized surgery; to the Americans, operating was unthinkable without it.

Some of the European surgeons who would operate at Romeral proved less meticulous, Martin reports, unwilling to spend much time scrubbing in, to wear surgical masks, even to wear gloves. Apparently they had not yet caught up with medical procedures that had become accepted practice in the United States. After Louis Pasteur and Robert Koch demonstrated the role of microorganisms in infection in the 1860s and 1870s, the British surgeon Joseph Lister had pioneered surgery practiced under antiseptic conditions—clean but not sterile. Sterile technique, pioneered in Germany and the United States at the beginning of the twentieth century, was a major technological advance that some Spanish and other European medical personnel would learn from the Americans.

"Without a sterilizer we could not open," Barsky laments. "It would mean that our orders to establish a hospital and get ready to receive wounded in forty-eight hours could not be carried out. All that energy, that will to make bricks without straw, would be for nothing if we had no autoclave." The IB leadership in Albacete had appointed Mildred Rackley as the American hospital's administrator. Now Barsky sent her off with one of the American drivers in an old Latil truck, a French make, to find an autoclave, an X-ray machine, water softener, a small operating room table, and more—a two-page list. "On her own," Martin adds. "This was sending her into a lion's den, but she set out bravely."

In the meantime, the *alcalde* summoned farmworkers from miles around to improve the bad road. "Carrying stones and dirt in small baskets," Martin writes, "the men dumped the stones in the runs and tamped the earth around them. At least the wounded would not acquire more fractures on the way to Romeral. Only the unconscious and the dead could have traveled without pain on that road."

Mule carts hauling food supplies slowed Rackley's progress. So did military police rerouting vehicles away from the Jarama battlefront. At Alcázar de San Juan, their truck broke down. It was the coldest night they had yet experienced in Spain. Rackley and her driver, a reliable professional chauffeur and mechanic named Carl Rahman, walked four miles to find a telephone. When they got through to Romeral, Barsky says, "We at the hospital sent out a salvaging truck and towed them back . . . in a black dawn dotted with flurries of snow. No autoclave. That was what worried us all. No autoclave, no hospital."

They could buy an autoclave in Madrid, but the capital would be difficult to reach with nationalist artillery shelling the roads. There was a Spanish hospital in Tarancón, a larger town thirty-two miles northeast of Lillo. Barsky sent Rackley there with instructions to push on to Madrid "only if she could not beg or steal an autoclave from the Tarancón hospital."

That hospital was "gruesomely overcrowded," Barsky reports. "The wounded were lying about the open patios; they could not be immediately admitted." The hospital director was a German surgeon named Kriegel; he'd been operating for thirty hours when Rackley and Rahman arrived and he refused to be interrupted. Eventually he came out to help. In a hospital storehouse he showed them a small autoclave. "Kaput," he condemned it. Rahman examined the machine. Its gauge was broken, which put it at risk of exploding. He decided it was repairable. They loaded it up and hauled it back to Romeral:

> Carl was shut up in a room alone with his problem, which was the chief concern at that time of everyone in the hospital. Word came from Carl: the autoclave would work but the linen and [surgical] greens would come out damp. An adequate vacuum couldn't be created. In bitter cold it is hard to deliberately put on a wet gown.

But that was what they would have to do, and that was what they did.

Although they were ready by 20 February, there was rebellion in the ranks. Not for the first time, some of the volunteers, used to holding meetings to hash out collective grievances, were complaining that Barsky was high-handed and undemocratic. Some agitated for him to be sent home. Martin went looking for the high-handed, undemocratic surgeon and found him cleaning the staff's stopped-up toilet. "He agreed to another meeting," Martin writes. "His shoulders slumped a little lower. He had lost weight during the search for a place to work who had no weight to lose."

Doctors, nurses, and drivers met in one of the new wards, sitting on the new beds. "The stale complaints were aired," Martin writes. She shocked them by announcing that if Barsky went home, so would she. The three or four prime agitators were prepared to lose their professional leadership; the others were not. Martin lectured them on their bad attitude "against a sick man and the only capable surgeon [among them] and for risking the prospect of more medical aid from America if this first group were to break up." Her lecture didn't win the argument, she says: the arrival of their first loads of wounded did.

The Jarama River flows due south from Madrid twenty-six miles through a sandy countryside of olive groves and stony hills to join the longer, southwestward-flowing Tajuña River at Aranjuez. The thin republican lines protecting that approach to Madrid were dug in on the west bank of the Jarama. In early February 1937, in what came to be called the Battle of Jarama, Franco's nationalists launched a major attack against the republican defenses. The attack was one lever of a pincer movement around Madrid, with Italian Blackshirts attacking simultaneously from northeast of the capital down toward Guadalajara. Hauling up all the way from Málaga, however, the Blackshirts were not yet in position. Franco, who resented the Italians' insistence on operating independently, had no intention of waiting for them. The primary goal of his assault at Jarama was to block the main highway between Madrid and Valencia, interrupting supplies and communications and thus forcing Madrid to surrender.

Fierce fighting continued through February in the wedge of hills, ridges, and valleys between and along the two rivers. Twenty thousand republicans, most of them militiamen, defended their positions against a larger and better-equipped nationalist force of Moroccan *regulares* and Spanish legionaries. Condor Legion ground forces—machine-gun, tank, and artillery companies—as well as aircraft also participated in the attack. The republicans called the German soldiers "blond Moors."

It was the first time the volunteers of the Abraham Lincoln Battalion saw battle. After Robert Merriman had given them their brief practice firing their greasy new rifles into a hillside, the four hundred Americans had been thrown into the republican lines on a hill overlooking the valley of the Tajuña. The British IB battalion had already been shot to pieces farther up the line, at a place called Pingarrón Hill. Of the original six hundred British combatants, some 225 had been wounded or killed. The Americans joined the Fifteenth Brigade on 16 February, writes Herbert Matthews, who reported on Jarama for the *New York Times*: "The object then was merely to hold the line, somewhere, anywhere, so as to stop that deadly drive toward the Valencia highway."

Merriman was Lincoln Battalion adjutant under a former U.S. Army sergeant, now a captain, named James Harris. Merriman kept a diary in Spain, a pocket-sized *dietario perpetuo* bound in red buckram that he had picked up in Barcelona on his arrival. The last entry before the Lincolns went into battle, written in blue ink, is self-consciously heroic in the Popular Front mode: "Men may die but let them die in a working-class cause. Men die and mean to die (if necessary) so that the revolution may live on. They may stop us today but tomorrow we still take up the march." No such rhetoric inflates the first battlefield entries, in pencil now when an ink pen would have been unhandy:

[February] 18—Early today air raid—bombs just missed us and how close! Edwards killed by bullet thru head while scouting. Was bawled out for not keeping men down by Gen[eral] Gal. Later in day another raid and came even closer. Some fight in air. We are definitely located. Went to inspect trenches after dark and artillery started up on us. Plenty tough and lost one man. Chelebian killed by shrapnel. Occasional firing and during night crossfire. Harris out.

This needs decoding. From inexperience Merriman had allowed the men to dig in too near the crest of the slope, making them vulnerable to sniper fire when they stood. One of them wrote home about the death of Charles Edwards, the first of the Lincolns to be killed:

Making observations from an outpost trench, Edwards warned the men around him:

"You got to keep your head down. There's a sniper shooting at us here."

When he too was told to keep under cover, he replied:

"My case is different. I'm an observer."

The next moment a bullet went through his head.

General Gal was János Gálicz, a Soviet-trained Hungarian and the commander of the Fifteenth IB, a well-tailored martinet and careerist hoping to make his name. Misak Chelebian was an Armenian from New York, a recent widower, the oldest man among the Lincolns, who spoke only broken English and whom the others hardly knew, killed instantly. Harris, the former U.S. Army sergeant, was a drunk; "Harris out" is Merriman's shorthand for having sent the drunken leader back to the hospital and replaced him as battalion commander.

Merriman added the later Jarama entries to his diary in March, after the battle, but they continue to convey the immediacy as well as the confusion of those urgent February events. "About 20th in the evening we received orders to move forward to support the Thaelmann Battalion," the retrospective section begins. The Lincolns climbed a hill and crossed the narrow tracks of a mine railroad to a flat-topped knoll with a wide view of the surrounding valley, where they were ordered to dig in facing the enemy trenches on a higher ridge a mile west. They'd been told to leave their packs and blankets behind, as if they were only advancing temporarily. They dug into the rocky earth with bayonets and helmets and scooped away sand with their bare hands. They dug all night, frustrated but staying warm, and by morning had a shallow, circular trench where they could defend themselves from attack in any direction. "Never did get old packs and blankets back for the men," Merriman laments.

By order on 23 February the Lincolns moved toward the road that ran north and south to the east of their position, Merriman notes, to "support the 24th Brigade Spanish and later we advanced between them and road." They took up a new position among the Franco-Belgian Sixth of February Battalion. From behind a stone wall above a notch between two hills, they watched the Sixth of February shoot and dynamite a *tabor* of Moroccans—the equivalent of a battalion, about eight hundred men—who tried to run a wild frontal assault down the hill and across the notch, ghostly in their gray djellabas. The Lincolns had wondered why the Sixth of February men had all lighted up smelly cigars as the battle was joined, suspecting them of feigning Gallic insouciance. Now they understood: the cigars served to light the fuses on the sticks of dynamite they threw. The seasoned Sixth of Februaries finished the battle by shooting into the writhing, moaning gray bundles scattered on the hillside.

As the sky darkened at day's end, two fifteen-ton Russian tanks clattered up the road. The Lincolns fell in behind them, Merriman writes, "forced a place for ourselves and moved forward" firing at the enemy lines until abruptly, hit by artillery, "tank (ours) burned and exploded throwing [armor] plates and shells all over." The other tank clanked away to the safety of the road and the battalion stood naked to its enemies. The men dodged into an olive grove, firing from tree to tree as they moved forward but finally reaching the edge of the grove before an open field, taking withering enemy fire and falling back.

Joe Gordon, a machine gunner, went forward with the infantry after his company's machine gun broke down and couldn't be repaired: "It was already dark," he recalls; "the firing was still heavy. One of our tanks had been hit, it was burning like all hell; it lit up a big area. Everything and everybody moved out of that area; the Fascists had expert snipers and besides we expected artillery bombardment." Gordon joined volunteers carrying shovels forward through enemy fire to men wounded in the open field ahead so they could at least dig in. Merriman estimated the Lincolns' casualties at twenty dead and forty wounded. "We could have broken through if we had been given support," he scribbled.

The climax of the Lincolns' first experience of bloody war came on 27 February, their eleventh day under fire, when they were ordered to participate in retaking Pingarrón Hill from the *tabor* of Moroccans that occupied it. The plan was Gal's, the culmination of his untiring search for a dramatic action that might turn the tide of battle, force the nationalists back across the Jarama whence they had come, and redound to his glory. Robert Colodny, a Lincoln veteran, calls it "an act of monumental stupidity."

Colonel Vladimir Čopić, Gal's toady, a fireplug Croatian careerist, now commanded the Fifteenth Brigade, which included the Lincoln Battalion. Čopić's idea of leadership was slavishly carrying out his superior's orders, however lethal.

Merriman's first assessment of the attack plan, summarized in his diary, was optimistic. A nationalist prisoner had confirmed the positions of the nationalist forces. Gal scheduled a late-night softening attack with aircraft, artillery, tanks, and armored cars; the attempt on Pingarrón Hill would follow. Merriman thought the "plan good and sounded like good use of all arms."

At seven that morning the weather was bad—low clouds threatening rain and impeding air support—and the attack was delayed until ten. An artillery barrage to precede the infantry charge started up at 9:50. The Twenty-Fourth Brigade of Spanish regulars was supposed to go forward at ten. "We waited," Merriman writes, "without promised machine-gun support, without telephone—artillery going to left and not helping us or 24th Brigade either. Armored cars (useless) behind hill, no tanks in evidence, no horses. 24th failed to move forward. Ceiling low, no planes." The Spanish had advanced a short way up the hill, taken heavy fire from the nationalists, and retreated back to their trench line.

Despite the Spanish balk, the order came up for the Lincolns to advance. Merriman called back to headquarters to report the deadly conditions. "Stated several times that 24th had not advanced," he writes. "Machine-gun fire on our boys too heavy for any action. Plan of attack fell to pieces all along the line. Our boys plenty brave." Whoever took the call passed it along to Čopić. After a delay Čopić phoned "and bawled me out for failing to move it as scheduled. I said the 24th had not yet moved and he said they were ahead of us 700 yards and we were seeing their second line. He gave us 15 minutes to make up the distance. He was never more wrong in his life."

Although the low clouds prevented air coverage, Čopić demanded they put out an airplane signal in the shape of a T with the vertical stroke pointing toward the enemy; they pinned it together hastily from white towels and underwear. The two men who climbed up onto the road to spread the signal were both cut down by machine-gun fire. "After all from Čopić," Merriman continues angrily, "I observed signal of 24th brigade and it was 100 meters behind our trench even yet. Nothing to do since our boys were in field and [I was] out of runners. 3 planes came instead of 20 and didn't do much."

When he climbed up to signal his men to begin the suicidal assault a bullet slammed into Merriman's shoulder and shattered it in five places. They pulled him back down into the trench. One of the men dressed the wound. He was "rushed to Colmenar," he writes, "even though I wanted to stop and have it out with Čopić. In Colmenar [it was] a butcher shop. People dead in stretchers in yard. Had to sit up. . . . Went to operating room. [Surgeons were] pulling bullets out of a man who had become an animal." Wounded but young and far from home, Merriman noticed a pretty nurse: "Viennese girl—swell, real stuff." And then again the gore: "Several doctors operating on stomach exploring for bullets while others died. Question of taking those who had a chance at all." An attendant splinted Merriman's arm with a board. An English officer who had been wounded alongside him, shot through the head and jaw, was waiting for him: "We were going to the American hospital at Romeral."

On the three-and-a-half-hour drive from Colmenar to Romeral, Merriman banged around on the floor of an ambulance while the wounded officer helped him hold up his arm. They found Barsky and his team operating in damp gowns, but Rahman made sure the autoclave kept working. "I cut through clothing," nurse Lini Fuhr recalls, "of boys I had danced with on the way to Spain."

The rest of the Lincolns fared no better assaulting Pingarrón. They met not only direct fire but also what Herbert Matthews calls "a truly murderous cross fire" from the right. "The result was almost literally a massacre." Of the Lincoln Battalion's 400 men, 127 were killed and 175 wounded. The attack failed. Čopić, after trying to have the Lincolns court-martialed for resisting his deadly order to attack, would go on commanding the brigade for the next eighteen months.

The British Battalion suffered terribly in the confusion of the battle. Jason Gurney, a sculptor from Chelsea, encountered a scene of absolute horror on an afternoon reconnoiter:

> I had only gone about 700 yards when I came across one of the most ghastly sights I have ever seen. I found a group of wounded men who had been carried to a nonexistent field dressing station and then forgotten. There were about fifty stretchers, but many men had already died and most of the others would be dead by morning. They had appalling wounds, mostly from artillery. One little Jewish kid of about eighteen lay on his back with his bowels exposed from his navel to his genitals and his intestines lying in a ghastly pinkish brown heap, twitching slightly as the flies searched over them. He was perfectly conscious. Another man had nine bullet holes across his chest. I held his hand until it went limp and he was dead. I went from one to the other but was absolutely powerless. Nobody cried out or screamed except they all called for water and I had none to give. I was filled with such horror at their suffering and my inability to help them that I felt I had suffered some permanent injury to my spirit.

As many as sixteen thousand men, republican and nationalist, died or were wounded in three weeks at Jarama—a number comparable to the casualties through January 1937 from the fighting at University City in Madrid. The nationalists held their forward line across the river, but the republicans blocked them from pushing any closer to the capital; the new positions would remain static throughout the war. The next battle, northeast of Madrid at Guadalajara, would test Mussolini's Italians—volunteers whom the Duce fancied to be a new Roman legion.

SEVEN

The Old Homestead

Like thousands of others in republican Spain during the war years, Robert Merriman soon found his shattered shoulder, wound and all, immobilized in a plaster cast. His cast extended out at a right angle to his body like a broken wing so that the shoulder joint could heal unstressed. The surgeons called it an airplane splint. And because the hospital had run short of plaster of paris—the lightweight, fast-setting gypsum plaster named after the historic gypsum mines under Montmartre, whose tunnels became the Paris catacombs—Merriman's cast was molded of much heavier lime plaster, the kind used in construction. He felt the weight.

Sealing open wounds such as compound fractures (the kind with exposed bone) under plaster was a major and lifesaving innovation of the Spanish Civil War. Earlier, during the Great War, a shocking 46 percent of American soldiers who suffered fractures were permanently disabled; 12 percent died. In contrast, in a series of 1,073 cases of infected factures treated and tracked by the innovative Catalan surgeon Josep Trueta during the Spanish war, 91 percent healed satisfactorily, with a rate of 8.5 percent disabled and only six (0.5 percent) deaths.

Sealing compound, infected fractures in plaster rather than leaving them open for disinfection was a medical innovation out of Lincoln, Nebraska. A Nebraska surgeon, H. Winnett Orr, one of the pioneers of American orthopedics, devised the technique in the 1920s after serving as a medical officer in the U.S. Army at hospitals in Wales and France. "We had our eyes opened to the very serious character of the war wounds," Orr writes in a memoir of his first exposure to war casualties in Wales. "It was almost beyond belief to see how very extensive was the physical damage done. The infections were appalling. Large open wounds involving bones and joints were bathed in pus. In those who had survived, there were some fearful evidences of the destructive power of gas gangrene."

Orr was an admirer of a colorful nineteenth-century Liverpool surgeon named Hugh Owen Thomas, the descendant of a long line of Welsh bonesetters. Thomas practiced among the poor in the Liverpool slums in Victorian times, when the standard treatment for arm and leg fractures was amputation. Thomas to the contrary emphasized immobilizing the broken limb—he invented the Thomas splint for that purpose—and his precept, "enforced, uninterrupted, and prolonged rest." A direct line connected Thomas and Orr: Thomas's nephew Robert Jones, who trained under his uncle in Liverpool, was appointed inspector of military orthopedics for Great Britain and Ireland early in the Great War, and recruited Orr among twenty American orthopedic surgeons who volunteered to help the British before the United States entered the war in April 1917.

Despite Jones's implicit endorsement, Orr's idea of cleaning, packing, and immobilizing compound fractures in plaster received a hostile reception from British and American surgeons in the military hospitals where Orr served. Covering an open wound with plaster, he was told, would leave any infection untreated and risk killing the patient. Only a captain, he desisted. His chance came at the end of the war. By then he was chief of orthopedics overseeing the main American hospital at Savenay, France, the transfer point for all American sick and wounded evacuated back to the United States. Between July 1918 and March 1919, Savenay processed more than 60,000 American casualties, 18,000 of them with bone or joint injuries.

"Within a few days after arriving at Savenay," Orr writes, slyly, "our supply of splints gave out. . . . With my own fondness for plaster as a fixative dressing, it came therefore into extensive use. Even a great many of our spine and fracture cases were put into plaster of Paris for transfer to the United States. . . . We never heard of any very serious effects as a result of this method. In fact the only complaint we had was that occasional cooties were found inside the casts." The office of the U.S. surgeon general commended Orr on the "most excellent condition" of the returning troops.

In 1927 Orr told an audience of orthopedic surgeons a different version of the story, acknowledging more timidity in bucking authority. "During a certain stage of my experience in France," he said, "it fell to me to send some thousands of men with bone and joint wounds from France to the United States in casts. If I had sent any of these on shipboard for transportation to the United States without making windows in the casts for the daily dressing of open wounds I should probably have been censured or worse, and at that time I should not have thought of doing so. Yet later observations show that most of those men would have had less suffering, fewer complications, and better ultimate results if they had been prepared according to the method now advocated, put in closed casts and left undisturbed during the entire period of transportation to the United States or longer."

Perhaps because his courage had failed him within the military, Orr began promoting his casting treatment after he returned to civilian practice in 1919. Over the next decade, one of his patients estimates, he wrote "almost two hundred articles . . . and delivered more than five hundred lectures, many of them illustrated with movies and lantern slides." Surgeons are a conservative lot. Most ignored his methods, but he made a decisive convert in Catalonia.

Josep Trueta was a surgeon on the staff of the Hospital de la Santa

Creu in Barcelona. Among other duties he served as chief surgeon for an accident insurance company. In Spain such organizations maintained medical clinics for the workers they insured. Trueta thus treated injured factory workers and victims of road accidents, which is probably why he noticed Orr's papers. He decided to try Orr's method: aligning the broken bones to their normal position ("reduction"), cutting away bruised or infected tissue ("debridement"), packing the wound with sterile gauze, and then casting the limb in plaster, covering the wound, and leaving the cast on for two months or more while the wound and the bones healed. "At first I treated only unimportant wounds this way," Trueta writes; "but encouraged by the results I used the method in severe compound fractures of the tibia and fibula with a very satisfactory outcome."

A practical advantage of the method was that it eliminated the daily nursing routine of dousing uncovered wounds with disinfectant. A disadvantage, Trueta notes, "was that the plaster cast soon stank unbearably from contamination"—the wound draining its "products of tissue disintegration," as the surgeon delicately calls them, into the gauze packing and soaking into the cast. Later, in the war, patients in Trueta casts would be banished together to stink up a dedicated ward or, in good weather, parked outside. They smelled like death warmed over, "but underneath," a prominent American surgeon discovered who toured the Barcelona hospitals in wartime, "when cleaned up, there were nice, pink, well-granulated wounds." (Granulation is tissue matrix, the new growth that fills open wounds as they heal.)

By 1929 Trueta had treated more than one hundred cases, which he summarized in a report to the Surgical Society of Barcelona. Like Orr's, his exciting success story "did not get a good reception. . . . In the seven years before the beginning of the Spanish war, I could not persuade more than a few surgeons to try my method."

In the meantime, Trueta conceived of a further application that extended Orr's method beyond fractures. "Towards the end of 1929," he writes, ". . . I decided by simple reasoning that if this method of treating chronically infected bones nearly always worked there was no reason why it should not be successful as a preventive treatment of infection in recent open wounds." Trueta realized he could use Orr's method to treat large wounds regardless of whether broken bones were involved: clean up the wound, pack it with gauze, cast it in plaster, and leave it alone to heal. Later, after he escaped Spain ahead of Franco's victory and found his way to England, a refugee stranger in a strange land, Trueta minimized Orr's contribution to shine up his résumé (he eventually won appointment as professor of orthopedic surgery at Oxford University). He hardly needed to do so: his innovations were substantial and transformative.

The war tested Trueta's new methods. As chief surgeon of the largest hospital in Barcelona, he applied his casting technique on a large scale, keeping a record of his results. He treated wounded militiamen and, once the bombing started, injured civilians as well; published two papers in Catalan medical journals; and wrote a textbook.

Even that wasn't enough for Trueta's fellow surgeons, however. It took the determined intervention of his colleague Dr. Joaquín d'Harcourt Got, chief of surgical services for the republican army, to command the use of Trueta's methods in the Spanish Republic's hospitals. D'Harcourt tested Trueta's system at Teruel, a major battle fought between December 1937 and February 1938, where he and his assistants followed the Trueta protocol in treating around a hundred casualties. "On returning to Barcelona," Trueta writes, "my friend told me how satisfied he had been with the results." Before then, Robert Merriman worked at granulating under his massive airplane-splinted cast.

Most foreign correspondents who reported the Spanish Civil War from Madrid stayed at the Hotel Florida. The relatively new hotel, with a wedding-cake marble façade and two hundred rooms with private baths, a modern luxury, had opened in 1924 on the Gran Vía at the Plaza de Callao, west of the city center. It was only a two-mile streetcar ride from the front lines in University City, but that was not its primary attraction to journalists. Its primary attraction was hot water. Such comfort, available hardly anywhere else in Madrid, came at a price: the Florida was directly in the line of fire from the nationalist artillery on Garabitas Hill in the Casa de Campo. Ernest Hemingway recalls people "paying a dollar a day for the best rooms on the front" of the hotel. "The smaller rooms in the back, on the side away from the shelling," where Hemingway stayed, "were considerably more expensive."

The war mustered its own capricious economics. Herbert Matthews describes a lunch "graced with a bottle of white Tondonia, 1918," because ordinary table wine had disappeared. The memory of that rare vintage was "one of the high spots of the war" for the *New York Times* correspondent. The vagaries of cigar stocks made up for the coarse food. "Cheap cigars disappeared early in January," Matthews writes. "So we smoked Coronas, Hoyo de Montereys, Partagas, and even rarer brands. In fact, as time went on the cigars got better. . . . I write of that period feelingly, for I love cigars, and while they lasted Madrid was a smokers paradise." But not much was dependable under wartime conditions. "One day the stores appear to be full of a commodity, and a few days later it has disappeared as if swept off the shelves by a giant broom. That happened to so many things—Scotch whisky, coffee, sherry, soap (we woke up one morning and there was not a piece of soap to be bought in the whole of Madrid). Matches vanished all the way back in December, and then all of a sudden it became impossible to buy flints to keep our lighters sparking."

Deprivations might be temporary or permanent. "One gets along somehow," Matthews writes. "Things seemed natural under the siege that were doubtless rather extraordinary." Among them was the fate of Madrid's cats. Matthews's wife was "impressed," he says, perhaps choosing the word carefully, "when I mentioned having eaten cat a few times during the winter for want of any other meat. It tastes a bit like rabbit and is rather agreeable on the whole. Certainly we weren't feeling like martyrs when we ate it."

If journalists and other visitors received exceptional treatment from a government anxious to win international support, the ordinary people of Spain also tasted the luxuries that centuries of elite domination had denied them, Matthews notes:

> The suffering of that first winter of war was very real. I could walk to the Telefonica every morning . . . without seeing much to realize that suffering, except the food queues. Along the Castellana, children were happily spinning tops, women gossiping cheerfully, men buying newspapers and entering cafes for their morning coffee and "churros," while crowded streetcars went by laden with workers. But those men and women I saw were not fashionable, or even bourgeois; they were ill-dressed, rough-looking proletarians, enjoying for the first time in Spain's history some of that wealth which a few aristocrats, landowners, and churchmen used to monopolize.

Matthews earned his keep that winter with vivid reports on the major battles around Madrid. After the February 1937 stalemate south of the capital in the Jarama valley, Mussolini's Italians tried to take Guadalajara, thirty-five miles northeast, to cut off Madrid from that direction. Had General Mola waited until the Italians were in position before launching his Jarama campaign, the two forces might have applied the pincers that would have crushed the capital. There was no love lost between the nationalists and the Italians, however, particularly after the Italians refused to launch a diversion north of Madrid during the third week in February when Mola's Jarama forces were exhausted.

The Italian commander, General Mario Roatta, having easily taken Málaga, expected an easy victory at Guadalajara as well. On 8 March 1937, despite cold and heavy rain, he launched an attack up the Zaragoza-Madrid road: two motorized divisions, the Littorio and Black Arrow, of some 35,000 men in 2,000 trucks with 200 artillery pieces, eight armored cars, and 81 fast light tanks. The poorly trained recruits had never seen combat. "In three days they expected to take Guadalajara," Matthews reports, "then push swiftly down the level plain to Alcalá de Henares [due east of the Barajas airfield], at which point the capital would be virtually cut off." Deep mud confined the Italians with their wheeled vehicles to the narrow roads, and their slow and toilsome advance despite their motorized carriage—five miles the first day, eight miles the second—gave the defenders time to shift forces north from Jarama to confront them.

The republicans attacked the Italians from the air on 12 March. Fifty republican aircraft emerging in surprise from low clouds un-loaded five hundred devastating 100- or 200-pound bombs along the Italian columns and followed up with strafing attacks. The Italians panicked, dropped everything, and ran. By the evening of 14 March the republicans had reclaimed the area, Matthews says, along with "an enormous amount of munitions, many machine guns, many trucks, eight cannons. . . . Even food and clothing had been abandoned, while some of the cigarettes they left behind reached Madrid that night and I found myself smoking Macedonias again."

Patience Darton, a twenty-five-year-old English nurse, had arrived from London by air at the beginning of March 1937, rushed out to nurse the sick and injured commander of the International Brigade's British Battalion. Tom Wintringham had been wounded in the thigh at Jarama, had then contracted typhoid fever, and was languishing in a dirty, poorly staffed Valencia hospital, where a bright, petite American rover named Kitty Bowler, with whom he was having an affair, cared for him as best she could. Darton had already signed on for Spain when the Wintringham case came up; her nursing skills had prompted her air delivery.

From an upper-middle-class English family brought low by the fail-ure of her father's publishing business, Darton had seen terrible poverty serving as a nurse and midwife in the London slums. Such public health work wasn't enough, she'd concluded: "It wasn't getting anywhere, we weren't even touching the edge of the problem." A lecture by J.B.S. Haldane that she'd attended in 1935 had politicized her. She, another nurse, and a male porter had been the entire audience in the room when Haldane arrived, nearly voiceless from too much public speaking. "He took one glance at the three of us cowering down the other end," Darton recalls, "and he came down and sat down, and said, 'turn your chairs round, and sit here in a ring,' and took off his collar and tie, which surprised us very much, you know, anyone doing that, and gave a marvelous lecture—he was a very nice person." Haldane talked about controlling tuberculosis not only with the sanatorium treatments of the day, which were beyond the means of the poor, but also with social improvements such as better food and sanitation. When the Spanish war began, though she "wasn't in the least politically organized," Darton decided, "they're doing something. They're just ordinary people there and they've risen and they're doing something, and I'm a nurse, I can do something too." She found her way to the Spanish Medical Aid Committee offices and enlisted.

"When the nurse arrived for Tom she caused a sensation," another young Englishwoman volunteering in Spain, Kate Mangan, recalls. "She was a lovely, earnest creature called Patience. She was tall, thin, angular and virginal. She had a mass of ash-blond hair done up in a bun, but usually covered by a white kerchief. Her face was pointed and eager, with a full mouth, rather large nose and very striking, very blue eyes. . . . She looked like the kind of beautiful hospital nurse one dreams of."

Darton was as competent as she was beautiful. From Valencia she wrote a friend a blunt evaluation of the conditions Wintringham was enduring:

> I found poor Tom in a very bad way in this terrible hospital. He was running miles of temperature and the place was so dirty, full of flies, and shit was all the way up the walls of the loo, which was blocked anyway. I took a dim view of that. He was looked after by this American

girl who didn't know anything. He was so wretched, dirty and prickly and horrible that I thought first thing I'd give him a tepid sponge bath.

Worse, Wintringham was emaciated; Spanish doctors still believed that typhoid patients ran the risk of intestinal perforation throughout their illness if they ate normally, and allowed them only enough food to keep them alive. Coming from an English teaching hospital that had investigated the question, Darton knew better. "If you don't perforate in the second week," she said, "you're not going to perforate—that phase is over, and you'd better be fed, because people were taking a long time to recover from typhoid because they were starved."

She and Bowler got busy, Bowler scouting Valencia for fresh food and netting to screen out the flies, Darton feeding and bathing the English captain. "A doctor came in furious and made me sign a form that I was responsible for killing him," Darton recalls; Spanish doctors believed that bathing, like eating, was dangerous to typhoid patients. Discovering that Wintringham's wounds had been sutured too tightly, causing tissue necrosis and infection, the reason for his high fever, she removed the sutures, drained the abscesses, and sewed him back up. She arranged to have him transferred to a private room at the more professional and cleaner Pasionaria Military Hospital elsewhere in Valencia. He was soon convalescing.

At about the same time, having finally finished *To Have and Have Not,* Ernest Hemingway arrived in Spain. He had sailed on the *Paris* on 27 February with a lucrative contract to report from Spain for NANA, the North American Newspaper Alliance, at a dollar a word—almost $13 today—in 500- and 1,000-word dispatches. He had lingered in Paris for a week untangling his sidekick and factotum Sidney Franklin, a young American bullfighter, from a passport problem. Then, with the Dutch documentary filmmaker Joris Ivens, he had flown from Toulouse to Alicante on 16 March 1937 to assist in shooting the final scenes of Ivens's documentary *The Spanish Earth*. The film, for which Archibald MacLeish and Lillian Hellman had written the scenario, was a covert project of the Communist International, and Ivens was a Comintern agent, but Hemingway and its American sponsors didn't know that. Nor did Ivens's Comintern connection ultimately matter; the film, which merely portrayed a village collective sympathetically amid dramatic battle scenes, would help raise funds to support the Spanish Republic's fight for its life.

The English poet Stephen Spender, twenty-eight years old in 1937, happened to be in Valencia at the time Hemingway was passing through. Despite his youth, Spender had already published four books of poetry and one of criticism and was well-known internationally. He had come to Spain primarily to locate and perhaps rescue a former lover, a young army veteran named Tony Hyndman ("Jimmy Younger" in Spender's autobiography, *World Within World*). Hyndman had joined the International Brigades and run off to Spain when Spender broke with him after a long relationship. To justify his presence in Spain, Spender had accepted a post in Valencia as head of English broadcasting at the Socialist Party radio station. However complicated his love life (he had married a young Oxford student, Inez Pearn, shortly after breaking with Hyndman, having proposed to her the day after they met), the young poet was actively anti-fascist and had been since his cabaret days with Christopher Isherwood in Weimar Berlin at the end of the 1920s.

To Spender's disappointment, the Valencia radio station director had no work for him after all; the republican government was dissolving all the ad hoc organizations of the early months of the war and restructuring their activities under central government control. Spender found Hyndman, who had fought with the IBs in the Jarama campaign. "He looked fit and bronzed and young in his uniform," Spender writes. "We went out into the square outside the café and then I realized that this physical fitness concealed an extreme nervousness. As soon as we were outside he said with great vehemence: 'You must get me out of here!'" Having tasted battle, Hyndman wanted no more of it. "He went on to explain that he had changed all his ideas. He had come to Spain on an impulse, but now he knew that he did not want to die for the Republic." Spender doubted that he could arrange Hyndman's release from the IB and return to England, but he agreed to try. Because Valencia was the temporary seat of the republican government, Spender stayed there, writing an occasional article and living with other journalists at the Victoria Hotel.

It was there, in mid-March, that Spender met Hemingway, who was passing through by car on his way to Madrid. In Alicante Hemingway had noticed families celebrating the Guadalajara victory even as they saw their sons off to war. "Coming into Valencia in the dark," he writes, "through miles of orange groves in bloom, the smell of orange blossoms, heavy and strong even through the dust of the road, made it seem to this half-asleep correspondent like a wedding. But, even half asleep, watching the lights out through the dust, you knew it wasn't an Italian wedding they were celebrating."

The novelist and war correspondent, thirty-seven years old, six feet tall and a solid two hundred pounds, seems to have impressed everyone in Spain who met him as massive. "A black-haired, bushy-mustached, hairy-handed giant," Spender describes him, adding that in his behavior "he seemed at first to be acting the part of a Hemingway hero." Spender wondered "how this man, whose art concealed under its apparent huskiness a deliberation and delicacy like Turgenev, could show so little of his inner sensibility in his outward behavior."

He saw through Hemingway's act on an afternoon walk. They stopped in at a bookstore. Spender wondered if he should buy Stendhal's *The Charterhouse of Parma*. "Hemingway said that he thought the account, at the beginning, of the hero, Fabrice, wandering lost in the middle of the Battle of Waterloo . . . is perhaps the best, though the most apparently casual, description of war in literature." Hemingway went on to discuss Stendhal, impressing Spender with his insight. "He saw literature not just as 'good writing,' but as the unceasing interrelationships of the words on the page with the life within and beyond them—the battle, the landscape or the love affair."

Spender then made the mistake of quoting Shakespeare, which caused Hemingway's curtain to drop again. "'Why do you talk to me about Shakespeare?' he asked with annoyance. 'Don't you realize I don't read books?' and he changed the conversation to—was it boxing?" Walking again, Hemingway told Spender that he had come to Spain "to discover whether he had lost his nerve under conditions of warfare which had developed" since his experiences in the Great War— meaning presumably bombing and strafing, since not much else had changed. By then they were approaching a *taverna*. "We went inside and found some gipsy players. Hemingway seized a guitar and started singing Spanish songs. He had become the Hemingway character again."

Something in Spender evidently made Hemingway, a man afflicted with an abscess of hidden anxiety, at least intermittently comfortable. So did Spain itself, a country he loved, and covering the war, his métier. Whatever the reason, the two writers got along. One evening, after a visit to the Pasionaria Military Hospital, they sat together in a café having a cognac with a pretty young English nurse named Patience Darton.

Spender's lean good looks and Hemingway's bulk dazzled her:

Spender is tall—about 6' 2" and too "Great God" for words. He is perfectly sweet and very gentle and is torn in two between his pacifist nature—he couldn't kill anyone and hates war—and his mind, which sees this war as the only hope for Europe against fascist domination. He's got bright blue eyes, like a new kitten, with just the same groping expression of bewilderment against this bloody world. Hemingway is a great burly chap with a thick neck and a roll of flesh round the back of it. He is charming and humble—seems really so. He had a jaw wound in the Great War and has a hesitation in his speech.

For amusement or flirtatiously, Hemingway fed Darton malarkey: his July 1918 war wounds, serious as they had been, were in the legs— shrapnel from an Austrian mortar round that killed the two Italian soldiers who happened to be standing between him and the explosion—and a little shrapnel in his scalp and hands, but no jaw wound. Charming he certainly was. "The thing you never get from his books," Orson Welles would recall of him, "was his humor. . . . He was riotously funny." Hemingway was even humble sometimes in Spain, people who worked with him there remember. And competent on his visits to the trenches and near the front lines with Ivens, the documentarian—there's a photograph of him helping a Spanish recruit clear a jammed rifle, his big hands expertly working the bolt.

Darton was surprised and pleased that the two men listened to her opinions:

> We were talking about books and I said how much I wanted the *Oxford Book of English Verse*. They both agreed and Stephen said he wanted to read right thru the Bible. Hemingway said "Have you ever done that? It's a hell of a good book—you find where all the others have pinched their titles from." Spender said he'd lost his feeling of the necessity of keeping a moral standard, and civilization and culture. He says the best thing for the world—the only hope for the world—was to fight it with its own weapons. I said I couldn't accept that, and they both agreed I was probably right.

Another Wintringham visitor during his convalescence was J.B.S. Haldane, back in Spain between terms teaching at University College London, where he was a professor of biometry—that is, biostatistics. Darton heard long talks between the two men, sometimes punctuated with shouting. Haldane had advanced by then from investigating poison gas to studying the craft of digging *refugios*. Spain, a nation rich in minerals, was correspondingly rich in miners. The accumulation by February 1937 of a substantial number of antiaircraft guns that the Soviets had supplied put an end for a time to the terrible German and Italian bombing raids of late 1936. Taking advantage of the reprieve, miners were digging and tunneling large-scale *refugios* in Madrid, Barcelona, and other republican-defended cities. Haldane studied them because he believed London would need such protection from terror bombing in the next world war.

Spender's former lover would spend time in a fetid military prison and acquire an ulcer from the stress, but the English poet saved him from a firing squad and eventually saw him sent home. Spender went home as well.

Hemingway, Ivens, and Franklin left for Madrid on 19 March, driven dangerously by a drunken four-foot-eleven chauffeur named Tomás; Hemingway wrote in one of his NANA dispatches that Tomás looked like "a particularly unattractive, very mature dwarf out of Velásquez put into a suit of blue dungarees." They arrived in one piece in Madrid on 20 or 21 March, Hemingway checking in to Ivens's hotel, the Florida. Franklin went to work hustling supplies. Hemingway and Ivens toured the Guadalajara and other battlefields, meeting and interviewing some of the victorious French and Italian IB troops and their leaders.

Mussolini's Roman legions, retreating from Guadalajara, weren't feeling victorious, if they were feeling at all. Hemingway wired a dispatch to NANA the next day that made vivid their loss:

> Along the roads were piled abandoned machine guns, anti-aircraft guns, light mortars, shells, and boxes of machine gun ammunition, and stranded trucks, light tanks and tractors were stalled by the side of the tree-lined route. Over the battlefield on the heights above Brihuega were scattered letters, papers, haversacks, mess kits, entrenching tools and everywhere the dead.
>
> Hot weather makes all dead look alike, but these Italian dead lay with waxy grey faces in the cold rain looking very small and pitiful. They did not look like men, but where a shell burst had caught three, like curiously broken toys. One doll had lost its feet and lay with no expression on its waxy stubbled face. Another doll had lost half of its head. The third doll was simply broken as a bar of chocolate breaks in your pocket.

Hemingway was "greatly admired in Spain," the contemporary American journalist Virginia Cowles observes, "and known to everyone as 'Pop.' He was a massive, ruddy-cheeked man who went around Madrid in a pair of filthy brown trousers and a torn blue shirt. 'They're all I brought with me,' he would mumble apologetically. 'Even the anarchists are getting disdainful.'" When the front was quiet, Cowles notes, Hemingway "used to prowl around trying to borrow cartridges to go out to the country and shoot rabbits"—a sign, she implies, of his fascination with death. He was pot hunting at a time when the Madrileños were near starving and the offerings were meager at Madrid's restaurants.

Not that Hemingway was ever short of supplies. Between his high Spanish reputation, which won him a government driver, an old taxi, and access to military gasoline, and Sidney Franklin's gifts at scrounging, he always had food and drink on hand. "There was a tall wardrobe in Hem's room," the American novelist Josephine Herbst remembers, "and it was filled with tasty items: ham, bacon, eggs, coffee, and even marmalade." Certainly people wanted to be around him, exotic and famous as he was, but no one was unhappy to share his food and liquor as well. "There was a kind of splurging magnificence about Hemingway at the Florida," Herbst writes, "a crackling generosity whose underside was a kind of miserliness. He was stingy with his feelings to anyone who broke his code, even brutal, but it is only fair to say that Hemingway was never anything but faithful to the code he set up for himself. He could give an ambulance [to the cause] but would not be able to stomach [someone] stealing jars of jam on the sly. It wasn't soldierly."

One reason Hemingway was exuberant, Herbst believes, was "the success of his love affair" with Martha Gellhorn. Hemingway's new girlfriend and protégé was due to arrive any day from Paris. A twenty-eight-year-old Missouri-born American journalist and friend of Eleanor Roosevelt, and already the author of two books, Gellhorn had encountered Hemingway early in January 1937 in Sloppy Joe's bar in Key West, Florida. The owner was one of Hemingway's fishing buddies; Hemingway bicycled to the open-air bar afternoons after he'd finished his day's writing to have a drink and read his mail. Gellhorn described him as she first saw him: "a large, dirty man in untidy, somewhat soiled white shorts and shirt."

Like Hemingway, Gellhorn was the child of a physician. Her father, George, a German immigrant gynecologist, had died the previous January 1936; she was visiting Key West with her brother Alfred and her widowed mother. Hemingway took Alfred to be Gellhorn's husband, the two on their honeymoon, and decided he could separate her from her "young punk" within three days. She was taken but not smitten: staying on when her mother and brother returned to St. Louis; hanging out with Hemingway and his second wife, Pauline, at their large, shaded Spanish colonial on Whitehead Street; writing to her mentor Eleanor Roosevelt that Hemingway was "an odd bird, very loveable and full of fire and a marvelous story teller." Why Pauline put up with the intrusion into her household of a smart, good-looking young blond ingenue is anyone's guess: probably because she had to.

After Key West, Gellhorn had returned to St. Louis to continue struggling with a novel she was trying to write. On the way, Hemingway chased her to Miami for a steak dinner and flirtation, then pursued her by letter and by phone. They finally got together in New York at the end of February, shortly before he left for Spain. By then she had decided to go as well. A friendly editor at *Collier's* magazine, Charles Colebaugh, credentialed her as a special correspondent; *Vogue* paid her for a commissioned article, "Beauty Problems of the Middle-Aged Woman," which she held her nose and wrote. "I am going to Spain with the boys," she told a family friend. "I don't know who the boys are, but I am going with them."

Gellhorn crossed the border into Spain at Andorra, the Lilliputian principality, only fifteen miles wide, set between France and Spain in the eastern Pyrenees. "She had fifty dollars and spoke no Spanish," writes her biographer, Caroline Moorehead. She boarded an unheated train to Barcelona, spent two days in the Catalan capital interviewing and observing, then caught a ride on a munitions truck to Valencia. There she connected with Sidney Franklin, who drove her up to Madrid in a car filled with "six Spanish hams, 10 kilos of coffee, 4 kilos of butter, 100 kilos of canned marmalade, and a 100-kilo basket of oranges, grapefruit, and lemons." Hemingway traveled in style. His new girlfriend, he had bragged to Joris Ivens in Paris, had "legs that begin at her shoulders."

(An alternative and probably more reliable version of Gellhorn's arrival has her traveling from Valencia to Madrid in the backseat of a chauffeured government car along with the young Federated Press correspondent Ted Allen. "I absolutely flipped for her," he told Gellhorn's biographer Bernice Kert—"the wonderful smile, the hair, the great figure." According to Allen, Franklin sat in the front passenger seat looking over his shoulder disapprovingly, and it's true that Franklin, an admirer of Pauline Hemingway, disliked Gellhorn.)

Taking a room down the hall from her lover, Gellhorn joined the crowd at the Hotel Florida. Among the Florida's habitués Hemingway mentions Herbert Matthews, Sefton Delmer, Virginia Cowles, Joris Ivens, Ivens's cinematographer Johnny Ferno, and others, including "the greatest and most varied collection of ladies of the evening I have ever seen." Besides the journalists at the hotel there were pilots and their patrons, including Antoine de Saint-Exupéry, André Malraux, and the Argentinian diplomat Ramón Lavalle.

Hemingway left John Dos Passos off his list, though they had been good friends earlier and colleagues in the production of *The Spanish Earth*. Their friendship ended that spring in contention over the fate of José Robles, Dos Passos's longtime friend and translator and a Spanish army aide to General Vladimir Gorev, the head of the Soviet military secret police in Spain. Robles had been mysteriously executed sometime in March by what Dos Passos would later call "Russian secret agents." They did so, Dos Passos would report in 1939, because they "felt that Robles knew too much about the relations between the Spanish war ministry and the Kremlin and was not, from their very special point

of view, politically reliable." Hemingway dismissed Robles's death, and
Dos Passos found his callousness unforgivable.

Hemingway's experiences at the Hotel Florida gave him material for
his fiction as well as his journalism. One night in the Florida elevator he
encountered a drunken three-musketeer trio of two American contract
pilots and a Spaniard—Frank Tinker, Harold "Whitey" Dahl, and José
"Chang" Sellés, whose mother was Japanese despite his Chinese nick-
name. Dahl, moving a haul of champagne to their seventh-floor rooms
while Tinker and Sellés finished checking in, managed to get stuck in
the elevator. "After about two minutes of this," Tinker recalls, "a huge
fellow with a mustache came along and wanted to go up on the elevator,
too, but as he saw Whitey was already on the inside he waited awhile,
expecting him to go either up or down. When Whitey failed to do either,
the large stranger opened the door and asked him, in Spanish, what the
hell he thought he was doing. Whitey, not understanding him, asked, in
English, why in hell he hadn't opened the door instead of standing there
with his mouth full of teeth." In "perfectly good American" Hemingway countered that "people shouldn't get into strange elevators unless
they were sure they could get out of them." The encounter ended as
Hemingway's encounters often did, with drinks in the writer's rooms,
112 and 113, at the back of the third floor at what Hemingway believed
to be a dead angle from the nationalist artillery on Garabitas Hill.

Hemingway folded the fighter-pilot trio into his ménage, particularly Tinker, who came from DeWitt, Arkansas, near Hemingway's
wife Pauline's family seat in Piggott. "It turned out," write the Arkansas pilot's biographers, "that [Hemingway] and Tinker had fished many
of the same creeks and streams, hunted the same territory, and knew
most of the same hangouts and local characters."

In Hemingway's 1938 short story "Night Before Battle," Whitey
Dahl becomes Baldy, "a man with a white curly sheep's wool jacket, the
wool worn inside, a pink bald head, and a pink, angry face," and the elevator incident enlarges into a comic scene edged with fear and the threat
of violence. Baldy is drunk and belligerent, drowning the shock of his

day's mission: he's shot down a Junkers-52, after which its Fiat escorts shoot the tail off his fighter, forcing him to bail out over the Jarama and free-fall six thousand feet before opening his parachute.

Virginia Cowles sums up the Hotel Florida crowd in a memoir:

> I don't suppose any hotel in the world has ever attracted a more diverse assembly of foreigners. They came from all parts of the globe and their backgrounds read like a series of improbable adventure stories. There were idealists and mercenaries; scoundrels and martyrs; adventurers and embusqués [deserters]; fanatics, traitors, and plain down-and-outs. They were like an odd assortment of beads strung together on a common thread of war. Any evening you could find them in the Florida; Dutch photographers, American airmen, German refugees, English ambulance drivers, Spanish picadors and Communists of every breed and nationality.

Franco had pulled back from Madrid after the Guadalajara debacle. Hemingway correctly assessed the Caudillo's situation in his NANA dispatch of 22 March. "Studying the terrain," he writes, "I believe an encirclement of Madrid is now impossible unless Franco gets huge reinforcements of a better class of troops than those who fought at Brihuega." In contrast, the republican government on 21 February had called up all men between twenty-three and twenty-seven years of age for compulsory military service. Hemingway judged that Madrid was "now fortified to such extent that it would be impossible to take it by direct assault." Since Franco needed to pacify the country as his forces advanced, imprisoning or killing his republican enemies, it mattered little where he fought so long as he held whatever territory he gained. So he decided to leapfrog north, to the Basque Country, to Vitoria and Bilbao on the Bay of Biscay and to little Gernika (as the Basques spell the name of that town, Guernica in Spanish), and subdue that region first.

Franco's move north led the republican government to believe it could further secure the capital. "If one started from the premise that the insurgents were on the run," Herbert Matthews says, describing the government response, "and the [republicans were] irresistible, the next thing to do was to lift the siege of Madrid, and the first step in that direction was to drive the rebels out of University City." Eventually, Matthews notes, the republicans would have to take Garabitas Hill, a redoubt from which the nationalists freely harassed Madrid with artillery fire. Fully aware of its importance, the nationalists had spent the winter fortifying that strategic Casa de Campo mount.

The republicans began their renewed Casa de Campo offensive on 9 April 1937. The Hotel Florida squad—Matthews, Hemingway, Gellhorn, Franklin, Ivens, Ferno, Virginia Cowles—set up in a ruined apartment house on the Paseo de Rosales within a thousand yards of the line of attack to watch the confrontation. "It was marvelous," Hemingway writes. "The battle was spread out before us. Government artillery, with the noise now of flying freight trains, was registering shell after shell of direct hits on an Insurgent strongpoint, the castle-towered church of Vellou, with stonedust roaring up in steadily jumping clouds." Government infantry advanced on a nationalist trench and government bombers passed forward overhead and bombed the trench line in what Hemingway called "great black flowerings of death."

Marvelous though the view was, the journalists were too close for comfort, Hemingway reports:

Just as we were congratulating ourselves on the splendid observation post and the non-existent danger, a bullet smacked against the corner of a brick wall beside Ivens's head. Thinking it was a stray, we moved over a little and as I watched the action with the glasses, shading them carefully, another came by my head. We changed position to where it was not so good observing and were shot at twice more. Joris thought that Ferno had left the camera at our first post, and as I went back for it a bullet whacked into the wall above. I crawled back on my hands and knees and another bullet came by as I crossed the exposed corner.

They moved to a safer position then, the third floor of a ruined house with a wall ripped away on the side facing the Casa de Campo. They camouflaged the camera with old clothes. "I was surprised to find how banal war became from a distance," Cowles writes. "Against the wide panorama of rolling hills the puffs of smoke were daubs of cotton and the tanks children's toys. When one of them burst into flames it looked no bigger than the flare of a match." Cowles's detachment may have been inexperience; Hemingway, who had been in battle, was engaged. "It's the nastiest thing human beings can do to each other," he told her, "but the most exciting."

Hemingway christened their observation post the Old Homestead. "We had a good time there every morning and afternoon," Herbert Matthews remembers. Not always. Up the stairs into the Old Homestead one day came J.B.S. Haldane, who greeted them "with his usual cordiality," says Cowles, "and looked around for a place to sit." Out of the general wreckage Haldane dragged a broken-down red plush chair into the middle of the room, sat down "in full view of the battlefield," braced his elbows on his knees, and raised and focused his binoculars. "Hemingway warned him it was dangerous to remain exposed, but Haldane waved him aside. A few minutes later Hemingway spoke again: 'Your glasses shine in the sun; they will think we are military observers.'" Haldane dismissed Hemingway's concern, Cowles writes, denying that there was danger:

Ten minutes later there was a loud whistle as a shell plunged into a flat next door. Two more screamed overhead and we all went down on the floor—all except Haldane, who scrambled down the stairs and disappeared. We were shelled for fifteen or twenty minutes, and when at last we got back to the Florida we found him sitting in the lobby, drinking beer.

"Hallo," he called amiably, "let's have a drink."

We did; and more than one.

The battle for Garabitas Hill ended badly for the republicans, who suffered nearly three thousand casualties. It temporarily slowed Franco's northern campaign, since he had to transfer reinforcements back down from that salient, but his forces in Madrid held on to their redoubt. Worse, they barraged the city with multiple daily shellings to punish the republicans for the temerity of their assault.

EIGHT

Not Everybody's Daily Life

When Franco opened his new front in Euskadi (Basque Country) and Asturias after the Italian defeat at Guadalajara in March 1937, the Condor Legion moved north. Nationalist control of the northern half of Spain had isolated the two mountainous provinces that fronted the Bay of Biscay, cutting them off from republican Spain. Germany wanted access to their bounty of iron ore; Franco wanted a front where his struggling forces could win victories and pacify the nationalist rear while he built up his main armies to renew his attack on Madrid. The red-bereted Carlist *Requetés*—royalist militias from Navarre, eastward in the Pyrenees—would carry the fight in the north along with Spanish and Italian infantry under the overall command of General Emilio Mola. And since the Basques were numerous on the ground but weak in the air, and the country was mountainous, the primary machinery for destroying the republican defenses would be German aircraft.

To that end, the Condors repositioned their bombers on forward air bases in Burgos, one hundred miles southwest of Bilbao, and their fighters in Vitoria, only thirty-four miles west of the Biscay provincial capital. These northern bases allowed Franco's air force to fly multiple sorties on the same day, delivering nearly continuous bombing and ground-attack support against Basque forces that lacked air cover. The Basques had just six fighter aircraft—fast but outgunned Polikarpov I-6 Moscas—plus seven ancient, slow, biplane Bruguet bombers. In March 1937, Germany reinforced the Condor Legion with fresh pilots and the first of a new generation of bombers, the Heinkel 111 and the Dornier 17, both faster than their predecessors and capable of carrying heavier bomb loads at higher altitudes—the He 111 about 3,300 pounds of bombs, the Do 17 about 2,000 pounds. Heinkel 51 biplane fighters and a mix of other aircraft, about 150 planes in all, with German, Spanish, and Italian crews, rounded out the force.

When the new bombers were ready, on 31 March 1937, Mola issued a brutal threat, printed in propaganda leaflets to be dropped by air:

> PROCLAMATION TO THE PEOPLE OF EUSKADI: I HAVE DECIDED TO TERMINATE RAPIDLY THE WAR IN THE NORTH. THOSE NOT GUILTY OF MURDERS WHO SURRENDER THEIR ARMS WILL HAVE THEIR LIVES AND PROPERTY SAVED. BUT IF SUBMISSION IS NOT IMMEDIATE I WILL RAZE ALL VIZCAYA TO THE GROUND, BEGINNING WITH THE INDUSTRIES OF WAR. I HAVE THE MEANS TO DO SO.

"Vizcaya" is Spanish for "Biscay." In 1937 Biscay was the only part of Euskadi still in the hands of the republicans—a half million people, their fighting men armed with bolt-action rifles and not much more.

The man who planned the Condor Legion's bombings in northern Spain was Lieutenant Colonel Wolfram von Richthofen, the Legion's chief of staff and operational commander, forty-two years old in 1937; the son of a Silesian baron, he was a fourth cousin of the Red Baron of Great War fame, Manfred von Richthofen. Significantly, Wolfram von Richthofen had been attached to the Italian Air Force from 1929 to 1932, charged in particular, writes a biographer, "to study the airpower concepts of the Italians, and especially to report on the ideas of the famous Italian airpower theorist, General Giulio Douhet." Douhet, the father of strategic bombing, had reacted to the grinding trench stalemate of the Great War with a vision of war carried high over the front lines to the enemy's homeland, where he imagined that aerial bombardment of civilian populations would drive them to rise up against their belligerent leaders and sue for peace.

Douhet's vision rationalized the deliberate targeting of civilian populations, aggrandizing the role of air forces in war. Germany had initiated that brutality during the Great War, bombing London from zeppelins. British fighters firing tracer bullets into the zeppelins' hydrogen cells eventually ended their threat. Germany turned to bomber aircraft then, and by the end of the war, between zeppelins and bombers, had killed about three thousand civilians in raids on British cities.

Although the Luftwaffe had repudiated strategic bombing in the mid-1930s, Richthofen understood its potential, particularly its capacity for instilling terror in both military and civilian populations. "Fear," he wrote in his war diary, "which cannot be stimulated in peaceful training of troops, is very important, because it affects morale. Morale is more important in winning battles than weapons. Continuously repeated, concentrated air attacks have the most effect on the morale of the enemy."

Durango, a crossroads town of ten thousand people twenty miles southeast of Bilbao, bore the first of the new wave of northern bombardments on the very day Mola issued his warning. "Mola threatened to raze Vizcaya," the historian Herbert Southworth summarizes, "and the Condor Legion bombed Durango, to show how it could be done." The tons of 500-pound bombs that the Condor Legion and the Italian Aviazione Legionaria dropped on Durango were deadly enough. They were high explosives, however, not incendiaries, and despite J.B.S. Haldane's observation about the greater destructiveness of high explosives in stony Madrid, high explosives alone could not raze a city, not at least in a single day's work. George Steer, a South African–born London *Times* reporter covering the war from Bilbao in much the same spirit of outrage as had Louis Delaprée in Madrid, reports 127 dead in Durango "not counting unexplained pieces" of bodies, qualifying his count as only the first day's recoveries. Another 131 wounded died later in Bilbao hospitals.

After the bombers departed, Steer writes, "in the silence, more horrible even than the noise, could be heard glass slipping prettily to earth, tiles crackling far away, rarely some queer balancing trick of a table five storeys up on a broken floor breaking down and the whole crashing to the cellar. Then silence, broken by a little moaning."

Mola's reluctant Italian conscript infantry brigades did not always advance, however, after Richthofen's bombers and strafing fighters had softened up the Basque defenses, while the poorly trained Italian pilots sometimes bombed the wrong targets and even their own lines. A frustrated Richthofen continued trying to coordinate his air forces with Mola's armies on the ground through the first weeks of April. "Each Italian performance is utterly untrustworthy," the German officer complained in his war diary. "And these are supposed to be our allies!" The solution to the problem, he judged cynically, was to dupe the Italians with easy victories: "We will use all our Feuerzauber forces to clear the enemy positions almost completely before the Brigada Mixta attacks. This cheap success should give them the necessary moral boost."

Using "all our Feuerzauber forces" meant increasing the destructiveness of Condor Legion bombings. On 25 April 1937, when the Legion bombed the Basque small-arms manufacturing town of Eibar, beyond Durango thirty miles east of Bilbao, it added incendiaries to the high explosives it carried in its bomb bays.

Picasso had not yet begun work on the mural he had agreed in January 1937 to create for the Spanish Pavilion. Between January and April, returning to painting after his long abstention, he painted the women in his life almost exclusively—Marie-Thérèse Walter and Dora Maar—in fond, realistic portraits or disguised as a plate of fruit or a candle on a table beside his comical self-referential jug. At the other existential extreme, he continued an exploration of monstrosity that he had begun a decade before, filling more canvases with the grotesque but curiously serene beach monsters that the critic T. J. Clark argues "speak to the singularity of creatures (meaning us) on two legs," their monstrosity "most deeply a device to make them nongeneralizable, nonrepresenta-tive." As each human is, however many were being inhumanly slaugh-tered in his homeland. Picasso might be safe in Paris, but he was born in the Málaga of Queipo de Llano's brutal February assault.

The beach monsters were a variation on the problem he would have to confront with his promised mural: how to make public art without generalizing away the uniqueness of its subjects. The scale of the pa-vilion wall that the republican officials offered Picasso would not have troubled him, but the subject matter and style clearly did. What should he paint that would represent republican Spain, his besieged homeland, to the world, and yet would not be dully generic, a visual cliché? Most public art fails for a reason: "public" and "art" are nearly mutually ex-clusive categories.

It isn't surprising, then, as his architect friend Josep Maria Sert re-calls, that "Picasso did not go to work on [the mural] right away. He took months to begin it. . . . But we often talked about the picture. Pi-casso liked to talk about it, about what he was going to do." Whistling in the dark. But then "one day"—one day in April—"we were given the measurements of the wall we had reserved for his picture and we discussed them." And now Picasso had at least a frame for what he wanted to do, if not yet a subject: "He said the picture was not going to be the whole length of the pavilion; the height [of the display area] was low and he wanted to have it in certain proportions. He promised to do this thing, but until the last moment we really doubted if he was going to do it at all."

Picasso had been thinking about composing a mural painting on the theme of the artist in his studio. What that theme might have to do with the Spanish Civil War he never explained. The relationship between observer and observed was one he had explored many times before, and in any case it was something he knew a great deal about. Which was more than could be said of his knowledge of aerial bombardment, as he himself acknowledged. And if such an aesthetic theme seems inapposite or trivial, let it be recalled that Joan Miró, who had also agreed to paint a mural for the Spanish Pavilion in Paris, was spending the winter painting an indictment of the poverty of the Spanish peasant in the form of a powerfully realized still life of an old shoe.

Once Picasso had the wall measurements, he drew a series of sketches across two days in April that incorporated them as well as his preliminary ideas for the mural itself. The most significant sketch, on blue paper, is dated 19-4-37—19 April 1937—and includes a perspective drawing of the pavilion room where the mural painting would hang. The painting itself is indicated by an empty frame; sculptures of human figures sketched standing to its left and right show its large scale. In the right foreground Picasso drew an artist with Marie-Thérèse's features wearing a broad-brimmed Rembrandt-era hat and holding a palette and a brush. The artist is observing the pavilion wall with its empty mural frame through an open window; to the left of the window stands an easel holding a canvas brushed with a zigzag line. Curiously, the artist is positioned in an adjoining room from which she looks into the pavilion room: she seems to be inside, but she's also outside looking in. Someone once asked Picasso why he seldom painted landscapes. "I never saw any," he answered. "I've always lived inside, myself." And getting out of inside, as Clark explores, out of the secure nineteenth-century bourgeois interior, is visually what much of Picasso's work is about—even if, as in his beach drawings, there were monsters outside.

Other sketches fill the left side of the 19 April sheet but abandon the perspective view, as if Picasso was also using the paper as a scratch pad for exhibition ideas: an outline figure larger than the artist raises a muscular arm in defiant salute, its fist grasping a hammer and a sickle; an even more muscular arm disembodied in the foreground repeats the hammer-and-sickle gesture; an accordion-folded drawing, like a small Japanese screen, lies unfolded on the floor; one tile-roofed corner of a stone building, realistically drawn, projects into the space below the win-

dow; beyond it a front view of the blank mural and its wall outlines the
mural with black dots above and to one side that may indicate lighting.

Most significantly for the work to come, a woman's head crowded
into the space below the easel streams downward at a steep angle, as if
she is looking out a window or floating into a room. Picasso is thinking
out loud, so to speak; not all these sketches can be (or need to be) expli-
cated. They report that he's decided on the size and proportions of his
mural. It's still blank—he doesn't yet know its subject matter—but he's
thinking about including a workman's sturdy arm raising high a hammer and sickle. Or perhaps the workman with the massively oversized
arm is an idea for a separate sculpture: Picasso would also contribute
several monumental sculptures to the exhibition, though none so bla-
tantly symbolic as this arm. Whatever else the sketches communicate,
they report very little progress: he knows the size of his mural, has a few
ideas to explore—but still hasn't found a subject.

The workman's arm raised high, with a real hammer and a real
sickle clenched in its fist like one double-ended tool, intrigued Picasso.
On the same day that he drew the arm on his exhibition sketch sheet, he
also drew it on a copy of the 19 April 1937 issue of *Paris-soir,* defacing
a story about the French foreign minister's desire to maintain friendly
international relations even with Germany and Italy. It served, then, as
an expression of Picasso's fervent disagreement with the French foreign
minister.

But Martin Minchom has identified an even more significant connection. "On page 3 of this same April 19 issue" of *Paris-soir,* Minchom
writes, appears "a startling little item entitled 'Madrid was subjected
to an extremely violent bombardment yesterday.' This could have
been dictated by [Louis] Delaprée's ghost, speaking of 'pools of blood'
on Gran Vía and its sidewalks, and of brain matter being splattered
around." Picasso would find the same news service story at greater
length on the front page of *L'Humanité,* a newspaper he read regularly.
The renewed shelling of Madrid was a consequence of the republican
failure to take Garabitas Hill.

Picasso, Minchom concludes, showed "no apparent interest in battles or the military vicissitudes of the conflict," but "violent death, the bombing of civilians and murderous lies" drew his attention and his passion; the renewed shelling of Madrid seemed to show that "otherwise isolated events were coming together to form an ominous series."

The crowd at the Florida Hotel found itself directly under the renewed Madrid shelling. It was a brutal assault—"a nineteen-day bombardment of the capital," as Ernest Hemingway describes it, "that was almost too bad to write anything about." Before he left town at 6 A.M. one day during the attack, Hemingway counted 32 shells exploding within 200 yards of the hotel. On another day, he writes, they "had over 300 shells come into Madrid so the main streets were a glass-strewn, brick-dust powdered, smoking shambles." Wherever he went at any time he found himself "unable to . . . avoid the sight of the dead and wounded and hoses washing streets and sidewalks, not clear of dust but of blood."

Then the hotel itself was hit. Early one morning "two terrifying thuds" woke Josephine Herbst. "A heavy wall of water seemed to be crashing down with an iron force. But the havoc was in me, where the flood was swishing and my heart had become no more than a helpless chip. My hands shook as I tried to find my clothes, then I gave up and, throwing on a dressing gown, ran into the hall. . . . People were running toward the rooms at the back, doors banged, and when Hemingway, fully dressed and fit, called out to me, 'How are you?' I opened my mouth to say 'fine,' but no sound came."

John Dos Passos responded more laconically:

The shells keep coming in. The hotel usually so quiet at this time is full of scamper and confusion. Everywhere doors fly open onto the balconies around the central glassedover [sic] well. Men and women in various stages of undress are scuttling out of front rooms, dragging suitcases and mattresses into back rooms. . . . Great exhibitions of dishevelment and lingerie.

Herbst, rushing back to her room, finished answering Hemingway—"But I didn't come here to die like a rat in a trap"—and found herself thinking that was exactly what she had come to do, if necessary. "I managed to dress and to walk out again, and seeing [the English journalist] Claude Cockburn with a coffeepot in his hand, walking with his head bent, pale but impeccable, I rushed up to him and took it from him." Downstairs, in a breakfast room toward the front of the hotel where the noise was loudest, sounding to Herbst like "thousands of rats . . . scrambling for their lives in the plaster of the walls," Dos Passos watched Cockburn plug in the coffeepot "that speedily blows out the fuse at the same time melting the plug." Someone brought coffee, Herbst continues, "and someone else some stale bread. A toaster came from somewhere." Herbst's memory has Dos Passos arriving after the coffeepot blew, "fully dressed and composed, even to a necktie."

What everyone remembers is the spectacle of a Frenchman in a shimmering blue satin bathrobe passing out grapefruit from his private store as his contribution to surcease: the Little Prince, Antoine de Saint-Exupéry, in Spain since 11 April representing *Paris-soir* to the tune of 80,000 francs for ten dispatches (about $85,000 today). Despite Saint-Exupéry's right-wing newspaper affiliation, the anarchist faction had supplied him with a chauffeured Rolls-Royce for his visits to the front. Along the way his anarchist driver played at sideswiping other chauffeured cars with the Rolls, ripping off fenders, a demolition-derby gambling game the chauffeurs had invented. The French writer, delighted with the mechanical mayhem, added pesetas to the pot to urge them on. Hemingway understood Saint-Exupéry's grapefruit gesture. "He had brought two bushel of them from Valencia and this was his first bombardment and he was handling it by giving away grapefruits."

Would you like a grapefruit? Saint-Exupéry asks in Hemingway's version of the scene. *"Est-ce-que vous voulez une pamplemousse?"*

Sometime during this period Hemingway found occasion to encourage Gellhorn to write about the war. So far, she says, she had done nothing "except learn a little Spanish and a little about war, and visit the wounded, trying to amuse or distract them." Then Hemingway confronted her, telling her

> that I ought to write; it was the only way I could serve the *Causa,* as the Spaniards solemnly and we lovingly called the war in the Spanish Republic. After all, I was a writer, was I not? But how could I write about war, what did I know, and for whom would I write? What made a story, to begin with? Didn't something gigantic and conclusive have to happen before one could write an article? [Hemingway] suggested that I write about Madrid. Why would that interest anyone? I asked. It was daily life. He pointed out that it was not everybody's daily life.

Gellhorn did begin writing about the war then, her first dispatch that late April a barbarous shard of everyday life, set in an empty square where "the shells are falling so fast that there is almost no time to hear them coming":

> Then for a moment it stops. An old woman, with a shawl over her shoulders, holding a terrified thin little boy by the hand, runs out into the square. You know what she is thinking: she is thinking she must get the child home, you are always safer in your own place, with the things you know. Somehow you do not believe you can get killed when you are sitting in your own parlor, you never think that. She is in the middle of the square when the next one comes.
>
> A small piece of twisted steel, hot and very sharp, sprays off from the shell; it takes the little boy in the throat. The old woman stands there, holding the hand of the dead child, looking at him stupidly, not saying anything, and men run out toward her to carry the child. At

their left, at the side of the square, is a huge brilliant sign which says:
GET OUT OF MADRID.

Monday, 19 April 1937, was a day crowded with coincidences. Picasso glimpsed his theme that day in the sketch he drew of the Spanish Pavilion setting for his painting. He read in *Paris-soir* of the renewed shelling of Madrid and the French welcome mat out for the Germans and the Italians and contemptuously defaced the front page with a hammer-and-sickle arm. Hemingway—while drunk, evidently, given the garble of the dispatch—also wrote of the renewed shelling, and in a phrase he is unlikely to have originated, speaks of "the martyrdom of Madrid." He had probably recently read Louis Delaprée's pamphlet, published in English and Spanish sometime after its French publication on 8 January 1937. Certainly Picasso had read it, in early January, when it catalyzed his *Dream and Lie of Franco* engravings. In case the painter needed reminding, a reprint went on sale in Paris in April, when he was intensifying his search for subject matter for his promised mural.

The most shocking image in Delaprée's pamphlet, Martin Minchom notes, "and probably in all of Delaprée's writing, is an electric flashlight illuminating a woman and dead child, which is also of course a central image in the *Guernica*. . . . One of the drawings connected to the *Guernica* has an even more explicit allusion to Delaprée's text, showing a woman with a sliced breast, from which a triangle of light illuminates the baby." Picasso was primed to respond to the bombing of Gernika by the stories, including Delaprée's, of the terror attacks on Madrid. "If Picasso reacted so furiously to the destruction of Guernica in April 1937," Minchom concludes, "it was surely because he felt: *they've done it again.*"

On that 19 April Monday as well, Norman Bethune formally resigned from blood transfusion work for the Sanidad Militar.

Since February, Bethune had become a tireless blood milkman rushing deliveries day and night to hospitals and aid stations; by March he was delivering up to one hundred units a day. Martha Gellhorn accompanied Bethune and J.B.S. Haldane on one run from Madrid to Morata, in the Jarama valley, during a lull in the fighting there. "The noise of the artillery," she wrote in a particularly felicitous phrase, "was still beating at the corner of the mountains" as they drove fast on the terrible shell-pitted roads. Gellhorn soon saw more than she had ever expected to see of wounds and surgery. One "fair, sunburned boy's" shrapnel wound "looked like soil erosion, ridged and jagged and eaten in" before the hydrogen peroxide with which the surgeon flooded it foamed its foulness away. Gellhorn knew soil erosion from her previous work writing about the rural disasters of the Great Depression for Harry Hopkins's Federal Emergency Relief Administration, the work that had first connected her with Eleanor Roosevelt.

Of her expedition with Bethune and Haldane she concluded, "None of it seemed real to me at all. I put this down not because I think it is important but because it is so, and because from the first day I have been here the business of making death, planning it or getting it or keeping it off, has struck me as by far the most unreal thing I have ever known in my life." After a long day's work, driving back to Madrid, "the blood had been delivered, and we had the orders for the bottles that were to be taken up the line next day. We did not talk. It was a smooth, black night, with high stars." They passed a line of tanks, "always ominous," but later, looking back at them in the dark distance, Gellhorn found the sight of them comforting: "It was as if six boats, with only their harbor lights showing, were tied together, riding a gentle sea."

Bethune's Instituto Hispano-Canadiense de Transfusión de Sangre would be responsible for 78 percent of all the blood transfusions performed on the republican side during the war—about 528 gallons of blood, enough for five thousand transfusions. Despite that great service, a cabal of communist officials in the Spanish government and several of Bethune's Canadian communist brethren began colluding in early April to expel him from Spain.

According to the Canadians, Bethune had broken down under the weight of his work into belligerent drunkenness and had to be relieved.

In fact, his biographer David Lethbridge writes, by early 1937 Spanish intelligence had formed "an entirely false picture of Bethune as a potentially dangerous renegade, politically ambiguous, possibly a double agent, possibly a spy, possibly a fascist sympathizer." The republican authorities came to that paranoid picture partly because Bethune had been observed making detailed maps of the frontline regions he visited, which of course he did in order to determine his blood delivery routes; partly also because he had taken up with a tall, beautiful strawberry blonde named Kajsa Rothman, a multilingual Swedish dancer and volunteer with whom he had fallen in love and who was working as his translator. Since the same authorities believed Kajsa to be a Trotskyist, the worst of all crimes in Stalinist circles in 1937, their convictions about her tainted their judgment about Bethune.

Once they decided that Bethune had to go, they worked out what one official preeningly called "a clever way" to expel the surgeon to avoid antagonizing Canadian donors to the Causa: they convinced him he should tour the United States and Canada lecturing to raise funds. He understood that he would leave Spain for the summer and then return. He had a new project in mind now that the blood service was up and running under Spanish military leadership: a children's village to shelter what were expected to be thousands of orphaned Basque children, refugees from Bilbao's inevitable fall. Once Bethune left Spain, however, in early May 1937, he was barred from returning. Even so, he continued fund-raising across North America through the summer and into the fall. Barred from Spain, he moved on in 1938 to China, to Yan'an, the end point of Mao Zedong's Long March, where he joined the Chinese communists fighting the Japanese. The following year he nicked his finger during surgery on a guerrilla fighter's septic wound and contracted fatal septicemia. He died on 12 November 1939.

A final coincidence on that 19 April 1937 Monday, an ominous one for the battle developing in Euskadi, was the arrival in northern Spain of twelve new Messerschmitt Bf 109s. The German Luftwaffe had detached the outstanding new fighter aircraft from its own small fleet of thirty and delivered them to Manfred von Richthofen to muscle up his Condor Legion to more effectively dominate the air over Euskadi.

Kajsa Rothman inexplicably escaped expulsion despite Spanish suspicions of her allegiance. By late April she had reinvented herself as Virginia Cowles's interpreter and Hemingway's occasional guide. Gellhorn biographer Caroline Moorehead reports in passing Rothman's successful infiltration of the Florida: "[Sidney] Franklin, an ebullient man, described not altogether fondly as 'buoyantly mindless,' who acted as Hemingway's majordomo, slept in one of the [Hemingway] rooms with the provisions, while a Swedish girl, who spoke seven languages and wore men's clothes, sometimes came and joined him."

Ilya Ehrenburg, the Russian novelist and journalist, met Hemingway for the first time in Madrid that spring. Ehrenburg was eight years older than Hemingway, and somewhat starstruck, but her naïveté gave way to friendship as they visited the front lines together and talked through the war. "I was with Hemingway at Guadalajara," Ehrenburg writes. "He understood military matters and quickly grasped the situation. I remember him watching the men bring the Italian army hand-grenades, red as large strawberries, out of the dugouts; he grinned: 'They've left the lot behind. It's just like them.'" Ehrenburg, like Spender, saw behind the Hemingway character the writer played, saw the real work the man did:

> If you had come across Hemingway by chance you might have taken him for a romantic bohemian or a typical dilettante: he drank, had various eccentricities, roamed the world, went in for deep-sea fishing, big-game hunting in Africa and appreciated all the finer points of bullfighting—nobody knew when he did his writing. But he was a hard worker; the ruins of the Florida were anything but a suitable place for a writer to work in, but he sat there writing every day; he told me that one must write doggedly, never give in—if a page turns out colorless, one must stop, rewrite it, five times, ten times. I learnt a great deal from Hemingway.

Robert Merriman, his left arm still immobilized in a heavy cast, and his wife, Marion, who had joined him from Moscow in March, met the Florida crowd at a gathering in Hemingway's rooms on 23 April. The Americans were planning a midnight radio broadcast home to encourage support for the Spanish Republic; Merriman had been asked to speak for the American IB volunteers.

Driving into Madrid from Albacete that morning, Marion Merriman had been impressed by the big Madrid bullring and the capital's wide, tree-lined boulevards, but when she and her husband left their car and driver and threaded through the dangerous streets on foot, the shelling had terrified her. By the time they reached Hemingway's rooms, she writes, she was "shaking badly. . . . Bob steadied me, then knocked on the door":

> "Hello, I'm Merriman," Bob said as Hemingway, looking intense but friendly, opened the door.
>
> "I know," Hemingway said. Bob introduced me, and the writer greeted me warmly.
>
> Then Hemingway and Bob fell into conversation about the war and the broadcast they planned. They were joined by John Dos Passos, Josephine Herbst, and a scattering of American volunteers who sipped Hemingway's scotch and compared notes and stories. I slipped into an old chair, still quite shaken by the action outside.

To her great relief, someone offered her a drink. She fell then to comparing her husband and the famous American writer. "Hemingway seemed complex. He was big and bluff and macho. He didn't appear to be a braggart but he got across the message, through an air of self-assurance, that he could handle what he took on." Merriman was younger than Hemingway by ten years and taller by several inches, a scholar in horn-rimmed glasses rather than a seeming adventurer in steel frames. "Hemingway was animated, gesturing as he asked questions, scratching his scalp through thick dark hair, perplexed, then scowling, then, something setting him off, laughing from deep down. He wore a sweater, buttoned high on his chest, and a dark tie, loosened at the neck." He needed a shave, "the scrubble roughing his cheeks and chin. He looked like he had had a hard night. He had a knot on his forehead, probably suffered in some roustabout skirmish."

Dos Passos caught her attention; an English major, she thought Dos Passos was a better writer than Hemingway, especially writing about war:

> But as a man, he didn't impress me. I thought he was wishy-washy. I couldn't make out everything he was saying, but his message was clear—for whatever reasons, he wanted out of there, out of Hemingway's room, out of bomb-shaken Madrid.
>
> I was scared too, with good reason. But somehow Dos Passos acted more than scared. I guessed it was his uncertainty, his facial expressions, his general attitude that this was a lost cause, given the superior strength of the Franco forces. Dos Passos criticized the Spanish Republic, for which Americans were fighting and dying.

Dos Passos had reason for his disillusion in the summary execution of his translator and friend José Robles, about which Hemingway had recently bluntly informed him; he was in fact about to leave Spain, his whole view of politics transformed.

At midnight at the radio station, with Hemingway acting as anchor, Merriman spoke first, a six-minute speech he had written at the hotel that afternoon. The Lincoln Battalion surgeon, Dr. William Pike, spoke next, Dos Passos third, then Josephine Herbst, then the new battalion commander who had replaced Merriman, a Pennsylvanian named Martin Hourihan. Hemingway wrapped up the broadcast. "Pleased with Hemingway," Merriman judged in his diary. "Disappointed with Dos Passos."

The next day, Hemingway left with Gellhorn for a pack trip up into the Guadarramas, partly to report, partly to take the lay of the land for a novel he had decided to write about the war. He describes the trip as "a hard ten days visiting four central fronts, including all high positions, hours on horseback, and climbing to important positions 4,800 feet high in the Guadarrama Mountains, which, with the snows melted, can be studied intelligently." The trip was five days, not ten—he left on the twenty-fourth and returned on the twenty-ninth—but it was hard enough, if also fruitful.

Robert Merriman is often said to have been Hemingway's model for the hero of that novel, *For Whom the Bell Tolls*. Marion Merriman writes more accurately that her husband "would serve as part of a composite for the professor from Montana, the fictional character Robert Jordan." Another part of that composite must certainly have been the Lincoln Brigade's tall, stooped, forty-year-old adjutant Hans Amlie, a North Dakotan whom Marion describes as "a big Swede . . . an old-time socialist and brother of a Wisconsin congressman." Herbert Matthews would interview Amlie in July, after Amlie was wounded in fighting near Madrid. "A mining engineer," Matthews describes him, significantly (for evidence of Hemingway's borrowing) misidentifying him as "from Montana." Amlie calls himself "a prospector," the *New York Times* reporter writes, adding that he "has roamed far over our West, Mexico, South America. He is not a Communist, not a Socialist, knows and cares nothing about politics, except that he hates Fascism as much as any human being could hate it." Robert Jordan shares many of these qualities—unusual among the largely East Coast and communist IB members—with Amlie, who also told Matthews, "It was perfectly natural for me to come to Spain. This is the only place in the world where people like me belong at the moment. Anyone who loves liberty and hates Fascism must come here!"

Off in the mountains, then, Hemingway perhaps had still to meet Hans Amlie. In any case his primary model for the character of Robert Jordan was himself. Jordan's thoughts about his father's suicide, which thread through the novel, confirm that connection: Hemingway's father had killed himself in 1928, an act Hemingway attributed to cowardice just as Jordan does his fictional father's. The writer was busy with his own work when Gernika's time came, but Picasso was charged and primed.

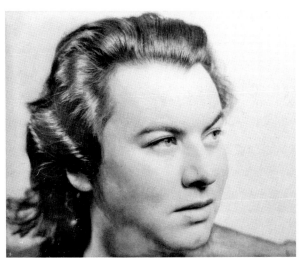

In July 1936 an attempted coup d'état by Spanish generals forestalled a People's Olympiad in Barcelona. Hastily organized people's militias fought back.

The American poet Muriel Rukeyser, in Barcelona to cover the Olympiad, saw her German lover Otto Boch off to fight and die for republican Spain, one of tens of thousands of foreign volunteers.

Nazi Germany supplied the rebel generals with planes to move North African merce-naries into Spain in the world's first large-scale airlift.

Symbolically attacking the Church and nobility that had long oppressed them, young militiamen "executed" a statue of Christ.

The Spanish people defended their cities to the rallying cry *¡No Pasaran!* ("They shall not pass!").

Brutal general
Francisco Franco led
the nationalist assault
on republican Spain.

With Franco's forces at the gates of Madrid, the first 3,000 American volunteers arrived
to support the loyal republican militias.

British biologist J.B.S. Haldane (*left*) investigated possible nationalist use of poison gas. He judged incendiaries and high explosives more deadly.

Canadian surgeon Norman Bethune (*left*) and his assistant Hazen Sise outfitted ambulances for delivering blood to the republican front lines.

The writer George Orwell volunteered to fight with a people's militia. His classic memoir *Homage to Catalonia* chronicled the civil war.

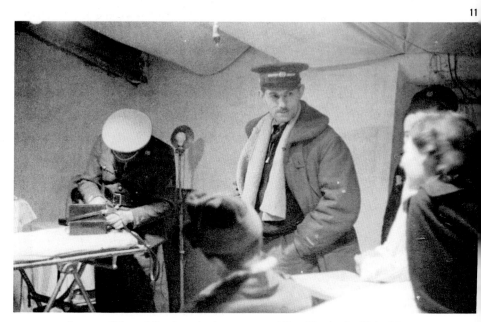

Surgeon Edward Barsky raised money at public rallies in the United States, organized hospitals in Spain, and operated on hundreds of wounded.

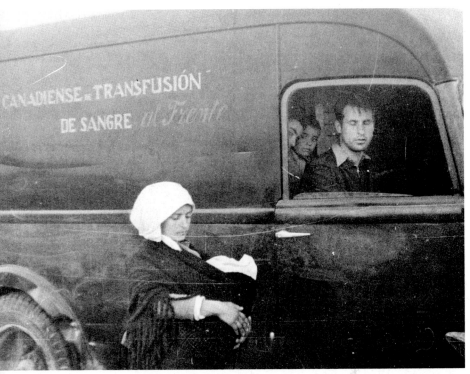

As Franco's planes strafed refugees escaping the overrun town of Málaga, Bethune and Sise desperately moved women and children to safety.

Hitler and Mussolini supplied Franco with air forces; large-scale terror bombing of civilians followed for the first time in the history of war.

The historic Basque town of Gernika (in Spanish, Guernica), near Bilbao, became the first city deliberately firebombed to destruction.

Pablo Picasso responded to the atrocity with his great painting *Guernica*. His mistress, the photographer Dora Maar, chronicled its creation. At the 1937 Paris Exposition, people crowded to see it.

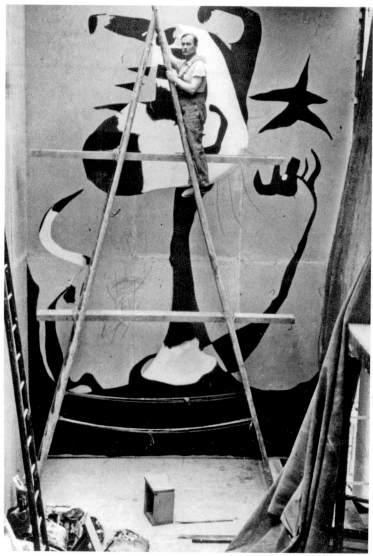

Catalonian artist Joan Miró painted *Guernica*'s counterpart, *Catalan Peasant in Revolt,* for the 1937 Paris Exposition as well. Subsequently the panels were lost in the confusion of war.

As Franco's forces closed in on Bilbao, the Basques evacuated
100,000 women and children to France and England by ship.

Martha Gellhorn and Ernest Hemingway covered the war for U.S. newspapers and magazines—and began a passionate love affair.

The English nurse Patience Darton (*right, front*) served in republican field hospitals. She and International Brigader Robert Aaquist (*right, rear*) fell in love and married.

At Brunete, twenty miles west of Madrid, tens of thousands died fighting Franco's forces to a stalemate, but Germany and Italy kept Franco resupplied.

By spring 1938, Franco's forces had cut Spain in two. Republican defenders attempted a surprise attack across the Ebro River.

22

A cave in a valley above the Ebro, with its own spring of fresh water, served as a field hospital blessedly safe from strafing German aircraft.

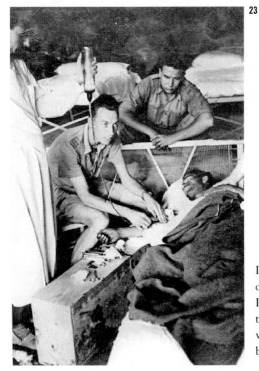

23

Inside the cave, volunteer doctors and nurses, Patience Darton among them, treated the wounded from the fierce battle raging below.

When she learned that her husband had been killed fighting, Patience Darton
moved to front-line nursing to assuage her grief.

After Franco's victory, German and Italian aircraft spelled out his name in formation at a celebration in Madrid. Franco's dictatorship oppressed the country until his death in 1975. Democracy followed under the restored Spanish king.

In 2013, Brunete resident Ernesto Vinas and the author inspected the old battlefield, still scattered with the remains of the Spanish "little world war."

NINE

A Sea of Suffering and Death

Monday morning, 26 April 1937, the Condor Legion's Wolfram von Richthofen conferred by telephone with his nationalist counterpart, Colonel Juan Vigón, about the day's bombing program. "After a short telephone briefing with Vigón at 6 A.M.," Richthofen noted in his war diary, "[squadron] D/88 is scheduled for Guernica [and] 2 villages at the west Marquina crossroads, to stop the Red retreat." A few paragraphs later Richthofen added: "Guernica *must* be destroyed if we are to strike a blow against enemy personnel and materiel."

Monday was market day in the historic Basque town of Gernika, twenty miles northeast of Bilbao in a green valley at the upper end of the Urdaibai estuary; a canal on the east side of town connected the town to the estuary and thence to the Bay of Biscay. Gernika had a distinguished history: it had been the meeting place of the Basque parish general assemblies since the Middle Ages. Founded in 1366, the old town had so far escaped bombing. Estimates of Gernika's population that sunny Monday vary from five to ten thousand. Some occupants had removed to Bilbao to escape the approaching battlefront, then about fifteen miles away to the east, but Gernika had also become a temporary refuge for retreating Basque militia. Three reduced Basque battalions were quartered near the town, and three field hospitals had been es-

tablished there, two in convents, one in a home for the elderly. Gernika's other military assets were few: an Astra small-arms factory in the
industrial district on the east side of town, a bridge across the narrow
estuary canal, a railroad station. With only three antiaircraft guns, it
was effectively undefended against air attack.

On Saturday, Basque president José Antonio Aguirre had appointed
a new town administrator, Francisco Lazkano. Given Gernika's dangerous proximity to the front, one of Lazkano's first acts was to cancel
the Monday market day, the *feria,* and block the main roads into town.
The country people came anyway in ox-drawn, large-wheeled carts,
following old lanes that circumvented the blocked roads. Many hadn't
heard that the market had been canceled, and in any case there was
money to be made from the billeted soldiers. The *feria* opened as usual
in the morning, the Plaza de los Fueros filling with farmers, livestock,
and produce, and continued throughout the day. The townspeople and
their country neighbors took their midday meal at local restaurants or
in the parks.

Noel Monks, an Australian journalist covering the war for the London *Daily Express,* transited Gernika at about three thirty that afternoon
as he was being driven out from Bilbao to visit the front at Marquina.
His driver's name was Anton. "Guernica was busy," Monks noticed.
"It was market day. We passed through the town and took a road that
Anton said would take us close to Marquina." They continued driving
for another half hour. Then:

> We were about eighteen miles east of Guernica when Anton pulled
> to the side of the road, jammed on the brakes and started shouting.
> He pointed wildly ahead, and my heart shot into my mouth when I
> looked. Over the tops of some hills appeared a flock of planes. A dozen
> or so bombers were flying high. But down much lower, seeming just to
> skim the treetops, were six Heinkel 52 fighters. The bombers flew on
> towards Guernica, but the Heinkels, out for random plunder, spotted

our car, and, wheeling like a flock of homing pigeons, they lined up the
road—and our car.

Seeing a bomb crater twenty yards off the road, half filled with
muddy water, the two men bolted over, dived in, and "sprawled in
mud . . . with our heads buried in the muddy side of the crater." Since
the Heinkels were flying more or less level with the road, their wing-
mounted guns couldn't easily fire into a crater. "The planes made several runs along the road," Monks writes. "Machine-gun bullets plopped
into the mud ahead, behind, all around us. I began to shiver from sheer
fright. Only the day before, [George] Steer, an old hand now, had
'briefed' me about being strafed: 'Lie still and as flat as you can. But
don't get up and start running, or you'll be bowled over for certain.'"

Tiring of the game, the Heinkels flew on. The two men ran back
to their car. A military car was burning nearby. They dragged out the
bodies of two men whom the Heinkels had machine-gunned and laid
them by the side of the road. "I was trembling all over now," Monks
writes, "in the grip of the first real fear I'd ever experienced." As he
calmed down and grasped that he was safe, exhilaration replaced fear.
Anton drove on. "At the foot of the hills leading to Guernica," Monks
reports, "we turned off the main road and took another back to Bilbao.
Over to our left, in the direction of Guernica, we could hear the crump
of bombs."

Monks assumed, probably correctly, that the Germans were bombing Basque reinforcements moving eastward from Santander, a coastal
town west of Bilbao still in Basque hands. The biplane Heinkel 52s
were not seen over Gernika that afternoon, nor did a group of bombers
appear until early evening, but their presence confirms the Condor Legion's heavy activity in the area that day.

The first bombs that fell on Gernika, hundred-pounders, dropped
around 4 P.M. from a single low-flying German twin-engine Dornier 17,
coming up from the south. The Do 17 was a light bomber that its pilots

had nicknamed the *Fliegender Bleistift,* the Flying Pencil; its long, narrow, tubular fuselage was supposed to make it harder to shoot down. A bombardier occupying a Plexiglas-windowed compartment in the nose controlled the release of the plane's two thousand pounds of bombs. A Gernika eyewitness reports three explosions from that first bomb run; a modern Spanish source reports twelve bombs. Three bombs seems unlikely. Other sources claim six bombs, perhaps meant for the railway station. "The bombs with a shower of grenades fell on a former institute and on houses and streets surrounding it," Steer would report from eyewitness accounts. (The grenades dropped with the bombs may explain the discrepancy in numbers among the various accounts.) Spotters rang the church bell to warn the town of a bombing raid. People ran for cover—to the cathedral; to the railroad station; to the bomb shelters, *refugios,* that had been hastily constructed in Gernika after the Durango bombing; to nearby farmhouses and woods. Its work done, the Dornier 17 flew on north, following the canal to the estuary toward the sea.

Twenty minutes later a flight of Italian warplanes approached Gernika from the north—three Savoia-Marchetti 79 trimotors, fast medium bombers with payloads of twelve bombs each, hundred-pounders. The Italians had been assigned to bomb the canal bridge and adjacent road on the east side of town, "to block the enemy retreat." Skittish or undertrained, they dropped all thirty-six of their bombs in one quick pass, missed their target, blew up a house and a few commercial buildings, and pulled away.

The next aircraft to arrive was a Heinkel 111B, another fast new German medium bomber, with an escort of five Fiat fighters. The 111B could carry three thousand pounds of bombs. "This third bombardment," writes the Spanish historian César Vidal, "was followed by a fourth and a fifth, also limited in scale. Indeed, at five o'clock and at six o'clock in the evening, another two German twin-engined planes also dropped their bombs over the town. If the aerial attacks had stopped at that moment, for a town that until then had maintained its distance from the convulsions of war, it would have been a totally disproportionate and insufferable punishment. However, the biggest operation was yet to come."

It came at around 6:30 P.M., half an hour before sunset: three squadrons of Junkers-52 trimotor bombers, the sturdy square-sided planes the republicans called *tranvias*—trams, streetcars. They "were so clumsy," Steer comments, "that they seemed to clang rather than fly." They were reliable aircraft, with corrugated duralumin fuselages and two bomb bays capable of carrying 3,300 pounds of ordnance, "the heaviest bombers that Germany had sent to Spain." They were loaded that night, for the small town of Gernika, with forty to fifty tons of bombs, almost as much as had been dropped throughout all Biscay that day. Fiats from Vitoria escorted them as well as the Messerschmitt Bf 109 fighters—twenty-nine planes in all. The Junkers-52s, Vidal writes, "made their attacks arranged in successive wedge formations of three airplanes, which meant an attack front of about 150 meters"—500 feet wide. Carpet bombing took its name from such wide attack fronts, planes advancing in formation across a town like a carpet being unrolled. With no significant Gernikan air defenses to destroy, the Fiats and Messerschmitts pulled away to occupy themselves strafing civilians as they ran to escape the rain of destruction; the pilots even played at machine-gunning the herds of sheep and their shepherds heading home from the *feria* on the roads outside of town.

Most of the buildings in Gernika were constructed of wood above the ground floor. For that reason, the Junkers, which had central and forward bomb bays, had been loaded with both high-explosive bombs and incendiaries—the HEs to make kindling, the incendiaries to light the fires. The HE bombs, 100- and 500-pounders, fell from the Junkers' central bomb bays. The two-pound incendiaries—tubes fourteen inches long and two inches in diameter of Elektron (an alloy of 92 percent magnesium, 5 percent aluminum, and 3 percent zinc) filled with thermite—were packed in droppable metal dispensers each holding thirty-six bombs. At a preset lower altitude an explosive charge blew open the dispensers to disperse their bomb loads over the target area.

Thousands of Elektron incendiaries fell on Gernika that night, skittering down like icicles broken off an eave. The thermite in the firebombs was a powdered mixture of aluminum and iron oxide. Ignited by a percussion cap in the impact fuse, it heated up almost instantly to more than 4,000 degrees Fahrenheit, burning for less than a minute but igniting the magnesium casing in turn through rings of holes drilled just above the impact fuse and at the top of the casing. The casing then continued burning for fifteen minutes or more, until all the magnesium was consumed: Elektron incendiaries, pure burning metal, were almost impossible to quench.

Back in Bilbao, the *Daily Express*'s Noel Monks had encountered the London *Times*'s George Steer and a Reuters News Agency man, Christopher Holme, in the Presidencia Hotel, where Monks was staying. The three journalists went to dinner at Steer's hotel nearby, the Torrontegui; a tramp steamer captain named Roberts, who was engaged in smuggling food to the Basques, joined them along with his young daughter Fifi. They had just eaten their first course—"of beans," Monks writes sardonically—and were waiting for the second course of bully beef "when a Government official, tears streaming down his face, burst into the dismal dining room crying: 'Guernica is destroyed. The Germans bombed and bombed and bombed.'"

Monks noted the time—9:30 P.M. "Captain Roberts banged his huge fist on the table and said: 'Bloody swine.'" Minutes later Monks, Steer, and Holme were racing toward Gernika in a Basque government car. In the night darkness they could see the reflection of the burning town on the clouds from ten miles away. Steer describes the climax of the bombing:

As the people not trapped in the *refugios* moved northwards before the general fire, the planes that raided Gernika came very low. It must have been difficult for them to sight their target in the smoke and grit which rose from the spreading campfire below. They flew at six hundred feet, slowly and steadily shedding their tubes of silver, which settled upon those houses that still stood in pools of intolerable heat; they slipped and dribbled from floor to floor. Gernika was compact as peat to serve as fuel for the German planes. Nobody now bothered to save relatives or possessions; between bombardments they walked out of Gernika in front of the stifling smoke and sat in bewildered hundreds on the roads to Bermeo and Mugika. Mercifully, the fighters had gone. They no longer glanced down to mutilate the population in movement and chase them across the open fields. The people were worn out by noise, heat and terror; they lay about like dirty bundles of washing, mindless, sprawling and immobile. . . . Fire was eating away the whole of crowded little Gernika.

Monks recalls helping some Basque soldiers move burned bodies, the soldiers "sobbing like children," as houses collapsed into the flames. He saw a crowd of panicked refugees corralled in the plaza almost surrounded by a wall of fire. "They were wailing and weeping and rocking to and fro." He moved around to the back of the plaza among survivors. "They had the same story to tell, aeroplanes, bullets, bombs, fire."

At least three hundred people, perhaps as many as a thousand, were killed that day in Gernika—machine-gunned, bombed, or burned to death. More than five hundred wounded were treated for injuries in Bilbao hospitals.

Richthofen recorded the bombing in his war diary on 30 April 1937, after his first visit to Gernika, which by then the nationalists had overrun. Even at that early date he was already contributing to the cover-up of the terror bombing that issued from Franco's headquarters as soon as Monks's and Steer's reports appeared in the London and New York newspapers on 28 and 29 April. The Germans and the nationalists had not yet fully coordinated their lies: Franco claimed the "Reds" had torched Gernika after a routine nationalist bombing, faking an atrocity, but in his diary Richthofen blamed smoky conditions for diverting his pilots from their supposed precision-bombing mission. Significantly, their asserted targets—the small-arms factory, the canal bridge—went undamaged. A Condor Legion report a year later summarizing the Legion's campaigns tells the real story: "We have had notable results in hitting the targets near the front, especially in bombing villages which hold enemy reserves and headquarters. We have had great success because these targets are easy to find and can be thoroughly destroyed by carpet bombing."

Steer, filing from Bilbao the day after the bombing, recognized its historic significance: "In the form of its execution," he writes, "and the scale of the destruction it wrought, no less than in the selection of its objective, the raid on Guernica is unparalleled in military history. Guernica was not a military objective. A factory producing war material lay outside the town and was untouched. So were two barracks some distance from the town. The town lay far behind the lines. The object of the bombardment was seemingly the demoralization of the civil population and the destruction of the cradle of the Basque race."

Richthofen intended nothing so grand, however. Fear and demoralization, certainly, but he was ignorant of the ruined town's history. When he toured it on 30 April to survey the destruction, he noted in his war diary, with a provincial's awe, that its "sacred oak . . . embodied the rights of Viscaya under the kings for more than a thousand years." And he added smugly that the Basque sacred oak "[was] not destroyed." The monument to ancient Basque democracy may not have been destroyed. Everything else was: more than 70 percent of all the buildings in Gernika were bombed and burned to destruction, a percentage comparable to the percentage of destruction that would follow in a direct line in less than a decade at Hiroshima and Nagasaki, metastases of the mass destruction first visited upon Gernika. Before that, Berlin would burn, too, and Hamburg, and Dresden, the new technology of aerial mass destruction coming back around to scourge its cruel pioneers.

"**W**hen news of the bombing of the town of Guernica reached us," the photographer Man Ray recalled of Picasso, "he was completely upset. Until then, and since the First World War, he had never reacted so violently to world or outside affairs." Picasso had found his subject.

A THOUSAND INCENDIARY BOMBS
DROPPED BY THE AIRCRAFT OF HITLER AND
MUSSOLINI REDUCE TO ASHES
THE CITY OF GUERNICA

L'Humanité blazoned across Paris on the morning of 28 April 1937. Ce Soir, the new evening newspaper founded by the French Communist Party and edited by Picasso's friend Louis Aragon, published photographs of the smoking Gernika ruins on 30 April. Picasso told one of his biographers, Pierre Daix, that the Ce Soir photographs had been the immediate impetus for the mural he would paint. He also probably saw a pamphlet of photographs of the destruction of Durango that was distributed in Paris beginning on 30 April, Martin Minchom notes.

At the beginning of the year, Dora Maar had located a spacious attic studio for Picasso at 7 rue des Grands Augustins, an eighteenth-century building behind an enclosed cobblestone courtyard on the Left Bank, a short walk from the Seine at Pont Neuf. The Spanish government had leased it for his exclusive use. There, on 1 May 1937, horrified by the destruction of Gernika and disgusted that Franco was blaming the republicans, Picasso outlined his initial conceptions of Guernica in quick pencil gestures on blue sketch paper.

The first of the sketches organized the basic elements of the work in what would turn out to be nearly their final form. These are, reading from the viewer's right to left: the corner of a room or a house with the hint of an opening door; a head extending from an upper window with an arm holding out a lamp; below the window a curving line that sweeps right, forward, and then around to the left near the lower edge of the paper to indicate the foreground; to the left of the window and filling the center of the image, the body of a dead or dying animal, lying on its back, its back legs raised in the air; some kind of horizontal figure lying in front of the animal; in the upper left quarter of the sheet, a smaller or more distant bull with a winged object on its back.

In 1935, Picasso had spoken of his interest in preserving photographically "not the stages, but the metamorphoses of a picture." A fortnight along in his creation of *Guernica,* Dora Maar would begin doing just that—for the first time, evidently, in the history of art. But in his 1935 comments he had added that "there is one very odd thing—to notice that basically a picture doesn't change, that the first 'vision' remains almost intact, in spite of appearances." Such would be the case with Picasso's first gesture drawing that first day of May: in its fundamental elements as well as in its spatial organization, it laid the foundation for the vast finished mural painting that would follow.

One exploratory variation came immediately: in the second of the five drawings Picasso sketched that Saturday in May, he moved the figures of the bull and the dying animal, now clearly a horse, to the foreground—the lower half of the sheet—and drew a horizontal line across the sheet to distinguish the lower-half foreground from the upper-half background. The background then accommodated another bull to the left of the building, and between the bull and the building, in a swirl of ambiguous lines, he drew what might be the ruins of a bombed-out town.

That variation divided the scene into two distinct horizontal panels and disconnected the animals in the foreground from the ruins in the background, making the drawing almost pastoral. It also required moving back and thus scaling down the building on the right side of the sheet and the figure holding a lamp in its upper window, which diminished their pictorial weight.

Picasso clearly wasn't happy with the arrangement of drawing II. He immediately abandoned it. In his next drawing, the third of the day, he let his control go and carry away with it the semi-realistic style that was constraining him. In this third sketch he drew with the loose, inartful, almost automatic style he had taught himself that mimicked the untutored gesture drawings of small children.

He filled the foreground with three flat, awkwardly outlined figures: a horse drawn vertically on the far right as if, defying gravity, it stood on the side of a building facing up; a second horse to the left of the first with a large teardrop-shaped wound in its belly from which curlicue lines pour forth that indicate intestines spilling out; and, occupying the lower left quarter of the sheet, another outline horse with a thick, bent neck, an inverted head with eyes at the bottom, ears at the top, and a mouth opening left which surmount a vestigial balloon body with four spiderlike legs that curve down to touch the lower edge of the sheet. A fourth horse sketched at the upper left retains the more realistically modeled extended neck and head of the second drawing. Looming over all, at the apex of the sheet, is the lamp of the lightbearer, held by a thick slab of arm extending back to the upper right corner, where the streaming, cometlike head with its Roman nose now begins to resemble Marie-Thérèse.

Reverting to a primitive or childlike line worked for Picasso that day as it so often had before, releasing him from the inhibition of realism. In this third drawing he partly solved the problem of filling the horizontal canvas without dividing it into foreground and background. The lightbearer, reaching out from right to center, connects the two planes of the drawing. So does the agonized horse. And by turning the horse on the far right vertically, even at the price of making it defy gravity, he gave himself an idea for a vertical figure that might fill the right-hand space—an idea that he immediately tested by adding another horse next to the first, this one mortally wounded and rearing up in pain, with bared teeth and a tear falling from its one visible eye.

And then, as if to celebrate, Picasso took another sheet of blue paper, numbered it IV, and drew a horse as a three-year-old might draw a horse, filling the sheet, a horse standing placidly on a ground of multiple pencil strokes—and added a small stick figure striding with its arms happily outstretched in the lower right corner where Picasso usually signed his name.

Having found his way out of the dead end into which he had drawn himself, Picasso next sketched a powerfully realistic horse going down in agony with its hindquarters grounded and twisted sideways and its forelegs stumbling, its neck extended and twisted back, and its mouth open as if screaming in pain. This gesture drawing, shocking in its power after the happy childlike horse sketch that preceded it, he labeled with the Arabic numeral 5.

In the last drawing of the day's series, executed in pencil and oil on a square piece of plywood, Picasso summed up what he had worked out so far: in the foreground a collapsing horse with a gash in its belly from which a little winged horse is escaping; behind the dying horse, a warrior in a Roman helmet lying prone and apparently dead, his hand still clutching a spear; behind the warrior a remarkably serene bull facing left and a house with a tile roof, with the lightbearer at an upper window as before, holding out a lamp.

And as if all that wasn't enough for one day, Picasso finished off his first day's work with a full-scale painting, *Two Nude Women on Beach,* one of his outdoor monster scenes, executed in ink and gouache on a 22-by-27-inch wooden panel.

The next day, 2 May, Sunday, Picasso refined the horse's head. In drawing 5, the horse had stretched up its neck and screamed in pain, but its open mouth had revealed neither teeth nor tongue. Now, in two alternative views of the horse's head in profile on blue paper, Picasso examined the options of locating the upper teeth inside the horse's mouth or, less realistically, outside its mouth, projecting from its muzzle. He simplified and stylized the head as well, and in keeping with the Cubist dislocation of the teeth, drew both eyes together on the near side of the head. In both sketches he gave the horse a prominent tongue, extended to embody the animal's scream. The tongue is a sharply pointed triangle, a dagger, borrowed for the occasion from his angry drawings of his dagger-tongued estranged wife, the ballerina Olga Khokhlova. As he had assigned the lightbearer Marie-Thérèse's features, so again was he mining his private emotional iconography to add complexity, ambiguity, and power to the images he was assessing for his painting.

In a third drawing that Sunday, on an irregular scrap of brown paper, Picasso gave the horse reason to scream, sketching its head with a mouthful of teeth above a Cubist depiction of an enraged fighting bull, one foreleg raised as if about to paw the ground, dagger tongue quivering, erect tail tipped with a smoky, flamelike swirl. He would salvage that tail for *Guernica,* and there extend the swirl of flame all the way to its base.

Finally, Picasso painted the horse's screaming head in gray and white against a black background on a two-by-three-foot canvas.

For the next three days Picasso did no work on *Guernica.* He was probably distracted by the violent clash between political factions that had broken out in Barcelona. Barcelona more than Madrid was Picasso's Spanish home, where he had attended art school, where he had lived as a young man, where his art was first exhibited, where his Blue Period evolved, where he found the prostitutes of *Les Demoiselles d'Avignon*.

The next five drawings for *Guernica,* all dated 8 May 1937, show him finding the basic form of his mural. The first drawing incorporates the bull; the dying horse; a dead, unhelmeted male figure with a broken spear; a mother pushing up on the right with a dead baby hanging from her lap, a variation of the scene he had read about in Delaprée's reports; behind these figures a building with a window and a quick line of gesture that indicates where the lightbearer will be; behind the building another quick gesture and a horizon line that seem to indicate a distant fire.

Then Picasso explored two of the figures from the previous drawing, the horse and the mother with the dead child. Preoccupied with the placement of the horse's teeth, he sketches a horse with a fore-and-aft jaw with upper teeth somehow on both the upper jaw and the lower. Then he experiments with dressing the mother in traditional Spanish clothing, including a mantilla that flares back like a cape to emphasize the monolithic right triangle formed by the mother's position thrusting forward and upward, with one leg rising from a squat and the other pushing off from behind; full, pendulous breasts emphasize the woman's maternity, her child dead, unweaned.

Picasso continued working through the weekend, as he had the weekend before. On Sunday, 9 May, he repeated and finished the figures of mother and child, executing a detailed drawing in ink. He filled in the light and shadow to shape the two forms in three dimensions: the child is more obviously dead for being more realistically drawn, the mother more obviously anguished.

And then, that same Sunday, the whole canvas emerges in a big composition study, drawn in pencil on a two-by-four-foot sheet crowded with figures. Reading from the viewer's right to left: a burning roof above a partly opened door; a muscular arm with a raised fist extending from a lower window of the next building; the mother and her dead baby; the dying horse; below the horse the dead soldier; behind the horse a wagon wheel; behind the wagon wheel a building with a tile roof, the lightbearer extending her torch from an upper window; to the left of the building a bull, its body in left profile but its head turned back to the scene of death and looking surprised; other buildings behind the bull, another raised fist extending from an upper window; a woman sitting in a doorway looking forlorn, holding the bodies of a dead man and a dead woman—a jumble of figures and events. At this point Picasso may have been considering a crowd scene set in a burning town. Many of the figures he will use in his finished mural painting are present, but the composition doesn't yet cohere.

On Monday, 10 May, Picasso worked on individual figures—the mother and her dead baby, sketched now descending a ladder; the horse twisted in death with its head on the ground; two variations on the horse's mouth and head, with a detailed drawing of its leg alongside; the head of a bull with a human face.

Tuesday, 11 May, brought major change. Confident now that he knew where he was going, Picasso stretched canvas on a full-sized wooden frame, 11½ feet high by 25½ feet long, and set it up in the big attic space at 7 rue des Grands Augustins. It was so large that it had to

be jammed in at a tilt under the sloping attic rafters and painted with
long-handled brushes, sometimes reaching from a stepladder. With
black paint and a narrow brush on that vast canvas, the artist drew
in the first full version of the painting. "Picasso worked fast," writes
biographer Roland Penrose, "and the outline of the first version was
sketched in almost as soon as the canvas was up." He sent for Dora
Maar, who arrived with her Rolleiflex and lights and took the first of a
series of photographs of *Guernica* in progress, the "metamorphoses of a
picture" Picasso had proposed in 1935. The reflection on the canvas of
one of her lights suggested the lightbulb that would appear in the upper
center of the painting.

A number of books and articles have described the process Picasso
followed in painting *Guernica*. Less well known are the many visual
references to other paintings that Picasso layered into the work. He did
so, I think, to anchor and extend *Guernica* into history, to deepen it with
the visual equivalent of allusion and metaphor. Almost every image in
the painting has its double and triple in previous works by a range of
well- and little-known masters, adding meaning much as the previous
uses of a word add meaning to its present sense.

The best-documented example of this layering process is the figure
of the lightbearer. She is female—Picasso added breasts at the window
to make sure that this was clear—and in the final painting resembles
Marie-Thérèse, although in some of his earlier sketches he had given
her Dora Maar's hair and features instead. One source of the image is
private: Dora Maar used to extend a lamp out an upper-story window
to see who was knocking when guests arrived after dark at Picasso's
country house at Boisgeloup, northeast of Paris.

From there the trail leads to Picasso's own work, in particular the
Minotauromachy of 1935, one of *Guernica*'s precursors, in which a virginal young girl holds out a candle to give pause to a huge-headed minotaur that has just killed a female matador with a sword. Peter Paul
Rubens's 1638 *Horrors of War* is another evident precursor of Picasso's
painting. If you reverse Rubens's image, it depicts, from right to left: a

partly opened door, a woman reaching up with both arms in horror, a nude woman reaching left across a soldier in armor with an upraised fist looped through a shield, and various figures of soldiers standing and fallen, one of whom holds up a torch.

Picasso clearly associated the soldier's upraised fist with the raised arm holding a hammer and a sickle that he had drawn on the front page of *Paris-soir* and had included in early versions of *Guernica*. As the painting developed he gradually replaced this overliteral salute to Common Front solidarity with a representation first of the sun and then of a sunlike eye with a lightbulb for a pupil. That representation, which seems to have originated in the reflection of Dora Maar's camera light on the canvas, also alludes to the *Ojo de Dios* of some Spanish churches, the Eye of God painted or inlaid on the interior of the dome that looked down on the congregants and saw and judged all.

Another torchbearer to whom *Guernica* alludes is the winged figure of Justice in Pierre-Paul Prud'hon's circa 1805 *Justice and Divine Vengeance Pursuing Crime,* a painting that includes a fallen male nude bleeding from a chest wound and a criminal running away left. A less obvious allusion, but a likely one, is to Jacob Jordaens's 1642 *Diogenes Searching for an Honest Man,* which bears compositional similarities to Picasso's painting—Diogenes at the center holding up a lantern, a figure on the left looking out an upper window, cattle looking on where Picasso would paint a bull, a horizontal format. Jordaens was a Flemish painter and a contemporary of Rubens, one of Picasso's favorite artists; Rubens sometimes hired Jordaens to paint reproductions for him. The story of Diogenes going about in daylight with a lantern looking for an honest man resonates with the lightbearer's action in *Guernica,* holding out a lamp to reveal the horror of the bombing of Gernika to the world.

Finally, and perhaps most surprisingly, the lightbearer with her lantern and her spiky hand at the window evokes the American Statue of Liberty with her torch and her spiky nimbus of light, a statue constructed in France and donated to the United States in 1886. The Spanish poet and critic Juan Larrea, who made this connection at a Museum of Modern Art symposium on *Guernica* in 1947, believed the allusion to Liberty to be unconscious on Picasso's part, but there were at least three smaller-scale but still monumental models of the Statue of Liberty in Paris: one in the Jardins du Luxembourg, one prominently mounted on a stone pedestal on the Ile aux Cygnes in the Seine near the Pont de Grenelle, and a third, the original plaster model, in the Musée des Arts et Métiers. It's probable that Picasso had seen them all, and his visual memory was immense.

Picasso worked intensely on *Guernica* throughout the month of May. Cigarette butts litter the attic floor in Dora Maar's sequence of photographs of the work in progress. She participated in the painting itself, adding many of the short vertical ticks on the body of the stricken horse that evoke the printed words of the newspaper reports they both were reading of the bombings of Gernika, Madrid, and other republican-defended cities and towns. Picasso had used a similar marking technique in painting his earlier newspaper collages, Pierre Daix notes.

"One day in the café," Sert recalls, "when the date of the Pavilion's inauguration was approaching, and we didn't know if we would have the canvas for the opening, [Picasso] said to us, 'I don't know when I will finish it. Maybe never. You had better come and take it whenever you need it.'"

During May, Max Aub proposed that the Spanish government pay Picasso for the painting. He had offered to donate it. Aub wanted payment exchanged to confirm the painting's legal ownership. Picasso agreed. On 28 May Aub sent a memo to his superior at the Spanish Embassy, the Spanish ambassador Luis Araquistáin, about the arrangement he made with the artist:

> This morning I came to an agreement with Picasso. In spite of our friend's reluctance to accept a subvention from the Embassy for the completion of *Guernica,* as he is donating the picture to the Spanish Republic, I repeatedly stressed the desire of the Spanish government at least to reimburse the expenses he has incurred in his work. I was able

to convince him and I have therefore made out a cheque to him for 150,000 French francs, for which he signed the corresponding receipt. Although this sum is of no more than symbolic value, given the incalculable value of the painting in question, it nonetheless represents, in practical terms, an acquisition of the same by the Republic.

One hundred fifty thousand French francs in 1937 would be worth about $98,000 today. It was no small sum, but Picasso donated several times that much to the Spanish Republic in the course of the civil war, and more afterward, privately, to its refugees. On Aub's authority, then, the francs exchanged hands to establish ownership.

In May as well, Picasso responded to rumors circulating in Paris that he was pro-Franco with his first public statement of political beliefs:

The Spanish struggle is the fight of reaction against the people, against freedom. My whole life as an artist has been nothing more than a continuous struggle against reaction and the death of art. How could anybody think for a moment that I could be in agreement with reaction and death? When the rebellion began, the legally elected and democratic republican government of Spain appointed me director of the Prado Museum, a post which I immediately accepted. In the panel on which I am working which I shall call *Guernica*, and in all my recent works of art, I clearly express my abhorrence of the military caste which has sunk Spain in a sea of suffering and death.

"The mark of the actual event," writes Daix of Picasso's painting, meaning the bombing of Gernika, "is in the horse, of *trompe l'oeil* newspaper collage, and in the immense canvas, which like the illustrated journals and magazines of the time, is almost without color." Which is true but incomplete. The canvas is large as a movie screen and the figures it projects—black-and-white as films still were, as newsreels certainly were, in 1937—are imaged not at normal scale but larger than life-size, as films image their moving subjects. Picasso enjoyed motion pictures; he saw them as not only entertainment but also a new technology, a new art form, and he borrowed from them as he borrowed from every process and technology he encountered. The implied camera that captures *Guernica* stands on the ground; it doesn't see the planes shuttling overhead; it records the reactions of the animals and the people below.

"The horror and inquisitiveness of the women" in *Guernica,* writes T. J. Clark, "—their bearing witness even at the point of extinction— have been given sufficient substance. What fixes and freezes them is felt as a mechanism, a rack. The bomb is the abstractness of war—war on paper, war as war rooms imagine it, war as 'politics by other means'— perfected. Here is what happens when it comes to earth." For all the people still alive in *Guernica* are women: "a machine for suffering," Picasso once called woman in a remark that most have taken to be callous, as it was, but which was also a secret revealed: "I am a woman," the Spanish artist, late in life, lowered his guard enough to explain.

A woman, yes, and a man, and an artist: the bull in *Guernica*, staring ahead with an aurochs's primeval opacity, "here a noble adversary," says Daix, "turning away from the killing which humiliates him," the bull has Picasso's eyes.

"Picasso continued [painting] his picture during May and June," Sert recalls, "and one day he brought it to the Pavilion. I think it was late June. I don't remember the date exactly. He brought it there. He was in love with his picture and he really considered it very important and a part of himself. . . . He brought the *Guernica* to the pavilion. He put it on the concrete floor and put it on a stretcher and put it on the wall."

TEN

Cuckoo Idealists

George Orwell, the British novelist and journalist, had spent a miserable winter as a militia volunteer on a freezing mountainside on the Aragon front, in Catalonia. Finally, in late April 1937, his unit was relieved. He headed for Barcelona in rags and worn-out boots, nearly barefoot and crawling with lice. "I wanted a hot bath," Orwell recalls in *Homage to Catalonia,* "clean clothes and a night between sheets more passionately than it is possible to want anything when one has been living a normal civilized life." He arrived in Barcelona on the afternoon of 26 April. His wife, Eileen, had been waiting there for him, but he had hardly settled in when the sporadic battling that came to be called the May Days began between political factions. The uproar that led Picasso in Paris to stop painting *Guernica* between 3 and 8 May put poor Orwell on a rooftop with a rifle for days, guarding the headquarters of the organization he had been fighting for, the POUM.

Ironically, Orwell had volunteered with the centrist and anti-Stalinist Partido Obrero de Unificación Marxista, the Workers' Party of Marxist Unification, almost by accident after his arrival in Spain in December 1936. The British socialist MP Jennie Lee remembered him turning up at the hotel where she was staying in Barcelona, "a tall thin man with a ravaged complexion," and asking her "could I tell him where to join up.

He said he was an author: had got an advance on a book from Gollancz, and had arrived ready to drive a car or do anything else, preferably to fight in the front line." Lee was suspicious and asked him for credentials. He told her he had none: "He had seen no one, simply paid his own way out." He allayed her suspicion, she recalls, "by pointing to the boots over his shoulder. He knew he could not get boots big enough for he was over six feet. This was George Orwell and his boots arriving to fight in Spain." Lee had sent this boot-proud political innocent along to John McNair, the local representative of the International Labor Party, which was affiliated in Spain with the POUM.

"I used to sit on the roof marveling at the folly of it all," Orwell writes of the May Days. "You could see for miles around—vista after vista of tall slender buildings, glass domes and fantastic curly roofs with brilliant green and copper tiles; over to eastward the glittering pale blue sea—the first glimpse of the sea that I had had since coming to Spain. And the whole huge town of a million people was locked in a sort of violent inertia, a nightmare of noise without movement." The streets were empty, the streetcars stopped where their conductors had abandoned them, but the firing was nearly continuous along the Ramblas and echoing from the buildings, "on and on and on, like a tropical rainstorm."

It wasn't even clear at first, Orwell says, "who was fighting whom and who was winning." As usual in Spain, the politics were as ornate as the grillwork. Ultimately the reason for the uproar was the same in Barcelona as elsewhere in republican Spain: the government was taking back control from the many ad hoc organizations that had sprung up at the outset of the war to hold off the nationalists under Franco. By now the Catalonian government was communist, with a decorative overlay of Common Front participation. It would prove to be implacably hostile to the POUM.

Along with five other POUM men, Orwell spent three days and nights on that lead-covered rooftop, outside a domed observatory above a movie theater, facing off against a squad of government assault guards in a similar position on a rooftop across the wide street. Both sides had agreed not to fire on each other, but Orwell knew that orders to fight might be telephoned up to either side at any time. When he wasn't bored, filling the hours reading from a stack of books he'd had the foresight to buy when he arrived in Barcelona, he was intensely aware that armed men were watching him. Trouble seemed to be starting once when one of the guards across the street began firing:

> I trained my rifle on him and shouted across:
> *"Hi! Don't you shoot at us!"*
> *"What?"*
> *"Don't you fire at us or we'll fire back!"*
> *"No, no! I wasn't firing at you. Look—down there!"*
>
> He motioned with his rifle towards the side-street that ran past the bottom of our building. Sure enough, a youth in blue overalls, with a rifle in his hand, was dodging round the corner. Evidently he had just taken a shot at the Assault Guards on the roof.
>
> *"I was firing at him. He fired first."* (I believe this was true.) *"We don't want to shoot you. We're only workers, the same as you are."*
>
> He made the anti-Fascist salute, which I returned. I shouted across:
> *"Have you got any more beer left?"*
> *"No, it's all gone."*

Later in the week six thousand republican assault guards arrived from Valencia to take control. As much as anything else, Orwell says, a growing food shortage put an end to the rioting. There were oranges in plenty but little more. By Friday afternoon, 7 May, the city had returned to normal, the shops along the Ramblas crowded and the streetcars running again. In disgust, Orwell realized he had wasted his leave and would have to return to the front.

Back to the line he went, brevetted a *teniente* now and in command of a mixed company of about thirty men, English and Spanish. Even the company's position was little changed, entrenched northeast of Zaragoza facing the nationalist trenches on higher ground about a third of a mile away. At least it was warmer; the cherry trees were blossoming in the no-man's-land between the lines. But Orwell was a tall man, six feet two; the nationalist snipers had the advantage of their position's greater height; and one day about ten days after he returned to the front, in the early morning, when he was standing at a corner of the trench parapet talking with Harry Milton, the only American volunteer in his unit, a sniper put a bullet through his throat. "I heard the crisp sound of a high-velocity shot," Milton recalls, "and Orwell [toppled] over. He landed on his back." Orwell was fascinated, at least in retrospect; the experience, he writes sardonically, was "very interesting":

> Roughly speaking, it was the sensation of being *at the centre* of an explosion. There seemed to be a loud bang and a blinding flash of light all round me, and I felt a tremendous shock—no pain, only a violent shock, such as you get from an electric terminal; with it a sense of utter weakness, a feeling of being stricken and shriveled up to nothing. The sand-bags in front of me receded into immense distance. I fancy you would feel much the same if you were struck by lightning. I knew immediately that I was hit. . . . All this happened in a space of time much less than a second. The next moment my knees crumpled up and I was falling, my head hitting the ground with a violent bang which, to my relief, did not hurt. I had a numb, dazed feeling, a consciousness of being very badly hurt, but no pain in the ordinary sense.

Milton administered first aid, pressing on the wound to staunch the bleeding. "My wound was not much," Orwell wrote a friend a few weeks later, "but it was a miracle it did not kill me. The bullet went clean through my neck but missed everything except one vocal cord, or rather the nerve governing, which is paralysed." His right arm was paralyzed as well. They lifted him up—blood poured from his mouth and he thought he must be killed—and laid him down. That was interesting, too. "My first thought, conventionally enough, was for my wife. My second was a violent resentment at having to leave this world which, when all is said and done, suits me so well. I had time to feel this very vividly. The stupid mischance infuriated me. The meaninglessness of it! To be bumped off, not even in battle, but in this stale corner of the trenches, thanks to a moment's carelessness!" Someone brought a stretcher. Orwell's arm woke up "and began hurting damnably" and he knew he was alive. Four comrades carried him on the stretcher a muddy, slippery mile and a half back to a dressing station, a morphine injection, and an ambulance, which banged and jolted him eventually to one of the Spanish army's big staging hospitals, this one in Lleida, on the Segre River about eighty miles due east of Zaragoza. Within a few days Orwell was up and walking around. He discovered a garden on the hospital grounds with a goldfish pond. He sat there for hours at a time, watching the goldfish swimming in circles, looking for an exit.

Ernest Hemingway and Martha Gellhorn had returned from their expedition into the Guadarramas on 29 April with full notebooks: *For Whom the Bell Tolls* would be set in the Guadarramas in the month of May 1937. They joined Joris Ivens, director of *The Spanish Earth*, in the impoverished village of Fuentidueña, where the poorest villagers lived in holes dug out of the hillside looking out on the vast expanse of the local *latifundista*'s fallowed fields. Ivens and his crew finished up filming. Everyone attended a farewell party at the Twelfth Brigade's base hospital north of Madrid, already nostalgic, dancing and drinking into the night before decamping for Paris. Hemingway spoke to the Anglo-American Press Club there and gave a nervous reading of his short story "Fathers and Sons" at Sylvia Beach's Shakespeare & Company bookstore at 12 rue de l'Odéon. James Joyce was in the audience. The two writers had been drinking buddies in Paris in the twenties, when Joyce's Irish insults would provoke some post-Vélodrome celebrants and the half-blind Joyce would inveigle his big American friend to fight them ("Deal with them, Ernest!").

The lovers sailed separately to America. Showing the colors coming off the *Normandie* on 18 May in a dockside interview with a *New York Times* reporter, Hemingway argued for an eventual republican victory. "If General Franco takes Bilbao the war will probably continue for another two years," he estimated, "and if he doesn't the war could possibly end late this fall or in the spring. The war has changed greatly. It is no longer a war of militia, but a serious war of trained troops, and the forces of the defenders of Madrid increase their strength every week, and time is definitely on their side." He based his estimate of which side would win on what he believed to be the impossibility of Franco's taking Madrid. Franco's turning north to occupy Euskadi and Bilbao didn't mean he had given up on Madrid, of course, but Hemingway had been inspired by the rout of the Italians at Guadalajara, where he told the *Times* reporter Mussolini had lost more men "than in the entire [1935–36] Ethiopian campaign." The republicans had lost even more while recovering little ground. After the interview the author flew down to Key West to collect his family and then sailed across to Bimini in the Bahamas to wrap up *To Have and Have Not* and to fish.

(Herbert Matthews judged Mussolini's response to his embarrassing loss at Guadalajara differently. "The Italian force here represents a good chunk of Italy's military strength," the *New York Times* correspondent wrote that summer. "The country cannot afford to lose it." To Matthews that meant Mussolini would have to maintain it, reinforcing and reequipping it as required. Italian prestige, he thought, had "suffered a terrible blow" at Guadalajara; "the reply to that defeat was necessarily greater intervention." That was true for Germany as well: whenever the republicans seemed to be winning, Italy and Germany increased their support for the nationalists. "It is all very logical and very obvious," Matthews concluded, "but sooner or later it must either stop or be made so overwhelming as to insure a quick victory for Franco. The other alternative is a European war.")

Gellhorn had lunch at the White House with Eleanor Roosevelt on 28 May, using the occasion to extract a promise of a screening of *The Spanish Earth* there when the film was finished. On 4 June the young journalist sat beside Hemingway, flown in from Bimini for the event, at a Carnegie Hall rally for the Spanish cause of the Comintern-sponsored Second Congress of American Writers. He was nervous and flushed in the summer heat but acquitted himself well, collecting thunderous applause from the overflow crowd.

George Steer's first report on the bombing of Gernika was published simultaneously in the London *Times* and the *New York Times* on 28 April 1937; with other reports, it aroused an international outcry against terror bombing. The Basque president, José Aguirre, broadcast an appeal that night for the rescue by evacuation of "the more than three hundred thousand women and children who have taken refuge in Bilbao." The next day Aguirre sent a formal request for aid to the president of the International Committee of the Red Cross in Geneva. By then, nationalist forces were occupying what was left of Gernika, and Franco's staff had begun promoting its absurd claims that the Basques had bombed themselves, dynamiting buildings and setting fires to manufacture an atrocity. Other than the fascist right, hardly anyone, in England or elsewhere, believed them.

Bilbao, winding along the basin of the Nervión River to front the Bay of Biscay, was surrounded on three sides and hungering despite efforts by private shipping to supply it by sea. Two English pediatricians, Richard Ellis and his wife, Audrey Russell, visiting the besieged city to assess the condition of the children there, found most of Bilbao's public services still operating but schools closed "owing to the incessant air raids." Condor Legion bombers had not yet hit the waterworks. No epidemics had yet broken out. Food was strictly rationed, "and though the food ships have run the blockade there is only ten days' food in hand for the city." People were living on beans, rice, cabbage, and 35 grams—

about one slice—of black bread per day. There was no coal "and owing to the air raids, little opportunity for cooking":

> In many cases it is obvious that the women have starved themselves to provide for the children. One pregnant mother who brought up five healthy looking children for examination was herself so weak she could hardly stand, and said, smiling, that perhaps she would find "time" to eat when her children were safe in England.

Ellis and Russell were surprised to discover that most of the children were in good health, if thin—"It was evident that even the poorer peasants have a high standard of care for their children, and that before the blockade almost all the latter were well developed and well fed." Only a few of the smaller children were starved to the point of marasmus—listless, emaciated, their bellies swollen with fluid. For most, the two observers write, "the period of malnutrition had not been long enough to cause permanent damage or muscular weakness, and . . . recovery under proper conditions should be rapid and complete." That was good news if relief could be organized.

The British government had resisted accepting Basque refugees. A National Joint Committee for Spanish Relief (NJCSR), represented by a large, sturdy, determined schoolteacher and former MP named Leah Manning, had been pressing the British authorities since February without much luck. The Home Office—the government agency that handles immigration—was actively hostile, and even a left-wing Labor Party member of the House of Lords proposed directing the children to France rather than to "cold and Protestant England." Steer's dispatches forced the issue.

"Bombardments of cities," Steer writes, "have always meant more to the British, who have to defend the greatest and most vulnerable of them, than to any other people." The reaction of the British people to the Gernika atrocity was outspoken revulsion. Reluctantly the British government agreed to admit four thousand Basque children as refugees and to protect any shipping, including nationalist, that was evacuating women, children, and men past military age from Bilbao. Steer judged that the evacuation of Bilbao would be "the largest evacuation of a people in the history of modern war. France was willing to take there women and children without limit; England to take as many children as private subscription could support, and that was 4,000; Russia, Holland, Belgium, Czechoslovakia would take others."

But if the British cabinet had acceded to popular opinion, the bureaucracy still resisted. "The Basques had no sympathy either from the Home Office or the Foreign Office," Leah Manning writes. "Both regarded the whole thing as a nuisance and myself as an officious busybody." The NJCSR had hoped to begin transferring children to England on 5 May. While the committee brought pressure to bear on the British bureaucrats, shiploads of Basque families diverted to France. Two ships carrying a thousand women and 2,300 children departed Bilbao for France on 6 May. Steer writes puckishly that "each child was issued with a tart weighing half a pound and a packet containing twelve cream caramels." Another three French ships departed on 9 May with four thousand men, women, and children aboard, "half of whom," Steer says, "were paying for their voyage and could maintain themselves abroad." Most of these refugees "belonged to the parties of the Right." The Basque government had promised not to discriminate between republican and nationalist, and it did not. Despite Basque evenhandedness, Franco was hostile to the evacuation. "In the evening before the [9 May] embarkation began," Steer confirms, "six insurgent bombers tried to hit the dock at Santurce [in Bilbao harbor]: the people went aboard at night."

The Home Office had imposed an extravagant requirement that the NJCSR guarantee ten shillings (half a pound, about £15 today) per child per week in support, and house and school the children only in private institutions. On 15 May the NJCSR hurriedly formed a Basque Children's Committee (BCC) to raise the necessary funds. The BCC cautiously projected evacuating and supporting only two thousand children, but Manning managed to boost that number to Steer's four thousand. Within days, in the middle of the Great Depression, a non-partisan, celebrity-studded British public appeal raised £17,000 (more than £1 million today) to pay for the operation.

The Home Office retreated to its next line of defense, authorizing transfer only of children between the ages of five and twelve. That would have again reduced their number from four to two thousand, and by now no fewer than twenty thousand Basque children had been signed up for removal somewhere beyond the war zone. Ellis, the pediatrician, was adamant about evacuating adolescents as well in the English contingent, writing in the *Manchester Guardian* on 19 May, "We want the older children to come, especially the older girls, for if Bilbao is taken and filled with foreign troops, these are exactly children of the age we want out of the place. . . . It is not many years since a victorious Moorish regiment marched past the General [i.e., Franco] with every bayonet decorated with enemy genitalia."

The prospect of being accused of responsibility for the rape and mutilation of adolescent girls at the hands of Berber tribesmen forced the Home Office to surrender. Finally, on Thursday afternoon, 20 May 1937, 3,889 Basque children accompanied by 219 women teachers and aides and fifteen priests boarded the Basque liner *Habana,* the pride of the fleet, and a private yacht that had been donated to the Basque government, the *Goizeko Izarra.* Once again the children were feted with food, one of them recalls, with results that should have been predictable:

> I went with my two sisters, one only eight, to the harbor at Santurce. Franco's planes came over about mid-afternoon, just to watch. On board they gave us wonderful food we hadn't seen for a year: *chorizos,* white bread, and we all ate too much, filling our stomachs to the top. Within an hour, the whole shipload was seasick.

The next morning the *Habana* and the *Goizeko Izarra* departed the harbor behind a Spanish destroyer, fell in line in a British military convoy a few miles out in open water, and sailed for Southampton. The Bay of Biscay was choppy, as always. "For two dreadful days and nights," Manning recalls with British candor, "Richard [Ellis], Audrey [Russell] and I slithered from one pool of diarrhea and vomit to another, giving drinks of water and assuring [the children] that it wasn't the fascists who had stirred up the waters against them." Children slept every-where on the crowded ship sailing north that Saturday night: fifteen hundred in berths, a thousand on mattresses on deck, the rest rolled up in blankets in the public rooms and even in the drained swimming pool.

Approaching the English coast on Sunday morning, Manning writes:

> I was awakened by the sounds of thousands of feet on deck, and going out was greeted with cries of *"Rubio," "Hombre,"* and asked perhaps five hundred times when we should arrive and whether they would really get white bread—and milk—and even meat, in England. Soon the boys were lined up dancing to the sound of a flute, when suddenly the whole ship listed to one side as four thousand children crowded the rails and deck and rigging to wave frantically to a blue strip on the horizon. *"Inglaterra! Inglaterra!"* I only trusted they would find the welcome there for which they hoped.

The port medical officer describes the "extraordinary spectacle" of "a vessel normally capable of carrying between 400 and 500 passengers steaming up Southampton Water with every inch of her decks covered with human beings." From the children's point of view, one of them remembers, "we thought we had entered a wonderland." The decora-tions from the 12 May coronation of George VI had been left up for them. "Everything was bunting, flags, music playing, people waving their handkerchiefs at us, so that we thought we were awakening from a nightmare or dreaming, and that the world to which they had taken us wasn't real. . . . There were thousands of people to welcome us, newsreel cameras, cakes and candies, buses to carry us. . . . They gave each of us a cup with the pictures of their new king and queen. It was wonderful."

The sojourn of the Basque children in Britain would not always be so wonderful. Steer would write sarcastically that "more distinguished persons were to notice that these war-terrified children sometimes stole apples, broke windows with stones, teased little girls"—but they were spared Bilbao's occupation on 19 June 1937 and the atrocities that followed at the hands of Franco's mercenaries. "In the end," Steer concludes, the evacuations "placed well over 100,000 Basque noncombatants north of the Pyrenees."

From Lleida, George Orwell had been transferred first to Tarragona and then, at the beginning of June, to a POUM sanatorium in the Barcelonan suburbs positioned below the mountain where Jesus is supposed to have rejected Satan's temptation to turn stones into bread. The Spanish communists had come to power with the fall of Largo Caballero's government on 15 May, Orwell writes, "and no one doubted that they would smash their political rivals as soon as they got a quarter of a chance." He found "a horrible atmosphere" in the Catalan capital in the aftermath of the May Days, "produced by fear, suspicion, hatred, censored newspapers, crammed jails, enormous food-queues and prowling gangs of armed men." Chief among the enemies the communists perceived was the POUM, because it rejected Soviet control. With a weakened arm and a thin, strangled voice, Orwell could no longer soldier. He saw no reason to stay in Spain eating up scarce food. His money was running out and he was sick of the war.

In mid-June he banged around from hospital to hospital all over Spain getting his medical discharge stamped, waiting at roadsides for hours for a lorry going his way that wasn't full of "men, loaves of bread or ammunition boxes," then "bumping over the vile roads [that] walloped you to pulp. No horse has ever thrown me so high as those lorries used to throw me." At one hospital, as he waited to be examined, "there was going on inside the surgery some dreadful operation without anesthetics—why without anesthetics I do not know. It went on, scream after scream, and when I went in there were chairs flung about and on the floor were pools of blood and urine." Operation without anesthesia was the punishment the military decreed for would-be deserters with self-inflicted wounds.

When Orwell returned to his Barcelona hotel with his discharge in his pocket, his wife saw him entering the lounge, met him at the door, and startled him by hissing, *"Get out!"* The POUM had been suppressed, its members arrested, even hotel employees turning them in. The couple found a café on a Ramblas side street where they could talk. Andrés Nin, the POUM's cofounder, had been picked up; they would locate him in a Barcelona jail and speak with him, but he was executed not long after on orders from Moscow. Since Orwell's wife was being watched—her room had been searched in her presence and Orwell's diaries and papers confiscated—he couldn't return to the hotel. She did; he found a ruined church where it was safe to sleep.

Orwell carried out one more mission, trying to save his POUM superior officer Georges Kopp, a Russian-born engineer who had also been arrested. Speaking up for Kopp meant exposing himself to military officials and the police as a POUM member, and his appeal was unsuccessful, but it had been brave of Orwell to try. Kopp did in fact survive eighteen months in a Spanish prison, after which he escaped to England, where Orwell's surgeon brother-in-law nursed him back to health.

"It was an extraordinary, insane existence we were leading," Orwell writes of their final week in Barcelona. "By night we were criminals but by day we were prosperous English visitors—that was our pose, anyway. Even after a night in the open, a shave, a bath and a shoeshine do wonders with your appearance. The safest thing at present was to look as bourgeois as possible. We frequented the fashionable residential quarter of the town, where our faces were not known, went to expensive restaurants and were very English with the waiters." In his anger and frustration at the crackdown, Orwell took to scrawling graffiti on restaurant passageways—*"Visca POUM!"*—*"Long Live POUM!"* in Catalan—"as large as I could write it." The British consul put their passports in order. They caught a morning train to Port Bou and crossed the border into France.

Six months later, writing *Homage to Catalonia,* George Orwell balanced his bleak experience of the war with an appreciation of the Spanish people, something almost all of the foreigners in Spain came to feel, an appreciation that would sound sentimental were it not so hard-won:

> This war, in which I played so ineffectual a part, has left me with memories that are mostly evil, and yet I do not wish that I had missed it. When you have had a glimpse of such a disaster as this—and however it ends the Spanish war will turn out to have been an appalling disaster, quite apart from the slaughter and physical suffering—the result is not necessarily disillusionment and cynicism. Curiously enough the whole experience has left me with not less but more belief in the decency of human beings.

A few months earlier, at the beginning of April, Stephen Spender had written similarly in a letter to Virginia Woolf:

> It is quite true that the politicians are very divided and quarrelsome but the real war and the real revolution are less an affair of the politicians who happen to be in power than is usual with such things. . . . The really encouraging thing about Spain is really the Spanish people and only the Spanish people. . . . This must be about the only War in which allies have come to fight in a country and have grown really to love the inhabitants, because I have never heard a word here against the Spanish people. They are so amazingly friendly and generous on every occasion.

For the rest of June 1937, Martha Gellhorn in New York had worked at trying to arrange for the immigration of five hundred Basque children into the United States and to start a book about Spain—too soon, she eventually decided—while collaborating on film postproduction with Ivens, Archibald MacLeish, Lillian Hellman, and the actor Fredric March. Gellhorn broached both subjects in a follow-up late June letter to Eleanor Roosevelt. She described a night of sound work at Columbia Broadcasting—Orson Welles had joined them to record the voice-over—when they made the scream of incoming shells "with a football bladder and an air hose and fingernails snapping against a screen, all tremendously magnified and it sounds so like a shell that we were scared out of our wits."

The children, Gellhorn went on to tell the First Lady—"those tragic little dark ones I know so well"—were waiting in St.-Jean-de-Luz, on the Bay of Biscay across the border in France. "There is passage money for 100 of them, and countless offers of adoption. As you know, they are welcomed in England and France, the governments there actually do the reception work." Not so in the United States: "Here, it appears, the Labor Department has decreed a $500 bond per child before they can get in, and also demanded the approval of the Catholic Charities. I find it incomprehensible, a Catholic lobby no doubt, but incomprehensible anyhow." It was incomprehensible because the Basques were Roman Catholic, just as Franco and his nationalists were. Their sin was siding with the republicans. "That must be the root of it somewhere," Gellhorn urged, "but it is pretty terrible. . . . It seems to me amazing that only America should offer no sanctuary to them."

Roosevelt scolded Gellhorn for "being emotional," but Gellhorn thanked her for "taking the time to tell me the other side"—presumably the political difficulty of helping the Spanish Republic against fierce American Catholic opposition. Instead of moving the children, Roosevelt argued, her young protégé should raise money to support them in France. Gellhorn barely restrained herself, agreeing that "emotional women are bad news" but insisting that "I don't know how else one can feel." How she felt, she told the First Lady, was "personally terribly helpless about everything."

The Roosevelts had agreed to receive Gellhorn's delegation on 8 July 1937. Hemingway and Ivens were intrigued when Gellhorn ate a stack of sandwiches at Newark Airport before they flew down to Washington. "We thought she was crazy at the time," Hemingway wrote his mother-in-law, "but she said the [White House] food was always uneatable." Which was saying a lot for someone just back from wartime Spain. "Mrs. Roosevelt is enormously tall," Hemingway writes, "very charming, and almost stone deaf. She hears practically nothing that is said to her but is so charming that most people do not notice it." He was dismissive of the wheelchair-bound president, "very Harvard charming and sexless and womanly, seems like a great Woman Secretary of Labor, say, he is completely paralyzed from the waist down and there is much skillful maneuvering of him into the chair and from room to room."

President Roosevelt surprised the trio of filmmakers regardless, telling them not to pull their punches; as Gellhorn paraphrases him, they should "make it stronger . . . by underlining the causes of the conflict." Hemingway summarizes the Roosevelts' advice more cynically: "They both were very moved by the Spanish Earth picture but both said we should put more propaganda in it." After the screening, which a small crowd of White House staff attended, dinner was served; the food, Hemingway says, "was the worst I've ever eaten. . . . We had rainwater soup followed by rubber squab, a nice wilted salad and a cake some admirer had sent in. An enthusiastic but unskilled admirer."

In her thank-you note Gellhorn apologized for Welles's narration of Hemingway's prose, "that awful voice which mangles it. . . . Ernest has borrowed some money (he is now quite broke with paying for the film and buying ambulances) and is going to pay to have that voice part done over, with someone who knows how to talk and has enough imagination to feel." Someone, no surprise, turned out to be Hemingway himself, his light midwestern timbre a nice match for his spare if somewhat stilted script. A Spanish-accented voice might have been better, but

Hemingway and Dos Passos, for one, had parted company permanently in a hostile confrontation on a train platform in Paris on the way home.

While Gellhorn returned to New York to continue fund-raising, Hemingway and Ivens flew to Hollywood. After a screening at Fredric March's house on 12 July and pitches by both men, the crowd of directors, actors, and screenwriters, Scott Fitzgerald among them, donated $17,000 ($279,000 today)—seventeen more ambulances for the cause. The ambulance chassis and power trains, twenty in total after a second fund-raiser the next day in Los Angeles's Philharmonic Auditorium, would be built at Ford in Detroit, with custom bodies added in Spain. Gellhorn had less luck in New York. The gentry treated her, she says, like a "cuckoo idealist."

The historian Robert H. Whealey counts the conquest of northern Spain as "one of the decisive turning points of the war." Franco, Whealey writes, already had "mining and agricultural regions that naturally generated foreign exchange: Morocco's mines; southwestern Spain's olives, sherry and pyrites; and the Canary Islands' tomatoes and early produce." Now he would also control "the rich northern iron ore fields of Vizcaya Province. . . . The Republican economy, in short, started out strong but weakened as the war progressed, while the Nationalists, although at a relative economic disadvantage early in the war, gradually improved their situation."

At the same time, Stalin began withdrawing his support for republican Spain. If he had gambled on establishing a communist state in southwestern Europe, he decided by June 1937 that his gamble had failed. He recalled his last ambassador to Spain that month. "By any reasonable measure," argues historian Daniel Kowalsky, "Stalin's intervention in Spain was enormously ambitious, yet it was an operational failure of roughly the same scale." Recent historians have argued otherwise. "The basic error in the wide-ranging historiography on this topic," Kowalsky counters, "has always been to view Stalin's position in

Spain as one based on strength rather than weakness. If framed within the context of failure, and defined more by impotence than puissance, Stalin's long-standing reputation as the villain of the Spanish Civil War may appear in a strikingly different light." Whatever else is true of Soviet participation in the Spanish Civil War, it was increasingly ineffective from the spring of 1937 onward. Against a rebellion of growing power, the republicans fought alone—but the International Brigades at least had not deserted them.

ELEVEN

Heads Down and Hope

With Tom Wintringham, the International Brigade officer, still convalescing from typhoid, Patience Darton began agitating in April 1937 for work more suited to her training. She was a skilled nurse and midwife, but the best the Spanish Medical Aid Committee could think to do with her was assign her two more typhoid cases. They were IB men, lodged in a decaying former convent where most of the doctors were pro-Franco. The Spanish staff had been throwing dirty dressings and worse out the back windows of the old building for years, Darton recalls, "so if you opened the window, a rash thing to do, it used to 'woof' as the flies all flew up." Cleaning up this feculent midden gave Darton a temporary challenge. She hardly endeared herself to the doctors when she recruited the hospital's medical students for the work. "We had a grand time sluicing this down with hoses and water, and having it taken away," she says, ". . . feeling very revolutionary."

Darton soon extended her revolution, Kate Mangan writes: "Her crusading fervor was at its height and she had plenty of scope for it. The hospital was an ancient, insanitary building, rife with all the germs of ages, an antique lazaretto of a place. When Patience first got there she found that the sick men had never been undressed but were lying in dirty sheets in their filthy uniforms." Nuns and Spanish girls didn't undress men, much less bathe them, even if they were wounded or sick. "The hospital had no change of linen," Mangan continues, "and no soap. [Darton] said that every day she expected to find them all dead, but only one died. . . . Patience got us to write slogans in Spanish and set [a healthy IB man] to making posters representing diabolical germs clinging to visitors' skirts or the dust on the ends of brooms."

Darton's complicated act of kindness rescuing an ill, depressed volunteer, Basil Murray, the son of Oxford classicist Gilbert Murray, inspired the captain of a British navy hospital ship to send Darton "crates and crates" of provisions, "butter and cigarettes and drink, and lots of lovely medical supplies, glorious things, bedpans and things—a very good lot of stuff," which she passed on to the committee in Valencia, reserving to herself only some of the cigarettes. Murray fell in unrequited love with her and changed his will in her favor before he died of pneumonia on the hospital ship on his way back to England. When Darton heard of it she asked the captain to tear up the will and throw it away. Predictably, a gift of provisions from the Royal Navy made the communists on the medical committee suspicious of her.

Abruptly, at the end of April, the committee sent its troublesome nurse to a hospital on the inactive Aragon front at Poleñino, fifty miles northeast of Zaragoza on the Flumen River, an upper branch of the Ebro. Although other members of the British Medical Unit were working at Poleñino, Darton had been misled into believing her transfer would be temporary. "It was nice to be with some English nurses again," she remembers, "but we hadn't got anything to do, [which] worried me frightfully." Winifred Bates, the Spanish Medical Aid Committee personnel officer in Spain, reported to the committee that when Darton "found that she had been tricked she behaved in a bad-tempered, high-handed way and quarreled with a number of comrades." She may have behaved badly, but she also, as always, went to work improving conditions. The hospital had taken over half of the Casa Pueblo, the Poleñino town hall—the town was anarchist and the Village Committee occupied the other half—and on her first day there she opened up its ample stores of gauze and fly-proofed the place.

With seven English nurses on hand and very little work, Darton decided they should train the Spanish girls, called *chicas,* whose duties had been limited to cooking and cleaning. "We were letting them do the skivvying," she recalls, "which was a thing I disagreed with profoundly. I thought we should train them. I mean, this was our chance to train them to do the things we could do":

> To them it was an enormous thing—we were modern women that they hadn't ever come across, you see. We didn't mind talking to men, we didn't mind throwing our weight around either, which we did a good deal, because you know what nurses are! And without thinking much about it, you see, but a Spanish woman couldn't have done that, and she couldn't have nursed a stranger—she couldn't have touched a strange man, let alone washed him or looked after him. For them it was a tremendous thing they were doing, to accept it, you see.

The May Days passed, far away in Barcelona. The surgeon at Poleñino was Spanish, a Dr. Aguiló, from Majorca, a republican, not a communist, highly skilled. "He could speak English and French perfectly," one of the other nurses remembers. "If we talked politics, as we ignorantly and frequently did, he would go to sleep until we'd finished. We once asked him how he knew when to wake up and he said, 'The noise is different.'" Aguiló could operate for as long as two days without stopping to sleep. They kept the pharmacy in his room and the only phonograph, 78 rpm and low capacity. They had only one record to play when they wanted to listen to music and on it one song, but they might have done worse. The song was "Smoke Gets in Your Eyes." The good doctor eventually married one of the British nurses, Mary Slater, Edinburgh-trained.

In the heat of Spanish summer, the nurses went swimming to cool off in the Flumen, which flowed with clear mountain water from the Pyrenees. The village leaders disapproved. "We were in an anarchist village," Darton says, "that didn't care at all for having us anyway . . . and they didn't like foreign nurses either, we were very 'uppish.'" Darton thought anarchists in general, despite their principles, were backward about women. "They weren't at all sure women should learn to read and write." About 60 percent of the Spanish population was illiterate. "There were no schools anyway and it wasn't the thing—it wasn't considered a good thing for people to learn to read and write, very dangerous. And how, it's true!" Even though the hospital served the community, the Village Committee stepped in to discipline the foreign Amazons:

> I'm still annoyed with them because we used to go and bathe in the river in perfectly respectable bathing dresses, proper built-up tops and things, well away from the village—very hot summer—and they didn't like this because they didn't approve of it—so they stopped us from doing it. They said we frightened the mules—and I haven't forgiven them yet!

By then, the beginning of July, the war was coming closer; from Poleñino they could hear artillery rattling in the distance and the distinctive crumping of bombs.

The American Hospital Unit under Edward Barsky fared better; at least it found plenty of work to do. Not long after Barsky's team had the hospital up and running well at Romeral, in mid-March 1937, orders had arrived to move the unit to Tarancón, fifty miles southeast of Madrid. "Ours not to reason why," Barsky quips. "Therefore we packed up and left only a skeleton crew behind to care for the patients who could not be moved. We parted with the old *alcalde* who had so patiently and helpfully attended to our innumerable requests; we waved goodbye to the peasants who were sleeping on straw because they had given their beds to the American hospital."

In Tarancón the army took away their ambulances for use on other fronts and shared out their equipment with two other hospitals where some of the surgical suites had no instruments at all. The battle of Guadalajara was under way by the time the American unit became functional. "Almost before we had things ready," Barsky writes, "the four hundred beds at the evacuation hospital in Tarancón began to fill up." On 17 March two hundred wounded converged on the compound within three hours. "Ambulance after ambulance arrived, each overcrowded with patients. The admitting rooms were soon so full that some of the patients could not get in at once. The floors of the passages were solid with wounded men. The operating room was in constant use; often all three tables were busy at once." In six days and nights, 17 to 23 March, they admitted more than six hundred patients, "most [of them] seriously injured [and] all cases requiring, at the least, urgent treatment." The wounded arrived sixty, seventy, eighty at a time; some had to be evacuated as quickly as they could be stabilized to make room for the next wave.

But the Guadalajara patients were different from the "cold, wounded boys" Barsky had encountered earlier at Romeral:

These men, even when they were on the point of death, were happy! They were even gay. Telling stories like eager boys of their successful rout of the Italians, smoking their captured Italian cigarettes (which I for one found rotten). They told tales of Italian field kitchens captured while the food was still cooking, of the capture of trucks loaded with valuable munitions and commissary. Men with the most gruesome wounds cracked jokes and the whole hospital had, believe it or not, a gala air. . . . These troops in Tarancón were victorious troops. I cannot prove it but I believe, and the doctors who worked with me believed, that victorious troops have a greater chance of recovery.

Eventually Barsky's team had time to dig deep, zigzag air-raid trenches like extended moats around the three Tarancón hospitals. They had buildings for garaging their ambulances and mechanics who "could somehow use their wits" to maintain their vehicles despite the lack of spare tires and parts. "We had an American mechanical laundry, complete with machinery, and two men trained in its operation from New York. This laundry was a true miracle in Spain. Washing hospital linen by the medieval Spanish method"—kneeling on a riverbank, pounding it with rocks—"had been one of the things which caused us the greatest difficulty."

They even had time one evening to celebrate one doctor's birthday with a dinner party. "We had a chicken, some very light wine, extra cans of sardines, bread, some tinned Danish butter and powdered coffee. Things went with a roar." Barsky, a moody man, cautioned them to rein in their happiness. The nationalists usually bombed Tarancón twice a day, morning and evening, and the bombers had been truant at that point for three days.

Sharing the honors with the birthday doctor, Barsky recalls, "was a very pretty young Spanish nurse, Carmen. She was sharing the honors because tomorrow was to be her wedding day." Barsky hadn't even finished cautioning the team when he was interrupted—first by "the tearing roar of planes," then by the "dry, gravel-like sound" of falling bombs. They were trained for such emergencies: they moved their patients into the trenches, carrying those who couldn't walk or crawl. The renewed bombing continued without cease all night and into the dawn.

Civilians streamed into the hospital from the town below, as if the hospital were situated in the hills above a dying Pompeii. Barsky got to work. "Many children. Screaming women. A mother in her black shawl holding a baby up to me. Looking into her eyes I saw that she did not know that it was dead. Looking into mine she read the truth, and shrieked—that cry of human agony which makes you believe in hell."

By midday, the bombers had found the hospital and began working on its demolition. Treatment stopped; everyone crowded into the trenches. "The hospital buildings crumbled before our eyes, slowly," Barsky writes. By midafternoon the building was a ruin. "It looked like the Roman Forum," Barsky says, "except that it smoked."

Tarancón had been destroyed, but the trenches had served, for the hospital at least. "We lost not a single patient. Our head nurse had been working constantly, administering aid to our soldier patients and to civilians as well. She was wounded slightly by shrapnel. But pretty Carmen, our little Spanish bride, had had her arm blown off at the shoulder."

They had already begun organizing another hospital near Saelices, fourteen miles farther southeast below Tarancón on the road to Valencia, in a rare setting. The rural estate had been the summer palace of the Spanish infantas, the daughters of the Spanish kings. Villa Paz's last occupant had been the Infanta Eulalia, born in 1864, an intelligent and modern woman. The infanta's *Memoirs of a Spanish Princess,* her fourth book, had been published in English the same month the war began, July 1936. With the coming of revolution, the low, white villa with its roof of buff-colored tiles had been opened to the locals' cattle and goats. The peasants had been too much in awe of it to occupy it themselves.

Of all the hospitals of the war, Barsky recalls, "I think we loved Villa Paz best of all":

> The Infanta's villa was an enchanting place. There were most romantic gardens with rare trees and sweet flowers, and there were nightingales in the trees. In the garden were many fragments of letters, torn bits of paper written on in many languages. Many of them were decorated by interesting crests. Around the grounds wandered huge wolf-hounds. The peasants said that these ghostly hounds would not leave the estate. . . . There were vast stables and grain lofts which we turned into wards. Inside the villa there was an enormous bed draped in regal brocade, the blanket woven with a rare floral design and the whole middle of it covered with a gigantic royal crest. Three of our nurses used to sleep in that bed together.

The team soon converted Villa Paz into a first-class hospital, American Hospital No. 1: 250 beds, good operating rooms, an X-ray machine, everything a hospital needed to function. "In the beautiful soft sunlight of early April," Barsky reminisces, "when the gardens were waking to life, our nurses scrubbed and scoured and whitewashed to bring about this transformation. With their own pay they paid to have the floors of the operating rooms tiled." They paid to have the buildings rewired, an electrical generator installed, screens built for the windows to keep out flies and mosquitos. They converted a stable into a long dining room with an attached kitchen; other stables and outbuildings became hospital wards. Two convalescing Spanish-American soldiers volunteered to teach the *chicas* to read and write.

Stories of individual hospital units, however colorful, may give a false impression of the scale of medical practice in the Spanish Civil War. Some two million men and women fought in the war on both sides; an estimated 200,000 were killed and many more injured. By May 1937 the International Brigades alone had fielded twenty-four hospitals providing some six thousand beds: six in Albacete, four in Murcia, three in Alicante, seven in Cuenca, one in Jaén, a huge complex of more than three thousand beds in Benicàssim at Castellon de la Plana, and small hospitals in Belalcázar and Madrid. A Swedish-Norwegian hospital opened in Alcoy. According to the British medical historian Nicholas Coni, "almost 18 percent of the IB doctors were female, a figure disproportionately high by comparison with the profession as a whole" and another indication of the liberal idealism of the Spanish war volunteers. Among the various IB medical units Edward Barsky's team, 117 strong, was the best equipped and the largest.

The Lincoln Battalion had settled in to picket duty on the Jarama front after the main lines had stabilized at the beginning of March 1937. Herbert Matthews visited there in late May, "to find the Americans playing ping-pong, baseball, and soccer just to pass the time away. They had dug in strongly on the crest of a hill in what had been an olive grove, and some of the dugouts were gems of comfort. Every now and then someone would get hit by the incessant dropping of stray shots, among which were a fair sprinkling of explosive bullets, not to mention a trench mortar shell now and then. But on the whole it was a quiet time, and I found them all healthy and reasonably happy, with plenty of zest left for fighting." Farther along, past Spanish trenches, Matthews inspected the English Battalion, where "rough old miners from Wales rubbed elbows with young aristocrats."

Matthews thought the front "idyllically peaceful" after the incessant shelling of Madrid that April and May. The grapevines were flowering all along the parapets, and a farmer or vintner among the troops had posted little signs every twenty yards asking his comrades, "Care for the grapes! They suffer when you hit them." So did the humans, needless to say, but grapes didn't take sides. When Matthews complimented one of the men on the quality of his trench work, the Irish-born New Yorker quipped, "Sure, we aren't going to pay rent after this war. We'll just build dugouts in Battery Park." Whether Matthews picked up the threat of class warfare in the Irishman's quip, he doesn't say.

On the afternoon of 3 June 1937 the implacable nationalist general Emilio Mola died, only days before his fiftieth birthday, when his twin-engined Airspeed Envoy crashed into a hillside twenty-five miles northeast of Burgos in dense fog. Mola and two of his adjutants were thrown a distance from the plane by the force of the crash. A shepherd, the only witness, raced to a nearby village for help. The army officers who arrived on the scene could identify Mola only by the general's sash he wore under his weatherproof coat.

The republicans, especially the Basques, despised Mola. He had coined the phrase "fifth column" and commanded the Army of the North. The Basques held him responsible for the destruction of Gernika and the ongoing starvation siege of Bilbao. In Valencia they celebrated with a bawdy review; the British *Daily Express* correspondent Sefton Delmer remembers laughing with a crowd at a strip joint near his hotel "at an earthy harridan doing her act as 'the widow of General Mola.' The 'artiste' was wearing nothing but a black diaphanous widow's veil. And as she sang the bawdy epic of what her husband, the General, had done to her and what he had left undone . . . she swung and twiddled her long and ample breasts in time with the music."

Picasso was not the only artist painting a mural for the Spanish Pavilion in Paris that June. So was the Catalan surrealist Joan Miró. Miró had finished *Still Life with an Old Shoe* on 29 May after having worked on that great, unsettling painting since late January. His biographer Jean Dupin calls it his *Guernica*. "From the very beginning of 1935," Dupin writes, "and for some years thereafter, no matter what Miró set out to do, his brush conjured up nothing but monsters. . . . Miró was not just letting himself go in these works; he made strenuous efforts to shrug off these visions, to escape from them. But they overwhelmed him: everywhere he looked terror was on the march."

Realizing that he could no longer work for only part of the year in France but must exile himself and his family there for the war's duration, Miró had settled in Paris in November 1936. He felt "very uprooted" there, he wrote his New York dealer, Pierre Matisse, the painter's son, in January 1937; "everything happening in Spain is terrifying in a way you could never imagine." He had finished all the preparatory drawings for a series of ten to twelve large paintings, and could "complete them very quickly," but not in Paris. "I left all my work material in Barcelona," he explained, "about a hundred things in progress. . . . Here it is impossible for me to improvise all that." But he was not without resources. Instead of the large paintings, he had "decided to do something absolutely different: I am going to begin doing *very realistic* still lifes," to "attempt to draw out the deep and poetic reality of things."

To return to realism, Miró returned to life-drawing classes at the modest Académie de la Grande Chaumière in Montparnasse. It gave him a place to paint, says Dupin, and perhaps as well "solace in the noise and numbers of the young at a moment when to be alone in front of a canvas or a sheet of paper had become unbearable." The nude drawing sessions, which Dupin calls "the clocked test of the artist's technical skill," forced Miró to quiet himself to direct perception. He drew and redrew the female body—the harbor and landscape of the world—that winter just as Picasso was alternating drawing one and then the other of his two mistresses. Though Miró's line was confident, the figures he drew emerged brutally distorted, as if they were swollen from the beatings Spain itself was taking.

"I will see what develops from this plunge into the reality of things," Miró had concluded his 12 January letter to Pierre Matisse, adding that it would "give me new impetus for the next works." Ten days later it did, when he sketched the basic components of *Still Life with an Old Shoe* over the masthead on the front page of the Paris newspaper *Le Jour.* "Let me tell you about the starting point for this still life," he recalls:

I was very depressed and disconcerted. I was living in Paris, in the Hotel Recamier on the Place Saint Sulpice. It was very close to the rue des Grands Augustins where I used to eat in a bistro called La Grenouille. As I was leaving the bistro one day, I found a broken bottle wrapped in paper on the ground. I said to myself, "I'm going to paint a still life with this." I was very likely thinking about van Gogh's *Still Life with Boots* when I put in the old shoe. I asked my wife to go and buy me an apple. I stuck the fork in it. When I did it, I wasn't thinking about the soldier sticking his bayonet into the enemy's body. I put in the fork because it was a utensil for eating the apple. I didn't intend the crust of bread to be a symbol of hunger.

The civil war was all bombings, deaths, firing squads, and I wanted to depict this very dramatic and sad time. . . . I was fully aware that I was painting something tremendously serious. . . . The composition is realistic because I was paralyzed by the general feeling of terror and was almost unable to paint at all.

Something about the broken bottle resonated with him. On 12 February, writing Matisse about the painting in progress, he crowed that "to look nature in the face and *dominate it* is enormously attracting and exciting":

As I work on it, I don't lose contact with the model for a single minute. I have put all the elements of the composition on a table. These are the various elements:

> *1 empty gin bottle wrapped in a piece of paper with a string around it.*
> *1 large dessert apple*
> *1 fork stuck into this apple*
> *1 crust of black bread*
> *1 old shoe*

I am going to push this painting to the limit, for I want it to hold up against a good still life by Velazquez.

Miró may not have been thinking about bayoneting the enemy when he pushed his ambitious painting "to the limit," but the fork he painted shares a muscular shaft with the massive forearm of the Catalan peasant he drew that spring in a design for a commemorative stamp. Nor is it common to impale an apple for eating with an instrument as large and broad as a serving fork with a single thick tine separated like a thumb from a palm of fingerlike tines. Miró's "crust of black bread" similarly is more a heel than a crust, its helmetlike end erupting toward the viewer in a cut face with black voids unmistakably located like the eye and nose sockets of a skull, while the torn upper edges of the paper wrapping the wine bottle blaze like a burning tower. Nauseous acid yellows and purples leaching from Miró's characteristic palette of primaries and punched out with black shadows compound the dissonance of this unsettling painting. In retrospect, at least, he would acknowledge its symbolism: "I later realized that without my knowing it the picture contained tragic symbols of the period."

"The work is going very well," Miró reported to Pierre Matisse on 21 March. "The still life will soon be finished; this painting is completely absorbing me, and I believe that along with *The Farm* it will be the capital piece of my oeuvre—which I nevertheless hope to surpass later." (*The Farm* was Miró's 1921 masterpiece, his "résumé of my entire life in the country," which Ernest Hemingway had bought for 3,500 francs— about $5,000 today—in Paris in 1925 as a birthday gift for Hadley Richardson Hemingway, his first wife.) "At the same time," Miró's letter to Pierre Matisse continues, "I am doing drawings, and in the afternoon I sometimes go to the academy to sketch nudes."

A month later, on 25 April 1937, the day before the Gernika bombing, Miró wrote Pierre Matisse again, announcing that "the Spanish government has just commissioned me to decorate the Spanish pavilion at the 1937 [Paris] Exposition. Only Picasso and I have been asked; he will decorate a wall 7 meters long; mine measures 6. That's a big *job*! Once the Exposition is over, this painting can be taken off the wall and will belong to me." Miró had his mural commission.

He had finished the stamp design a month earlier, mailing Pierre Matisse a photograph of it on 7 March. It depicted a red-cheeked, red-nosed Catalan workman in a traditional red Catalan barretina cap, his massively enlarged right arm, thick as his body, raised in a republican salute, his clenched fist larger than his head. Although the workman's face is drawn in profile, his right eye, emphasized with a black circle, looks out from the plane of the canvas to confront the viewer, wide open and challenging.

"The stamp cost one franc," Miró recalls. "The same painting was used to print a limited edition poster where the figure was enlarged and the following text appeared: 'In the present struggle I see the spent forces of fascism on one side and, on the other, those of the people, whose immense creative resources will give Spain a drive that will astonish the world.'" He realized the risk he was taking in declaring himself publicly, Miró adds. "I was standing up against everything I considered antiquated and vesting my hopes in something that seemed to me more human, more genuine. After painting this, I was really afraid."

Having put his life in danger by standing with the republic, Miró was prepared to unleash his full fury in the mural. Since he lacked a large studio, he decided to paint his mural onto the material that formed the interior walls of the pavilion. The space that he had been assigned, fully two stories high, faced the open stairwell that led from the third-floor exhibition area down to the second floor. The side walls of the stairwell would be illuminated with quotations from the writings of the great Spanish poet and novelist Miguel de Cervantes. Miró's mural could be viewed from the stairs.

Work on the pavilion had begun only in March. Given the brief months available for design and construction before its scheduled opening in July, its architects, Luís Lacasa and Josep Lluís Sert, had opted to use standard materials in standard dimensions: an exposed metal H-beam skeleton; a ground-floor foundation of rubble faced in brick; entrance and exit stairways of reinforced concrete; wooden slab or cement ceilings; walls of glass or corrugated asbestos lined with compressed excelsior.

The surface on which Miró intended to paint was a coarse composite of compressed sugarcane fiber bound with waterproof glue called Celotex, textured like felt and just as absorbent. Celotex was manufactured in large rectangular sheets, and the six sheets taped together at the seams that would cover the stairwell wall measured a heroic 18 feet high by 12 feet wide. Those would be the dimensions of Miró's mural, vertical in contrast to Picasso's horizontal *Guernica* on the ground floor.

Miró began painting at the beginning of June, working from a two-tiered wooden scaffold assembled from two fifteen-foot ladders leaned together to form an A-shaped support, with lower and upper decks of two-by-twelve boards inserted crosswise through the ladder steps. If his commemorative stamp design inspired the composition, as he told Sert, he clearly made a point of not repeating himself: the workman in the mural, which would be titled *Catalan Peasant in Revolt,* is no salt-of-the-earth fellow raising a fist in working-class solidarity but a vast beaked, screaming head stretched up on a narrow, starved neck. Its left arm is a spindly flare, but its right arm wields a vicious sickle—less a political symbol than a tool of husbandry repurposed as a deadly weapon cocked to disembowel a belly or hack off a head.

In its menace, Miró's mural differs from Picasso's. With the exception of the bull, Picasso's surrogate, and the torchbearer—both of them witnesses rather than participants—all the figures in *Guernica* are victims. Miró to the contrary presents his Catalan peasant charged with rage, armed and ready to fight. *Catalan Peasant in Revolt* alludes to a much earlier conflict than the fundamentally defensive war that the Spanish republic was currently waging: it invokes the Revolt of the Catalans, the Reapers' War, which began in May 1640 when a militia of several thousand armed peasants marched into Barcelona and proclaimed a Catalan Republic. For the next two decades the Catalans fought beside the French against Hapsburg Spain, but ultimately gave way to superior forces. Defeated, they lost to France the corner of Catalonia that runs from Andorra to Perpignan, an area the size of Rhode Island. "Peace had come at last," writes the historian J. H. Elliott, "but, as part of its price, the new frontier between Catalonia and France was henceforth to be the southern chain of the Pyrenees, and the Catalan-speaking lands were divided forever." Miró knew his people's history. Did he mount his reaper's massive, enraged head on so narrow a neck to incarnate the risk of Catalonia's renewed rebellion? The reaper's thin underpinnings, like Picasso's wide canvas of victims, hint at disturbing forebodings of defeat.

Sert doesn't characterize the public's reaction to Miró's mural, but perhaps both works, Miró's and Picasso's, echo in the public's response to *Guernica* that Sert reports:

It was curious to observe in the months that followed—and I lived there constantly—in reviewing the exhibits in the pavilion, to see the reaction of the people. The people came there, they looked at this thing and they didn't understand it. The majority didn't understand what it meant. But they felt there was something in it. They did not laugh at the *Guernica*. They just looked at it in silence. I watched them pass by.

After spending four months on picket duty on the Jarama front, stalled there largely because of the hostility of General Gal—János Gálicz, the martinet Hungarian Fifteenth International Brigade commander— the Lincoln Battalion had been relieved in mid-June 1937. Weeks of drenching rain and miserable cold had made for grim living as the front went inactive, but the weather had warmed with the arrival of spring. New recruits filled in the ranks reduced by the slaughter of 27 February under Gal's deputy Vladimir Čopić on Pingarrón Hill. On 13 June, one International Brigader recalls, the Lincolns had "retired to a series of villages to the east of Madrid" from which they enjoyed "the luxury of baths, haircuts, and passes to Madrid" for a renewing two weeks before joining a new, all-American battalion, the George Washington. They prepared for battle on a major front about to open fifteen miles west of Madrid.

The battle on the broad, open prairie west of the Guadarrama River outside the small town of Brunete would be the first time in the war that the republicans had initiated an attack. It was intended, one of the participants writes, to "drive back or cut off Franco's position in the western suburbs of Madrid, from whence his artillery was able to disrupt industry and to terrorize the population." With the 350 remaining men of the Lincoln, 150 Lincoln replacements, the 525 officers and men of the new George Washington, 250 men from the American cadres of the Canadian Mackenzie-Papineau Battalion, 120 medical personnel, and smaller contingents of transport drivers and mechanics, the Lincoln and Washington Battalions would enter battle 1,800 strong.

Herbert Matthews drove out from Madrid to see the Americans on Sunday, 4 July 1937. "That was a particularly pleasant holiday for me," Matthews recalls:

It started with ham and eggs for breakfast at the American Transport Unit's camp outside Fuencarral. Ham and eggs are enough in themselves to make a red-letter day in this country. They were playing baseball when we arrived, and the game had a finish that ought to go down in history. The score was 4–2, ninth inning, two out and bases full. Mike Radock, the "Babe Ruth" of the outfit, strode up to the plate waving a mighty bat, while his comrades shouted and danced with excitement. The pitcher wound up. A hush suddenly descended—and then it was broken!

But, alas! the interruption was the warning bell of the camp, calling the drivers to muster immediately and go out on a job.

"Get rolling! Get rolling!" a sergeant was shouting.

After all, as the Spaniards say, *"estamos en guerra,"* ["we are at war"] and discipline is discipline. Seventeen drivers had to go away, taking their July fourth dinner with them. The rest of us had a happy and boisterous meal under the trees—an excellent meal, washed down with a bottle of beer and ending with two portions of ice cream apiece.

The Lincoln and Washington Battalions had not fared so well, having marched sixteen miles the previous night moving into position for battle. Matthews drove over to see them, "wondering sadly how many would be alive and well for the next holiday." In the next twenty-four hours they moved forward another six or seven miles. As an International Brigade army of fifty thousand men marched out from the Guadarramas, the battle for Brunete banged open at dawn on 6 July.

How many would survive, Matthews found out soon enough. Three miles north of Brunete the Americans attacked the village of Villanueva de la Cañada that first day and took the village but lost thirty men. Sid Quinn, a Glasgow grocery clerk, remembers a savage confrontation with

Franco's mercenaries during the struggle for the village. "A group of civilians were pushed out of the village towards the end of the fighting,
mostly women and children. We wondered what was happening until
we saw they were being used as a living shield, they were screaming. It
was ghastly to watch it. They were old men, babies, toddlers, and they
were shot down by us because we couldn't stop. Every last one of them."

Wednesday, 7 July, the Americans struggled down to Brunete itself,
the two battalions separating. "Thursday, the eighth," Matthews writes,
"another advance was made. They were staggering from weakness, for
there had been no food and almost no drink since the drive began. On
that afternoon, tired though they were, the Washington Battalion drove
a column of rebels back across the Guadarrama River and on to the top
of a hill, which was known as Mosquito Ridge." They named it for the
bullets, a veteran would recall, whining down like mosquitos from the
defending nationalists' guns.

There before Mosquito Ridge and across the wide battlefield the
Condor Legion attacked the republican forces, including the Americans: Messerschmitt Bf 109B fighters flying top cover for Heinkel 111
bombers while He 51 biplanes strafed the nearly defenseless lines from
below five hundred feet. "The biplanes came in waves of nine-across
formations, wingtip to wingtip," writes historian Walter Musciano,
"each carrying six 22-pound fragmentation bombs and dropping them
simultaneously." Musciano says that "the resulting carnage demolished
the morale of the surviving troops," but it did not demolish the morale
of the Washingtons. "All that night they rested on their positions," Matthews testifies, "gathering their last remnant of strength. Jack Weiss,
who was wounded the next day, swore to me that not a single soldier
thought of going back or had lost the smallest part of the enthusiasm
with which the offensive had started."

Friday, 9 July, the Americans charged up Mosquito Ridge:

As they surged upward, a sharp machine gun barrage met them and it
was obvious that they were facing the heaviest sort of odds. During the

night the rebels had entrenched above them, and were shooting down. They had machine gun nests; they were still fresh and desperate. And still the Americans came on. They spurted singly and in groups, yard by yard, taking what cover they could. A flanking movement was tried, but cut off. Hour after hour passed, but still they kept trying. It was their fourth day without food, and with precious little rest. The ranks were thinning—twenty killed, about eighty wounded out of two hundred men. Darkness was approaching, and at eight o'clock human endurance could go no farther. They had got three-quarters of the way up the ridge, and were hanging grimly on with a pitifully thin line, when a Spanish battalion came to relieve them.

The charge up Mosquito Ridge should have been the end of it, but it was only a beginning. The battlefront shifted back and forth during the next week as republican and nationalist forces gained, lost, and then recovered ground, with terrible losses on both sides. (Of the British battalion's 331 men, for example, only 42 survived Brunete unwounded.) Penelope Phelps, a nurse whom the Spanish called "English Penny," from the North London working-class district of Tottenham, assisted the New Zealand surgeon Douglas Jolly in treating the flood of Brunete casualties in the field hospital the army had set up at a nearby road junction. "I realized he was the best surgeon with whom I had ever been associated," she recalls:

> He operated swiftly and dexterously however complicated the situation. . . . For five days and nights we had only brief snatches of sleep and that on blood-soaked stretchers not occupied by the wounded. We were sustained by mugs of black coffee, bully-beef sandwiches and cigarettes. I had begun to smoke as did all other colleagues, male and female.
>
> We now had heat and flies instead of the cold to contend with. The atmosphere in the operating theatre was stifling and the floor slippery

with caked blood. But still the news was good, our troops had taken Villanueva de Cañada. . . . Then came the Fascist counter-attack and with the weight of armor, planes and big guns against us, Brunete was lost, but our soldiers resisted every subsequent attack, day after day. In the operating theater the flow of casualties and the heat and flies continued unremittingly.

Supplies ran short. They ran out of general anesthesia—ether and chloroform—and switched to local or spinal anesthesia or sedation instead. When they used up the last of the sterile surgical gowns, Phelps draped the surgeons in sheets that the local people had donated. One night, with three operations under way, the generator failed. The surgeons had to operate by flashlight, Phelps recalls. The buildings burning in nearby Villanueva de la Cañada added their firelight.

At the end, in late July, German and Italian fighter aircraft, bombers, and artillery dominated the battlefront. Roddy MacFarquhar, a Glasgow railway clerk with the Scottish Ambulance Unit, remembers "a terrible artillery barrage" on the final day of battle that went on nonstop for six hours, quartering the battlefield yard by yard. "All we could do was to keep our heads down and hope that we might survive it." After the barrage, in the darkness, MacFarquhar and his comrades found a welter of bodies, "living and dead," piled around the forward machine gun in no-man's-land.

The historian Linda Palfreeman reports "roughly 16,000 casualties at the battle of Brunete, 6,000 Nationalist and 10,000 Republican. An estimated 1,000 Republican troops were killed, over 7,000 were wounded and a further 3,500 were sick. The truth was that although the Republican army had inflicted thousands of casualties in the Nationalist ranks, its own losses, in terms of both men and equipment, had irrevocably weakened the Republican cause."

At the end of the first long year of the Spanish Civil War, the medical services at least were thriving. Jolly told Moisès Broggi, the Catalan surgeon, that with such inspired inventions as mobile autochir* surgical units and blood transfusion services, "considerable and transcendental improvements were being made in surgery."

But as always in war, the improvements advanced by involuntary vivisection—by necessary but terrible experimental interventions on the bodies of living men. Fortunately, even in their exhaustion, the doctors and nurses who served in the war brought a full measure of compassion to their work as well. As Germany and Italy continued to support the nationalist rebels with men and matériel, they would need all the strength and compassion they could wring from their weary souls. "The horrible tragedy we are going through may stimulate a few isolated geniuses and give them greater vigor," Miró would write. "But if the powers of regression known as 'fascisms' extend their sway and drive us any farther in the direction of cruelty and incomprehension, it will mean the end of all human dignity."

---

* "An auto-chir," Edward Barsky explains, "is a surgery on wheels. In it a surgeon, if he trains himself to stand still, can operate in perfect comfort under the most adverse conditions. He can move in his auto-chir as close to the front lines as he dares. Around the completely modern operating table are cases for instruments, and in back of the operating table is located a modern autoclave. Our auto-chir had its own batteries to supply current for its own lighting and sterilizing systems, a reservoir for water, and a place to scrub up" (Barsky, n.d., p. 97).

PART THREE

The Thing That Is Trying to Ruin the World

TWELVE

Only the Devil Knows

Patience Darton opened her way to the front lines in late August 1937 when she slapped the Spanish cook. Darton and the eight other idled British nurses had been transferred by then to a hospital in Fraga, a village halfway between Zaragoza and Barcelona—"a marvelous little town," she wrote home, "very old and beautiful . . . right in the mountains on the steep sides of a valley with a river." Fraga might be beautiful, but their situation hadn't changed—"too many of us doing nothing," Darton thought—and her frustration probably animated her outburst.

"Patience was not diplomatic," recalls one of the other nurses, Margaret Powell, a daughter of Welsh farmers. "She had a row . . . with the young and lazy cook and she was probably in the right though she shouldn't have slapped him. That was the end, and Antonio said, 'It's her or me.' She was worth twenty of him but of course she had to go." Luckily, there were International Brigaders nearby and doctors among them looking for nurses.

Darton's own version of the story omits its intemperate climax:

One day a couple of doctors came over from the International Brigades on the scrounge—they'd heard about the nurses and they came and

took two of us. We didn't mind, we were all ready to be abducted. . . .
They had a better organization and they needed nurses, and we obviously, I mean I was still fed up about this—there were nine of us—
doing nothing. All English, all trained, I found it outrageous. So I was
all for it, and off I went.

The second nurse whom the doctors recruited was Lillian Urmston, another British volunteer, a steelworker's daughter from Staly-
bridge, near Manchester. The two nurses joined the IB just in time to
work with the wounded from Belchite, a nationalist garrison town
about thirty miles south of Zaragoza where Franco's forces had resisted
grimly and been destroyed. Ernest Hemingway, back in Spain after his
summer of filmmaking and fund-raising, reconstructed the early September nationalist defeat for the *New York Times* in a 13 September dispatch. Along with three Spanish brigades, Hemingway learned from
his interviews, the IB had first taken Quinto, on the Ebro about twenty
miles downriver from Zaragoza. Then:

> They had marched twenty miles across country to Belchite. They had
> lain in the woods outside the town and had worked their way forward
> with the Indian-fighting tactics that are still the most lifesaving that
> any infantry can know. Covered by a heavy and accurate artillery bar-
> rage, they stormed the entry to the town. Then for three days they
> fought from house to house, from room to room, breaking walls with
> pickaxes, bombing their way forward as they exchanged shots with the
> retreating Insurgents from street corners, windows, roof tops and holes
> in the walls.

The Brigaders had "become soldiers," Hemingway thought, since
he had last seen them the previous spring. "The romantic have pulled
out; the reluctant ones have gone home along with the badly wounded.
The dead, of course, aren't there." Those who were left were "tough,

with blackened matter-of-fact faces; and, after seven months, they know their trade." Among them he found his friend Robert Merriman, recovered from his shattered shoulder. Merriman was lightly wounded again in the Belchite assault, but had fought on until the cathedral where the nationalist garrison had made its last stand was taken.

In these two battles, Quinto and Belchite, thousands had been wounded or killed. The surgeons at the republican field hospital set up in four wooden huts twelve miles outside Belchite performed 160 operations in twelve days. The Lincolns alone suffered more than 250 casualties. The republican artillery barrage had destroyed Belchite as thoroughly as Condor Legion bombs had destroyed Gernika the previous April. But the Belchite assault, unlike Gernika, had not been a surprise attack on civilians. The town was utterly ruined, however, and remains abandoned to this day.

A tall, blond, Cape Town–born British physician and physiologist named Reginald Saxton led the IB medical unit to which Patience Darton had been assigned. The unit worked out of an improvised field station near Huesca, forty-five miles northeast of Zaragoza. "We were all living loose on the countryside, in three huts, by the side of a river," Darton recalls. A typhoid epidemic that autumn made life almost unbearable for the foreign volunteers. (Since typhoid fever was endemic in Spain, Spanish soldiers were largely immune, and the first antibacterials, the sulfa drugs, were just then being tried out in Britain and not yet available in Spain.)

"It has been raining for days and days," a young British medical secretary with Saxton's unit, Rosaleen Smythe, wrote in her diary, chronicling the course of the epidemic. The river was rising and had reached the hospital doors. The buildings leaked and they lacked sanitation—no clean water, no fires, no heat, no toilets. The wards were filling with influenza cases. "Existence is a misery. Rain is coming in. Rats run across the floor." The weather turned to frost and bitter wind. Smythe thought the nurses—Ada Hodson, Patience Darton, Lillian Urmston—

"splendid," however, spirited enough despite the terrible conditions to laugh at the faces one of them made when she tried to drink the mixture of tea, coffee, and cocoa that passed for a stimulant among the IBs.

As the epidemic subsided, the medical team moved the recovering typhoid cases to a convalescent hospital in Valls, a small town in the mountains inland from Tarragona, the old Roman port city on the Mediterranean fifty-two miles down the coast from Barcelona.

Triage, from the French *trier,* "to sort," though not an invention of the Spanish Civil War, was improved and widely applied then. One of the doctors who recruited Darton after she slapped the cook was a twenty-eight-year-old Latvian-born surgeon named Len Crome, a naturalized British citizen. Crome, the Fifteenth Brigade medical chief, was responsible in part for implementing the IB's triage system, a counterintuitive method of sorting patients for treatment. In civilian medical practice, triage had long meant sorting patients according to the severity of their injuries and treating the most severely injured first. Crome and his colleagues adapted the triage process to the different requirements of war: with medical personnel in short supply and manpower urgent on the battlefield, the wounded who needed immediate lifesaving treatment—whose air supply was compromised, whose bleeding was severe—might still be treated first, provided they could be stabilized quickly. But casualties would primarily be sorted into the lightly wounded who could be restored to duty with minimal treatment, those more seriously wounded whose treatment could be delayed, and those most likely to die, who might receive only palliative care.

Crome reported to General Walter, the Thirty-Fifth Division commander, who disguised his urgent concern for his troops behind a stern stoicism. ("Walter" was the nom de guerre of Red Army general Karol Świerczewski, who became "Goltz" in Hemingway's novel *For Whom the Bell Tolls.*) The surgeon vividly recalls Walter's pungent response when he first proposed triaging the Brunete wounded. "Headquarters was in an olive grove a kilometer or so from the front," Crome writes. "The ground was under constant shell fire and was frequently raided by low-flying planes. Most of the officers were working in slit trenches but Walter and his adjutant Alek sat up above by a field telephone in a camouflaged tent." Crome reported to the tent, where Walter questioned him:

> "Well, comrade, what are things like at the front?" I told him. "And what is the situation in the hospitals?"
>
> "We get a lot of wounded and not enough doctors to deal with them."
>
> He became grave, blinked heavily and went on quietly. "Yes, it's war. . . . And what is the morale like? What are the people saying?"
>
> I explained that some of the doctors wondered if it might not be better to help first the lightly wounded who had a better chance of recovery rather than waste much valuable time on hopeless cases, such as severe head injuries. I had no answer to this myself and wanted to have his opinion.
>
> This came with no uncertainty: "I never knew that you were such cannibals! Tell your doctors from me that if I ever hear such talk again they will be sent one and all to the front lines, and without rifles! You will be the first to go. And when you are wounded you may well wonder if your injury is light enough to warrant treatment."

Whether triage was introduced without Walter's knowledge, or he eventually acquiesced, it had become standard practice by the time Patience Darton joined the IB that autumn.

The International Brigaders suffered another three hundred casualties when they attacked Fuentes de Ebro, near Zaragoza, in October 1937. By mid-October, with the fall of Gijón, Franco had conquered all of northern Spain, and at the end of the month, acknowledging its shrinking territory, the republican government retreated from Valencia to Barcelona. It officially integrated the International Brigades into the Spanish republican army on 1 November 1937, and thereafter Spanish replacements began to fill in for IB casualties. By the beginning of 1938, some units of the International Brigades totaled as many as 90 percent Spanish.

Franco responded to the Spanish government's move to Barcelona by intensifying the bombing of the Catalan capital. Lacking radar, still in its earliest stages of development in Britain, Germany, and the United States, the republicans used listening posts to warn them of incoming planes—microphones positioned at the focus of large sound-collecting horns. The nationalists devised an evasive tactic that J.B.S. Haldane, who continued to visit Spain during university vacations as a technical consultant to the republican government, describes in his 1938 book *A. R. P.,* a study of air raid precautions based largely on his experiences during the Spanish war.

A series of night attacks began in December 1937. The bombers approached Barcelona from the nationalist bases on Majorca and usually bombed the working-class areas near the harbor. To evade antiaircraft fire as the city's defenses improved, Haldane writes, the planes "rose to a great height, shut off their engines some miles out to sea, and glided down towards their objective, so that they could not be detected by listening posts." They switched on their engines just in time to begin their bombing runs, limiting their time over target to a bare minimum. Radar would make the technique obsolete, but silent bombing worked against the republicans in the Spanish Civil War.

Of a particularly devastating assault on Barcelona that winter, Haldane writes bitterly, "Though they were carried out by only 6 Savoia 'planes in each of two visits, about 300 people were apparently killed. These included 83 orphan children in one house. While I am aware of the glorious record of the Italian Air Force . . . it is not every day that they can kill 83 orphans with one bomb. Their average is very much lower."

By late 1937 the Catalans had created a network of more than a thousand air-raid tunnels under the Barcelona hills—enough tunnels, Haldane learned, to shelter some 240,000 people. That December he toured one still under construction. More than a mile in length, it had been dug into and under a hillside, about fifty-five feet belowground, with a winding ramp giving access. It measured about seven feet high by four feet wide, and—cut into the hard, baked Spanish soil—it needed no support. Workers were tiling it and installing electric lighting.

Barcelona's tunnels, with toilets and kitchens, lined with benches where whole families sat out the repeated nationalist bombings, saved lives. The streets, as Haldane writes, were a different story. "The danger is greatest from a bomb which bursts immediately on hitting the ground. In this case many splinters* fly out sideways, and cause appalling casualties in a crowded street. . . . The hot gases from a bomb not only burst its case but push away everything in the neighborhood, with an almost inconceivable force. The air in front of them is pushed forward at a speed of about four thousand miles an hour, twenty or more times the speed of the most rapid hurricane. A man standing within ten yards of a large bomb will be torn to pieces, and the pieces thrown for hundreds of yards. A brick wall is not merely knocked down. It is shattered into a hail of projectiles which may kill people at a great distance." Despite shelters, Haldane reports that nationwide, up to May 1938, the number of Spanish children known to have been killed by bombing was 10,760, in a country where children were considered so precious that their parents were willing to starve themselves to feed them. "The number of adult civilians killed," the British scientist estimates further, "is probably at least four times as great. Besides this a larger number have been wounded, many being permanently mutilated." Civilian deaths from Franco's bombing raids throughout Spain would total around 54,000 men, women, and children among more than 100,000 civilian casualties from bombing alone.

"**F**ranco was preparing a new attack on Guadalajara for December 18, 1937," Herbert Matthews writes, "with Madrid as the final objective. The Republicans forestalled him with a surprise attack at Teruel

---

* That is, shrapnel.

on December 15." Teruel, a hundred miles due east of Guadalajara, is a mountain town and provincial capital, of variable temperature in the summer at three thousand feet altitude but bitterly cold in the winter. The winter of 1937–38 was the coldest in Spain in twenty years.

The force of forty thousand republicans attacking Franco's nationalists at Teruel and drawing him away from Madrid was to be entirely Spanish, with the International Brigades held in reserve. Robert Merriman understood that casualties would be heavy in the battle against Franco's superior artillery and aircraft. Anticipating a shortage of medical services, he called Edward Barsky to Valencia for briefing. Barsky says Merriman told him, "Doctor, you're going to be needed, but it will be an even chance if you get there. You'll surely get stuck in the mountains, and you may freeze to a man, but you've got to get there—you're all the medical corps there is." An orderly handed him an envelope, Barsky says. "It contained our orders. They were: *Proceed at once to Hija and join the Fifteenth Brigade.*" In Barsky's assessment, "Teruel would prove to be the most severe and crucial struggle of the whole bloody war."

Barsky's journey up and over the mountains to reach the battle lines near Teruel was a nightmare. He wasn't alone, although the claustrophobia of his descriptions of the ordeal sometimes makes it sound so. A wealthy young New Orleans poet and volunteer, James Neugass, Barsky's driver, enumerates the thirty-vehicle convoy of the twenty-five-bed field hospital that stretched out behind Barsky's staff car:

> We have the bed-truck and supply truck, four big evacuation ambulances ["ambs"] with four stretchers each and room for fifteen light wounded in their compartments; five light six-wheeled front-line ambs, each with two stretchers and room for ten light wounded; surgical and dental auto-chirs; light commissary truck; bug-hatcher [lice disinfectant] and shower wagon, and the staff car, which is mine.

By late December 1937 Barsky's convoy was halted in Alcorisa, seventy miles northeast of Teruel, the staff working in the provisional hospital there and waiting for further orders to advance. Hurry up and wait, as military movements always do. There was a dance on Christmas Eve at a local schoolhouse; the nurses changed from their blue ski pants into skirts for the occasion. "The floor was crowded with International drivers," Neugass reports—"always to be recognized by their pistols—Spanish *soldados* on leave, village boys and grandfathers. The orchestra played *jotas* with an occasional Bavarian-sounding waltz." No hangovers the next day, he laments: "The medical alcohol ran short."

From Alcorisa, the worst of the mountains lay ahead.

Ernest Hemingway reported from Teruel that month, this time in the thick of battle, observing out of a frontline dugout above the river along which the town lay, the Turia:

> Friday while we watched from a hilltop above the town, crouching against boulders, hardly able to hold our field glasses in the fifty-mile gale which picked up the snow from the hillside and lashed it against our faces, government troops took the Muela de Teruel Hill, one of the odd thimble-shaped formations like extinct geyser cones which protect the city.
>
> Fortified by concrete machine-gun emplacements and surrounded by tank traps made of spikes forged from steel rails, it was considered impregnable, but four companies assaulted it as though they never had had explained to them by military experts what impregnable meant. Its defenders fell back into Teruel, and, a little later in the afternoon, as we watched, another battalion broke through the concrete emplacements of the cemetery, and the last defenses of Teruel itself were squashed or turned.

Hemingway, determined to believe that the republicans would win the war, saw the Teruel breakthrough as further proof of their superior morale despite the obviously superior numbers of tanks, artillery, and aircraft that Franco commanded. It followed, Hemingway hoped, that "across a country cold as a steel engraving," the battle for Teruel "may be the decisive one of this war."

Edward Barsky's hospital convoy, with Barsky's car in the lead and James Neugass driving, left Alcorisa on the last day of 1937, following the Fifteenth Brigade's motorized battalions. "Once more our motor-cade, a chain made up of most uneven links, took to the road," Barsky writes. "It was colder, rougher and steeper than anyone had imagined. We were menaced by the speeding lorries rushing down the mountains to get fresh troops to take back to the front." As they climbed in low gear, their radiators boiled over. They had to melt snow for water to refill them, a tedious job at best. Their motley collection of cars and ambulances survived on ingenuity, not spare parts, which were rare, and on "spare tires more precious than gold."

Down the narrow mountain road careened the menacing trucks:

> With everybody's brakes screaming and with a skid like the gnashing of teeth, my car just barely managed to avoid collision with a lorry, empty, tearing downhill full speed. I got out to do a little old-fashioned American bawling-out but somehow my conversation with the driver got off to another tune.
>
> "How are things further up?" I asked him.
>
> "If you mean the road, you will never get up it. If you mean at the front, it is the most furious fighting of this war." As he climbed back to his seat I acknowledged his salute. *"Salud,"* we said, both together.

They stopped to thaw themselves at the house of a peasant couple farther up the mountain. The hospitality of the Spanish never failed to surprise the international volunteers, who mention it repeatedly in their letters and memoirs. No sooner were they settled, crowded around the arched fireplace, than the grinding and roaring of heavy engines invaded the mountain silence. Robert Merriman strode into the room and looked them over. "What are you waiting for?" he asked. "Orders," Barsky answered. "You'll be needed!" Merriman encouraged them. The IBs had to be called forward after all to help the republicans with the nationalist counterattack; Merriman was leading the Americans. He didn't stay ten minutes. "There was no conversation in the little *casa* now," Barsky broods. "We had, I think, only one unspoken thought. The troops were going into severe action, Spaniards and Americans with them, men we knew and men we might never know, but they were going into action *without medical aid*. Each one of us knew by remembering things we might wish to forget exactly what that might mean."

Later that night, farther up the mountain, they found themselves alone on the road. Barsky wondered if they were lost. They encountered a stalled car that had careened into a gully and was partly covered with snow. Barsky scraped away a window, looked in with a flashlight, and discovered Len Crome, "drowsy with cold," waiting for his chauffeur to return with help. Crome had Barsky's orders. "They read, as we had known they would read, to proceed at once to the front and to choose a situation for a front-line hospital, 'as near Teruel as Dr. Barsky may deem expedient.'"

At 3:30 A.M. they made it over the pass and headed down the mountain. "Average speed three miles an hour," Neugass notes. By 4 A.M. they had slowed to one mile an hour. "Car went off road only once, but each time seems to be the last. . . . Snow is six to eight inches deep on the road with ice underneath. Chains would do us no good. Entire convoy of brand-new Diamond-T's which delivered the Brigade to the Front stuck below pass on way back." The staff car's radiator was leaking and had to be filled hourly, with laboriously melted snow.

Barsky took over driving. Neugass clomped ahead in the snow to show him the road. The going seemed to get better. Then they skidded, twice, once nearly fatally. On a third skid, Barsky recalls, "careened at a dangerous angle," the Harvard ambulance, coming up behind them, nearly ran them down. "We could not have seen a worse sight. This meant that the whole unit would be stuck in those mountains during this storm." Undergraduates at Harvard University had taken up a collection to pay for an ambulance, the largest and heaviest of the more than seventy, including Hemingway's custom Fords, that Americans donated to the republican cause in the course of the war. On the mountain in the swirling snow, the medics were lifting cars out of ditches, turning them around by hand, and setting them right on the road again. They managed to lift the Harvard ambulance despite its weight, turn it around, and point it downhill.

Colder and colder, below zero and dropping toward eighteen below. In the night darkness they had passed a small town. Now in the afternoon light Barsky decided they should return there rather than continue trying to move forward. "Even in Romeral I had amputated frozen feet," he writes ominously. He had allowed gangrenous feet and legs to freeze before surgery, using the winter cold for natural anesthesia.

Crome rode with Barsky now. Their car and then the small Ford ambulance they drove next both skidded into the deep roadside drifts and wedged, beyond salvage. Fine, he and Crome would walk back to the town they had passed while the others dug out and hauled out whatever they could move. "We had no boots, just shoes," Barsky writes. "We were not heavily dressed and our clothes were dirty and cold and sweaty. We had been fighting to get up those mountains now for over thirty hours." They left the others and trudged back alone.

Time passed. The two men took turns walking in each other's footprints. They weren't even sure they were on the right road. "We both knew that if we once stopped we would never go on. I wondered who ought to shoot whom? It would not be the thing to leave a buddy to freeze; those boys up the road had at least a bit of shelter in their wrecked cars."

Debating whether to discuss "this somewhat delicate matter" with Crome, Barsky decided he would let the question settle itself. "If I gave out, or if he did, it would be time enough to make the decision. Our revolvers were still dry."

The snow blew in drifts:

One of us fell. The other kicked him to his feet.

"It can't be far now," said one.

"The hell you say!" said the other.

Was this perhaps the time to settle that recondite social point? Keep stumbling on alone and think it over thoroughly.

"Do you see something?"

"Yes, or I think I do."

"Well, come on, that much further anyway."

The thing we saw was a big snowdrift, but out of this snowdrift came smoke. You could have said we smiled frozen smiles. It was the auto-chir. We cleared a spot on the glass window and looked in. The nurses never got tired of talking about the anxiousness in our dirty, bearded faces. They said we looked like the heads out of two El Greco crucifixions. Well, why not? For inside the auto-chir those nurses were making tea!

In the small town of Aliaga, a natural fortress in a blind canyon, guarded by three great cliffs, Barsky routed out the *alcalde*. "He listened to my story. . . . Due to his initiative the mayors of all the surrounding towns turned out crews and snow plows and a large force worked all night on the roads." The next morning they left for the front, "tormented by the thought of what our delay might have meant."

By nightfall they had reached Mesquita, near Teruel. Near enough. "Open trucks rolled into the town patio," Barsky concludes—"open trucks which had come forty kilometers over the sort of road we ourselves knew so well—open trucks in that weather, filled with wounded men. Dr. Byrnes and I went to work in an operating room which was hastily set up. I think that for us we established a record. We operated for fifty hours."

The Teruel diversion wasn't enough. Nothing the republicans did was ever enough, not with Italy and Germany supplying Franco, the Western democracies remaining bystanders, and the Soviet Union in full withdrawal. At Teruel, a Scottish volunteer recalls, "you began to realize the massive difference in strength between the two armies. It was to get more apparent as time went by, but it was really noticeable at Teruel, they could bring up more and more men."

They did: men and tanks, men and artillery, planes that bombed and strafed. "For the first time an artillery barrage comparable with those of the World War was laid down," Herbert Matthews reported from Teruel on 23 January 1938. "At the American brigade's headquarters it was estimated that in the sector its battalions held there was not five feet of ground that did not receive its shells. . . . It was the greatest attack of the war. No fewer than ten waves of men surged forward— brigade after brigade, fresh troops and more fresh troops—until human endurance could bear no more."

So the tide of battle turned. By late February Franco's nationalists had surrounded and retaken Teruel and the republicans were retreating. The nationalists counted 14,000 dead, 33,000 sick or wounded; the republicans that many and 50 percent more. Total casualties, perhaps 140,000, a midsized city of the injured and the dead, fighting over a frozen plateau on a section of the moon—Sefton Delmer's image.

Barsky and his little hospital retreated with the rest, even though, as he writes, "the roads were practically impassable, choked with tanks, troops, artillery, refugees, goats and donkeys." The retreating troops gave way to let them pass. An obstacle loomed. "The road led through the narrow streets of a little Spanish hill town. Plaster houses built three and four stories high right up to the narrow street. Beyond the houses, mountains. Through this tunnel all, everything, the army and the moving hospital had to pass." Barsky pushed to the front of the line, and saw the last obstacle he expected to see: the street packed with sheep, "a solid agglomeration of wool and meat as impassable as lava." *Men are more than sheep,* he thought, and acted:

> I started to beat up the bleating rear of that solid flock. I saw at once that I was hopelessly blocked that way. The artillery of the enemy was din in our ears. All my patients were in the ambulances well in back of me. This delay caused by sheep could easily mean the destruction of us all; the capture of everything; the wounded as well as our precious tanks and artillery. The line had begun to stop. Then I thought of something. About five of us opened all the doors of the houses and like sheep dogs we herded those animals inside. We broke in doors that we couldn't open and left a man in each doorway to keep the sheep inside, while the army and the hospital passed by.

Crome came up, Barsky recalls: "He was surely a welcome sight." The two doctors found a few moments to be alone. What Crome had to tell the American was less welcome. "'It's bad, Barsky,' he said, with tears in his eyes, and his voice broke a bit. 'Very bad. I'm glad you didn't unpack. I'm afraid it's the end here, the lines are broken.'"

THIRTEEN

History to the Defeated

Behind the lines in Valls, nursing at the Casa de Reposo, Patience Darton fell in love. Robert Aaquist, a German Jewish Brigader from Palestine, was recovering from typhoid when Darton met him—"very young," she describes him in a letter home, "only 23" (but she was only twenty-five), "but a natural leader of men." Everyone loved him, Darton adds. The other Brigaders had elected him their political delegate. Tall, slim, with a high forehead, Aaquist was earnest and dedicated. They had long talks about political philosophy—he was an ardent communist, she a skeptic—"and became used to depending on one another without realizing it."

That was in January 1938. By early February Aaquist was smitten, though Darton didn't know it yet. "I met Patience, the most wonderful girl I've ever met," the young Brigader wrote his parents. "We take walks together every day, all the trees are in bloom." Then battle intervened. Aaquist went off to fight at Teruel and took a bullet in his left shoulder. It only clipped the bone, but along the way in, it shattered his cigarette lighter. The lighter added shrapnel to the wound.

Assigned to Teruel herself, Darton found Aaquist among other wounded IBs at the big IB hospital in the coastal town of Benicàssim. "So I rushed over and we were terribly glad to see one another again,

ever so much more than I realized I would be." When Aaquist understood that Darton was going on to Teruel, he was disheartened. She
estimated he'd need a month to heal, promised him she'd be back in
ten days to pick him up, climbed into an ambulance, and rode off. She
wrote home:

> Curiously enough I found I was sitting gazing out of the window, see-
> ing nothing and singing loudly, happy as hell, and I couldn't think why.
> I'm happy, anyway, in Spain, except that I always worry about the war
> and the international situation. . . . But this was quite a different thing.
> I was just absurdly happy, I didn't know what about, till I remembered
> that Robert had said he wouldn't go to the *Casa de Reposo* unless I were
> there. You don't know how moral and high minded and conscientious
> [he is] and how unlike him it was to let any personal consideration
> count at all. . . . I got quite a shock when I realized what a lot it meant
> to me and gave myself a good lecture on the subject. I realized then that
> I'd fallen hopelessly in love with him.

Idolizing him, thinking herself unworthy, Darton couldn't believe
Aaquist might reciprocate her feelings. It didn't help that he awkwardly
signed his letters with a comradely "Red Front!" when they wrote each
other during their brief separation. A fearful experience on a night in
late February convinced her to bring them together. Exhausted, sick
with pleurisy and with an infected arm, she found herself stuck in an
ambulance parked in the Teruel *plaza major,* hoping to survive the
latest nationalist assault. "Lots of machine gun stuff simply whipping
around the place," she recalls, "ricocheting everywhere, mortars—and
I never have liked mortars—and nowhere to go. I mean, I couldn't get
out of the damned thing, I was sitting crouched in the ambulance and
it felt very, very thin indeed, and of course, terribly cold." When the
driver returned from the errand that had delayed them she convinced
him to detour through Benicàssim on his way to deliver her a hundred
miles up the coast to Valls. In Benicàssim, at the hospital where Aaquist

was convalescing, she asked the doctor in charge, a dedicated Viennese communist named Fritz Jensen, to transfer him to Valls. Jensen agreed. Darton thought Jensen must have assumed she was pregnant. She didn't disabuse him.

"It was dark when I got to Robert's hospital," Darton wrote home, "and he wasn't in his ward, so I went out to look for him in the Sala de Cultura and in the dark I met him. I couldn't see him but I just knew it was him and said hallo Robert and he said hallo Patience." Unlike Muriel Rukeyser and her Otto Boch, Darton and Aaquist could speak to each other without a dictionary in hand. He knew some English, she'd been learning German to facilitate her IB nursing, and they had both picked up Spanish. Aaquist had been among a group of several hundred Palestinian Jews when he came to Spain to fight fascism; he and his family had emigrated from Hamburg, Germany, to British-mandated Palestine in 1934.

Aaquist was as determined to transfer to Valls, to Darton's hospital, as she had been to arrange it. They made the rounds of Benicàssim together to collect the other necessary permissions. "He got leave to go," Darton writes, "but he couldn't come that night and so I went in the ambulance. When we said goodbye we found we were kissing and I said oh Robert, he said you angel both in such surprise and then the ambulance went on with me struck all of a heap."

Hitching his way, Aaquist caught up with Darton in Valls the next evening. Despite his wounds he had walked the last ten miles rather than wait for one more passing truck. In his crowded hospital ward that evening, they only shared a jar of jam, a rare and welcome dessert. Deliriously they spent the next day together, discovered at evening that they were starved, and walked three miles into town to a café, where "I ate 11 eggs and he ate 16, not to mention *ensalada*, and *mistela*, a rather good drink." (*Mistela* is alcohol-fortified grape juice.) Darton continues:

> We floated or flew back I don't remember how and found a fiesta going
> on, which seemed too commonplace and *mundial* so we sat outside in the

dark and laughed and talked and kissed. By that time we were rather convinced that the other one wasn't disgusted at mere kissing. I think it must have been the eggs we had eaten. No angel could eat 16 eggs, I thought. You'd be surprised at the amount of things we discovered for the first time—why poets write poetry and the birds sing, and the world was beautiful, and god made men and women and little oddments like that. It was just like being at the beginning of the world, and it still is.

The next two weeks were rapturous with talking and walking and making love. Someone accused them of immorality. "We were staggered," Darton says. "It just seemed funny, like someone speaking another language. . . . We were made for one another, two parts of the same whole so what the hell." In that early spring of 1938 Darton recalls the peach trees blooming, "all these acres of pink peach trees over the bare ground, and lots of little bulbs, lovely little bulbs, little daffodils and things, and squirrels."

Love made a space for them, but love doesn't conquer all. That spring was desperate with nationalist breakthroughs and republican retreats. Posted to separate fronts, the lovers stayed in touch by letter, writing when they could. Darton recalls the chaos of retreating with the hospital loaded onto trucks. "One of the times we were machine gunned, we'd got quite a lot of refugees in the truck with us." They had jumped off the truck and run from a strafing plane whose spray of bullets caught and killed a two-year-old. The child's mother "wouldn't believe it, she couldn't believe it, that one moment she was holding her live child and the next moment there was a dead baby in her arms." The hospital found temporary shelter in a railroad tunnel and operated from there until the republican lines were overrun once again. There were many such tunnels in mountainous Spain that served as hospital sites despite their obvious drawbacks of cold and tunneled wind and darkness. Sheltering hospitals and hospital trains in tunnels was another innovation of the Spanish Civil War that responded to the evolving challenges of air attack.

In mid-March 1938 the nationalists began a major offensive in Aragon, the province in northeastern Spain inland from Catalonia that extends from the French border to below Teruel. Franco was pushing toward the Mediterranean. The American writer Alvah Bessie, one of the final wave of volunteers to join the International Brigades, found "every town along the Mediterranean shore . . . empty and deserted" at the beginning of April, when he arrived in the region from France. "The road was jam-packed with peasants evacuating toward the north. Their faces were impassive, dark with the dust of the roads and the fields, lined and worn. Their eyes alone were bright but there was no expression in their eyes. Looking at them you knew what they were thinking: 'Franco is coming; Franco is coming.'"

That was when Robert Merriman disappeared. The Lincolns had not fared well fighting rearguard actions during the retreats. At the beginning of April they lost Gandesa, a market town in a long valley perpendicular to the Ebro River, fifty miles inland from Tarragona. At Gandesa the nationalists took some 140 Lincolns prisoner, reducing the battalion's strength to about 120 men. Retreating at night through the olive groves toward the river, hoping to escape down the river road to Tortosa, this disorganized rump stumbled into an encampment of nationalist infantry. The guard yelled "*Rojos! Rojos!* [Reds!]" They froze in place. "High above we hear footsteps on the terrace," one of the Lincolns, John Gerlach, recalls, "and a few seconds later we hear a command: '*Manos arriba! Manos arriba!*' [Hands up!]" Instead of surrendering, they ran. "Soon we are near the main road where we rest momentarily and make certain there is no one about. We listen. Behind us only darkness. No more footsteps. No shouts or shots. Only silence!" But Merriman and their other leader, David Doran, had broken in a different direction. "There is no record," Gerlach says, of what happened to them, adding in benediction: "They delivered themselves into the night in the greatness of their faith."

In San Francisco, not knowing if her husband was dead or a prisoner, Marion Merriman sought word of him for months through personal and journalist contacts and with U.S. State Department help. Only when the foreign volunteers were withdrawn from Spain in October 1938 with no word forthcoming did she accept that he was dead.

After traveling to the United States to raise funds for the republican cause, Edward Barsky returned to Spain in March 1938 promoted to surgeon-in-chief of the International Sanitary Service, responsible for all twenty-four International Brigade hospitals. He moved to Barcelona in mid-March just in time for a relentless two-day terror bombing the Condor Legion inflicted on that city. "The subways were crowded with men, women and children who lived there and ate there during the whole forty-eight hours," Barsky writes. "The stench in these subways was terrific, the combination of sweating humanity with all the body odors, with stinking olive oil and food, all overtoned with the actual smell of fear and horror." J.B.S. Haldane reports panic among the bombarded Barcelona population, the first he had seen—"About a quarter of the population ran out into the country," he notes—but Barsky remembers continuing resistance: "All these emotions seemed welded together with a spirit of determination; it was remarkable to hear the Catalonians utter curses and avowals of fighting to the bitter end despite the horrors under which these people were living. The children were taken out of the town, up in the hills and kept there."

Barsky's new problem, besides coordinating personnel, supplies, and transportation in polyglot conferences among officers speaking Spanish, French, German, or English, was evacuating the many IB hospitals north into Catalonia as the nationalists thrust toward the Mediterranean. He had a few weeks during which to prepare, but the order when it came was still a shock. One of his assistants called him from Albacete yelling in German that Barsky should have warned him he had only ninety-six hours to move all twenty-four hospitals—reading from the order—"to places designated by Dr. Barsky."

"I was thunderstruck," Barsky recalls. "I could barely get up from the chair. One phrase kept flying through my mind: 'To places designated by Dr. Barsky.' I knew we had almost four thousand wounded soldiers. How could I put up four thousand wounded soldiers? Where could I put up four thousand wounded soldiers? Where would I get blankets and mattresses and all the other things which would be essential?" He had a thousand medical personnel to move into Barcelona as well, into a starving city, under bombardment, with no places for them to sleep or eat. What could he do?

Barsky assumed that the Spanish trains would be slow, making it necessary to do the transfers in stages and thus buying him a few days. He and his staff went out searching for buildings. They commandeered a convalescent hospital in a nearby town, 200 beds with room for 200 more; a large building and a cavalry barracks in another town, space for 1,200; a convent in yet another town, space for 1,500 more; and a "filthy old monastery" northeast of Barcelona crowded with refugees, whom they had to expel. Some of the monastery buildings dated back to the eleventh century. Its rooms were small; walls had to be torn out to open space for wards. The doctor assigned to set up the monastery hospital refused to take in the wounded until the renovations were done. Barsky, whose authority was military and therefore absolute, ordered the man to be ready when the first five hundred patients arrived—that night. "If everyone doesn't get in," he threatened this doctor bluntly, "I'm going to have you shot."

Once the monastery hospital was functioning, Leo Eloesser, the Stanford thoracic surgeon, who had arrived in Spain in mid-November 1937 and had already served at Villa Paz and Teruel, directed it as surgeon in charge. The antiquated monastery water supply was typhoid-ridden, Eloesser found. With an epidemic fulminating, he treated the contaminated tanks with potassium permanganate, which disinfected the water while dyeing it deep purple, and hung "Not Drinkable" signs from the taps. Barsky arranged for a daily truck to deliver water for drinking and washing. "That epidemic was put down in record time," the physician writes proudly; "in three weeks there were no new cases." There had been ninety cases in all, with twelve deaths.

In the confusion of the retreats, Alvah Bessie had trouble locating the remaining men of the Fifteenth Brigade. He finally found them in the hills above Tortosa, including three of those who had just escaped Gandesa, lying on the ground wrapped in blankets, naked and shivering. They had swum the Ebro to escape, they told Bessie. The Ebro is a wide, cold, fast-moving mountain river. "Other men had swum and drowned."

Bessie then looked down from the hillside:

Below us there were hundreds of men from the British, the Canadian Battalions; a food truck had come up, and they were being fed. A new Matford roadster drove around the hill and stopped near us, and two men got out we recognized. One was tall, thin, dressed in brown corduroy, wearing horn-shelled glasses. He had a long, ascetic face, firm lips, a gloomy look about him. The other was taller, heavy, red-faced, one of the largest men you will ever see; he wore steel-rimmed glasses and a bushy mustache. These were Herbert Matthews of *The New York Times* and Ernest Hemingway, and they were just as relieved to see us as we were to see them.

The two correspondents passed out welcome packs of Lucky Strike and Chesterfield cigarettes. Bessie thought Matthews seemed bitter, "permanently so." In contrast, "Hemingway was eager as a child. . . . He was like a big kid, and you liked him. He asked questions like a kid: 'What then? What happened then? And what did *you* do? And *then* what did you do?'" Matthews was discouraged about the war, Bessie judged. Hemingway "did not seem to be. . . . Hemingway said, Sure [Franco] would get to the sea, but that was nothing to worry about. It had been foreseen; it would be taken care of; methods had already been worked out for communication between Catalonia and the rest of Spain; by ship, by plane, everything would be all right." In his 1939 memoir *Men in Battle,* Bessie has Hemingway running on in that vein for another full page, a cruel caricature of a man hoping for the best for a people he admired and loved. With unsuspecting generosity in the hills above Tortosa that day, Hemingway hands Bessie another pack of Lucky Strikes, adding, "Here, I've got more."

Whether or not Matthews was bitter, he was certainly discouraged. "When it was all over," he writes, "the Lincoln Battalion started up again, as men struggled in one by one, with forty Americans and thirty-five Spaniards. More than 400 were gone: killed, wounded, ill, prisoners, or deserters."

In mid-April Franco's forces broke through to the Mediterranean coast at Vinaròs, north of Valencia, and cut Spain in two.

Vinaròs lay just twenty miles below the delta of the Ebro River, which flows from its source near Santander in the Cantabrian Mountains of northern Spain 578 miles southeastward along the southern foothills of the Pyrenees to enter the Mediterranean a hundred miles south of Barcelona. On its way, southeast of Zaragoza in the Catalonian boot heel, it follows a great bend northeastward, then carves through forested mountain gorges before descending to the Mediterranean littoral. The nationalists were now deployed to the south of the Ebro below that great bend, the republicans to the north, defending Catalonia.

At the beginning of May 1938, in a renewed effort to achieve a diplomatic end to the war, the prime minister of the Spanish Republic, the physician Dr. Juan Negrín, issued a thirteen-point plan that "solemnly declare[d] its war aims to its fellow countrymen and to the whole world." *Aims of the Spanish Republic* included "the absolute independence and complete integrity of Spain. . . . The liberation of our territory from the foreign military forces of invasion. . . . A People's Republic . . . based on the principles of pure democracy [with] universal suffrage. . . .

A radical agrarian reform. . . . Renouncing war as an instrument of national policy. . . . Complete amnesty." Franco rejected these enlightened principles out of hand. "He and all Spanish nationalists would rather die," the Caudillo told German ambassador Wilhelm von Faupel, "than place the fate of Spain once again in the hands of a red or democratic government."

Negrín and his generals understood then that their only alternative was to fight, however grave the odds. Franco had turned his armies down toward Valencia, once again preferring to secure his rear before pushing on north into Catalonia. To divert an attack on Valencia, the republicans began planning a major counteroffensive across the Ebro, muscled with a force of more than eighty thousand men and all the planes, tanks, and artillery the Spanish Republic could muster—not many. Between mid-March and mid-April, during the brief second prime ministership of French socialist Léon Blum, some additional armaments had come though from France.

The George Washington and Abraham Lincoln Battalions were merged into one unit after Merriman and Doran were killed, and a tall, self-taught Brooklyn intellectual with a booming voice, Milton Wolff, was appointed commander. (The Spanish predictably called him *El Lobo*.) The new Lincoln-Washington Battalion was rebuilt that spring with green wood: Spanish replacements, some four hundred of them, who arrived in May. They were innocents, untested adolescents between sixteen and twenty years old. The hardened Brigaders called them *la Quinta del Biberón*—the baby-bottle recruits. "Many had never shaved," Bessie writes pityingly; "most were conscripts from farm, factory, and office. . . . All seemed to be at that stage of adolescence where they were more girls than they were men. . . . They were ill at ease; they seemed unhappy; certainly few held any convictions about the war and now had left their homes, their parents, for the first time in their lives." They were cannon fodder. For six weeks the Lincolns trained them as best they could.

Dignitaries visited the republican encampments to boost morale, among them the leader of the Indian Socialist Party, Jawaharlal Nehru, then forty-nine, and his twenty-year-old daughter, Indira Gandhi. The republicans built rowboats for the river crossing inside abandoned churches and hid them under the trees in olive orchards. The river crossing was intended to be a surprise attack. "The men all knew," Wolff assesses the surprise factor, "and the Fascists knew but couldn't believe."

Robert Aaquist had returned to duty, training with the XI Brigade for the Ebro crossing, but through the spring he and Patience Darton managed to meet every six weeks or so. When he saw that she had lost weight, he began calling her his "pancake," addressing her that way in letters; between meetings they wrote each other almost daily. By mid-May they had married, not legally but informally, by IB custom. Darton echoes Wolff's assessment of the Ebro preparations: "They were building roads all round, organizing the thing very strongly to fight back to go across the Ebro. And we knew this, it was an open secret. We were all ready, we were longing for it. We wanted to get back, we wanted to recover the ground."

Twenty-four hours before the crossing, Bessie writes, advancing into position, the Lincolns emerged from a ravine in the late-night darkness to find the staging area alive with activity:

> The roads were jammed with trucks, moving in complete darkness, loaded with small pieces of artillery, ammunition, tandem machine-guns, sections of pontoon bridges all ready to be put together. We began to have some understanding of the scope of this operation and it cheered us; we saw more bridge sections, huge barrels lying beside the road under the trees, boats; we saw mule-trains carrying smaller cases, machine-guns; dispatch-riders on motorcycles weaved in and out among the marching men and the *camions,* miraculously avoiding collision. . . . We left the road and cut into a wide dried stream bed that flowed down to the Ebro. Two hours before dawn we camped on this stream bed, dropping to sleep with complete exhaustion on the sharpened pebbles.

After that final day's rest, at fifteen minutes past midnight on Monday, 25 July 1938, the first rowboats pushed off the north shore of the broad, swift river. The moon was new and the sky was dark. The river would have been a cool, humid presence in the summer heat. Each boat carried "eighteen to twenty fully equipped men," Edwin Rolfe reports, ". . . rowed across by Spanish sailors and fishermen, men from Galicia and the conquered North." Some boats hauled sections of light footbridge, *pasarelas,* mounted on cork floats. On these the defenders could walk across the river single file, three thousand men per hour. Then engineers would assemble the pontoon bridges, strong enough for trucks and tanks. "Once the crossing had been made the fighting began," Rolfe continues, "but so great was the surprise that the first landing parties quickly overcame the resistance of the enemy at every important defense post on the riverside. The inland push began."

Crossing by daylight in the second wave, the Lincolns had been bombed and strafed by a single, sky-blue Italian bomber, an observation plane, which they cursed. They encountered no other nationalist forces that morning, but they heard Franco's planes bombing the shores of the river behind them, "bombing the bridges as they were constructed; we felt somewhat trapped, but we could still advance; only there was no way of knowing how far we could advance before we would meet the first of their counterattacks." Evidence that the nationalists were ahead, an ambulance passed them returning toward the river, "its cab and body jammed with wounded men in fresh white bandages; they lifted their fists in greeting and we cheered them."

Until Franco could move his forces up to counter the republican attack, he applied his mass of German and Italian aircraft and artillery to slow its forward motion. By the end of the first day, all the boats used in the Ebro crossing had been sunk. Nationalist aircraft dropped up to ten thousand pounds of bombs per day on the Ebro bridges, which the republican fortification units then hastened to rebuild. Artillery found the republican forces as well, "with a conscious knowledge of where we were," it seemed to Bessie, "—to left, to right, ahead, behind, crashing like enormous garbage cans heaved by gigantic men." A British Brigader, Robert Cooney, remembers that "quite a few of the fellows tied a piece of string around their necks with a piece of wood on it so they could bite on it" to stave off panic during the relentless bombings and barrages. "The planes came over us so low that you could actually see the bombs coming out. We'd no real anti-aircraft equipment, only machine guns. You'd not a lot of time to duck for cover."

Earlier in the summer, expecting major casualties, the IB medical services had identified sites for field hospitals on both sides of the Ebro. The most secure of these was a hillside cave shelter overlooking a narrow valley about eight miles northeast of the river, outside the village of Bisbal de Falset. A young British hospital statistician named Nan Green, who worked there, calls the Santa Lucia cave "a natural wonder with a huge rocky overhang, set in the side of a steep hill," with pines growing above and below. "Because of the deplorable state of the roads," Green explains, "the People's Army medical services had developed the custom of bringing its most seriously wounded men to improvised hospitals as near to the front line as possible, to avoid the jolting and sometimes lethal transport to the Base."

Under its massive overhanging lintel, the cave shelter opened like a dark mouth a hundred feet wide, with an interior ceiling ten feet high that extended deep into the hill to a back wall from which flowed a spring of fresh water. This natural cave had sheltered animals and humans since prehistoric times. The lintel and the hill from which it projected guarded the shelter from overhead bombing, and the narrowness of the valley prevented aircraft from diving in for strafing attacks. For once, Franco's air forces were powerless to murder the wounded in their hospital beds.

"One day," Darton remembers—it was 24 July, the day before the river crossings began, the date on her orders—"we suddenly were sent for, a whole lot of us in different sections, to go to kilometer something on the Bisbal de Falset road, where they'd got a set-up, a huge cave." The medical service had packed 120 beds into the Santa Lucia shelter as well as an operating room and a kitchen. There, and on the valley floor below, everything the Spanish and foreign-volunteer physicians had invented and tested during the war came together: the triage system, blood storage and transfusion, field surgery, plaster-casting wounds and fractures. "In the valley below," Darton confirms, "we had the tent which wasn't so safe and nice as our cave, but where the ambulance would get to, and then the stretcher bearers had to carry [the wounded] up quite a steep place to the [operating] theater and to the cave, once they'd been sorted out into 'serious,' 'medium' and 'wait, it can go back.'"

Leah Manning, the stout British former member of Parliament, visited the cave hospital on 26 July and idealized it in her report back to the Spanish Medical Aid Committee in London. "I suppose that in all the history of modern warfare there has never been such a hospital," Manning writes. "It is the safest place in Spain, beautifully wired for electric lights and with every kind of modern equipment." The reality was less glamorous, Darton recalls:

> The cave was very uncomfortable; it was very dark, very low and all uneven. The metal beds were all higgledy-piggledy over the floor and you could barely see—we hadn't got lights. We had lights for the [surgical] theatre, run off of one of our ambulances, but we hadn't got lights in the cave [ward], and we had to do our work by little tiny oil lamps, ordinary tin [sardine] cans with wicks in them with oil. It isn't much light; a miserable little fickle light, and you couldn't see across the cave, and you kept banging yourself on those iron beds.

Worse than the lighting problem and the banged shins, far worse, was the condition of the wounded hauled up from the river, sorted at the triage station on the valley floor, and then hand-carried around on the access ramp into the cave:

> We had an awful lot against us. They had a lot more artillery on their side than we had and we were near to—we were obviously very near

a lot of good mortars, because we had a lot of mortar wounds, and they're much bigger, they're much more smashed-up things. . . . And mortars take great chunks out of people if they survive at all, huge lumps have been hurled out of them, much more smashing up stuff than bullets which go through you. . . . We tended to get people at night because the shelling was so enormous they couldn't move in the day. So for the first time, we got people rather long after the battle, we got them sometimes hours after they'd been wounded and some, of course, we couldn't save because of that—they were already too bad.

Amid the welter of IB languages, which might have been a barrier, Yiddish turned out to be a blessed lingua franca—most of the Jewish IBs knew it, and since Yiddish derives from medieval German, many of the other Europeans at least recognized cognates. In contrast, Darton remembered to the end of her life the plight of three Finnish IBs whom the stretcher-bearers brought in, seriously wounded:

Nobody could speak anything to them. Nobody speaks Finnish. They were all very bad chest wounds. In those days we didn't know that you could operate on chest wounds, we used to strap them up tight and sit them up, but they were miserable. They couldn't breathe. . . . And they were all three dying. And we couldn't get anyone who spoke Finnish and they weren't Jewish. Oh! I'll never forget them, they were such beautiful creatures, great blonde things, you know, unable to say anything.

The IB doctors and nurses also treated the enemy wounded in their cave hospital, even offering blood transfusions despite the prejudices of the Spanish soldiers against mingling their blood with the enemy's, especially the *Moros'*. Darton recalls one Moroccan prisoner, wounded in the neck, who needed a transfusion. "God how he hated us," she says, "he used to give terrible looks to us, he didn't trust us at all, he expected we'd kill him the same as they killed people. . . . The [Spanish] chaps got together and said they weren't going to give the blood of the women of Spain to the Moor"—meaning the stored blood delivered to the battle-front from Frederic Duran Jordà's Barcelona collections. Yet they did. So also had the Spanish republicans protested when their own military carried out limited terror bombings earlier in the war.

The road that passed above the cave hospital led to the battlefront. From the cave vestibule, day and night, Darton watched truckloads of the last republican draft—"children," she remembers, "fifteen- and six-teen-year-olds in the last call-up, going up to the front." It was more than she could bear, she thought, although there is always more to bear in war, particularly when your side is losing:

> And we saw what happened when they got to the front—these terri-ble smashed-up people, streaming in. And to hear those kids singing as they went up—it was terrible when I thought what was going to happen to them, and it got me down frightfully. We were working terribly hard, it was very uncomfortable, very dark in that cave and almost everyone who came in was pulseless and seriously ill. . . . I was on nights . . . and this darkness and the discomfort and the seriousness of it—I thought it wasn't worth it, I thought no war is worth all this, this misery and this horror.

Perhaps no war is, not even that first desperate war against fascism to which the Spanish people were abandoned by the democracies and by the Soviet Union as well, so that of Spain's 24 million souls, fully half a million died directly, or from hunger and disease, or immediately af-terward in Franco's hundred thousand vindictive executions.

The more that Patience Darton could bear at least came on quickly, at the end of the first week of the Battle of the Ebro. The tall young British nurse, Robert Aaquist's cherished "pancake," received a letter dated 31 July 1938 from Sergeant Bert Ramin, Forty-First Battalion Machine-Gun Company, addressed *Esteemed Comrade*. "I ask you above all to accept these lines calmly," the letter began, and continued: "On 27

July 1938 Robert was killed, struck a mine and died immediately. A few days before, he charged me with notifying you in the event of his death. At the same time I am sending all his letters to you, yours to him as well as his parents' and ask you to notify them of his death." Sergeant Ramin went on to praise his comrade: "We know what we have lost in him."

In the next days Fritz Jensen, the Viennese physician, hearing of Patience's grief and exercising war's curious compassion, arranged her transfer to the battlefront. "The move to the front was like a sort of therapy," she would say appreciatively. Before she left the cave hospital, however, Santa Lucia, the waters of which are said to heal afflictions of the eyes, Darton wrote Robert Aaquist's parents in Palestine with news of his death. She wrote of her love for him and of his for her; she told them he had loved them and had cherished the photographs they had sent. She assured them, "these last eight months were full of joy for him." Patience Darton, one among forty thousand international volunteers, changed her mind then about the worth of war, of that war at least, war as one man she knew had fought it, as she was fighting it. *"For me and for many,"* she wrote of her husband, interred now in a common grave among his comrades, *"he was a revelation of how to live and fight against the thing that is trying to ruin the world."*

The Fall of the Curtain

The Battle of the Ebro raged on through the summer and autumn of 1938, grinding to a nationalist victory only in mid-November with little ground gained but with republican resources exhausted. By then, the Internationals—the few foreigners left among what had become a largely Spanish force—had departed Spain. Juan Negrín, the last premier of the Spanish Republic, had announced their repatriation as a gesture of goodwill at a 21 September 1938 meeting of the League of Nations, and they had left, reluctantly, after parading through Madrid in October. "I saw La Pasionaria through floods of tears," Patience Darton recalls, "waving from a balcony. The Spaniards all around us were crying openly, hugging and kissing us—it was all so terrible. What could *I* do against the fact that we were being made to leave Spain? I had to accept the decision of the Spanish Republican government."

Needless to say, Negrín's gesture had not inspired Franco to expel his German and Italian mercenaries. To the contrary, after his prodigal Ebro campaign he traded large interests in Spanish mines for German war supplies sufficient to finish out the nationalist conquest.

Past the Ebro, Franco's forces pushed into Catalonia. Barcelona fell on 26 January 1939, Valencia on 30 March. On 1 April 1939 the Spanish Civil War ended in republican defeat. In May the nationalist armies paraded Franco's victory on Madrid's Gran Vía while Spanish, Italian, and Condor Legion aircraft in formation overhead spelled out the Caudillo's name. Reprisals followed: firing squads manning machine guns, long years in prison, slave labor put to draining swamps and building monuments. "Our regime," Franco announced grandly, "is based on bayonets and blood, not on hypocritical elections."

After the Paris Exhibition closed in November 1937, *Guernica,* Picasso's masterpiece, began an odyssey of touring and exile. It was exhibited in Scandinavia, in England, again in France, and then in the United States, where it remained on display in New York at the Museum of Modern Art until 1981, after both Picasso's and Franco's deaths, when it was returned to Spain. Today it hangs in the Reina Sofía in Madrid, still a shock to encounter in its complexity of violence and suffering and its monumental scale.

Miró's *Catalan Peasant in Revolt (The Reaper)* suffered a crueler fate. "Miró's mural was sent to Valencia," the art historian James Soby writes, "where its masonite panels were soon lost and possibly destroyed. The loss is serious, since no one who saw the mural in place in the Spanish Pavilion is likely to forget its strong and poignant efficacy as a symbol of oppression."

Otto Boch wrote Muriel Rukeyser from the front, a few letters in German "speaking of his soldier's life." Rukeyser tried repeatedly to return to Spain, her editor Rowena Kennedy-Epstein reports, "to write on the 'end' of the war, just as she had written on its 'beginning,' to write of the refugees crossing the Pyrenees [after the republican defeat] and 'the buffer zone'—what she called 'a paradigm of all boundaries'—but she was never allowed to return." She appears not yet certain if Boch is alive or dead as late as October 1941, when she published a poem, "Long Past Moncada," which wonders "Whether you fell at Huesca during the lack of guns, / Or later, at Barcelona, as the city fell."

At some point Rukeyser learned the details of her lover's death. In 1972, during the Munich Olympics, she published a brief remembrance in several German newspapers offering "further information" about

Boch to "any of his family and friends." What she learned she recounts in a memoir of her 1936 visit, published in *Esquire* in 1974. Boch had enlisted in the Thaelmann Battalion and fought on the Zaragoza front. He was killed in 1939, Rukeyser writes, near the end of the war, "on the banks of the Segre River, at a machine-gun nest where six hundred out of nine hundred were killed that day. It is in the Franco histories. Their intelligence worked very well. They knew every gun position."

Edward Barsky's life could fill several more books. After he left Spain in January 1939 he returned to his work as a surgeon at New York's Beth Israel Hospital. In 1941 he helped form a Joint Anti-Fascist Refugee Committee (JAFRC) and served as its chairman. The writer Dorothy Parker led a JAFRC fund-raising campaign, which listed among its sponsors Albert Einstein, Leonard Bernstein, Paul Robeson, and Orson Welles. By 1943 the JAFRC had raised almost $400,000 (about $5 million today) for the relief of Spanish Civil War refugees. That major humanitarian effort ran afoul of the anticommunist witch-hunters of HUAC, the U.S. House of Representatives' notorious House Un-American Activities Committee. Investigating the JAFRC postwar, HUAC found Barsky and other JAFRC leaders in contempt of Congress in 1947 when they refused to turn over their financial records and membership list. Barsky served six months in federal prison, after which the New York State Board of Regents compounded the insult by suspending his medical license for six months. The U.S. Supreme Court upheld that suspension in 1954, prompting the liberal associate justice William O. Douglas to dissent: "When a doctor cannot save lives in America because he is opposed to Franco in Spain, it is time to call a halt and look critically at the neurosis that has possessed us." Like the Yale classicist Bernard Knox, who had fought with the IBs and served with distinction in the U. S. Army during World War II, Barsky had been what Knox had learned to call "a premature anti-Fascist"—"an FBI code word for 'Communist,'" Knox writes.

Despite his government's harassment, Barsky continued to practice at Beth Israel and continued his human rights work as well. In the

1960s, as a member of the Medical Committee for Human Rights, he helped provide emergency medical services for civil rights workers in the American South, just as he had done on the New York docks in 1936. Barsky died at eighty in 1975. His remarkable memoirs, which I have quoted here at length, remain unpublished.

Ernest Hemingway, Martha Gellhorn, George Orwell, J.B.S. Haldane, and Alvah Bessie left abundant records of their own subsequent lives. Simply listing their names speaks to the importance of gifted men and women assigned to a small but pivotal war at a hinge of history, to their conviction and their forlorn hope that success in this small war might forestall a more terrible conflict than any the world had yet suffered.

After arriving back in London in December 1938 with not a penny to her name and in borrowed shoes, Patience Darton found work as a nurse until the Second World War opened with the German invasion of Poland in September 1939. Her gifts for nursing and organization began then to be recognized. She lectured on combat nursing and devoted herself as well to refugee relief, much like Barsky in the United States. In 1944 she began working in medical procurement for the UNRRA, the United Nations Relief and Rehabilitation Administration, which distributed food and relief supplies to a starving Europe in the wake of the war.

Darton had hoped to go to China in 1939, much as Norman Bethune had done, to support the Chinese communist guerrilla war against the Japanese, but the China Medical Aid Committee in London wasn't sending nurses. After the communist victory in 1949, which established the People's Republic, she found occasion, working as a translator in Beijing in the 1950s, marrying a fellow translator who was an IB veteran, and bearing a son, her only child. In 1958 she returned to England. She and her husband later divorced.

Through all those years, though Darton spoke freely of her war experiences in Spain, she rarely mentioned Robert Aaquist, nor had she returned to Spain. She did return in November 1996, with her son, named after Aaquist, and with her biographer Angela Jackson. By then she was ill with lupus and frail. Hundreds of Brigaders attended the homage that month. The Spanish government was awarding them honorary citizenship. Darton took the stage with them, the only woman among them. Jackson describes her end:

> The next morning, she was admitted into hospital, impossible to rouse from sleep and slipping deeper into unconsciousness. I was at the hospital with Patience and her son throughout the following night. She never fully regained consciousness but held tightly onto my hand. Perhaps there was some comfort in it. If not for her, then for me. I wondered how many times she had held the hand of someone as they lay dying during the long nights in Spain. The next day, 6 November 1996, aged eighty-five, she died.

Jackson remembers then reading a letter Darton wrote to Robert Aaquist. Dated 23 July 1938, it was almost certainly the last letter the tall, confident English nurse sent her Brigader husband before he encountered the mine that tore his life away. She's regretting that they've had so little time together:

> When we are together again we will make up for it. We will rest and eat, and eat and rest; occasionally, we will talk. But most of the time you will be in my arms and we will just make love and argue. We may go so far as to kill a few lice now and again. My arms are aching to hold you, dearest. I do want you so much. I am going nearly mad waiting here.

These are old stories. What survive are documents, paintings, methods, technologies—and bones in a basement, bones scattered across a peaceful field.

Half Moon Bay, California
April 2012–March 2014

ACKNOWLEDGMENTS

The Alfred P. Sloan Foundation generously supported my work and travel for this book. Special thanks to Sloan president Paul L. Joskow and the Foundation's officers. Foundation vice president Doron Weber guided the work from beginning to end.

My agent, Anne Sibbald at Janklow & Nesbit Associates, represented me ably, as she always does. With this book I return to Simon & Schuster, where Jonathan Karp is president and publisher and my supportive and perspicacious editor is Ben Loehnen.

In Spain, Almudena Cros shared her expertise in Madrid, Ernesto Vinas in Brunete, and Angela Jackson in the Priorat. Maria Oianguren Idigoras and Andreas Schäfter, of Gernika Gogoratuz, guided me in Gernika. I could not have written about Picasso's process without the artist Jane Rosen's lessons in seeing through touch.

Stanford University Librarian Michael Keller generously arranged access to Stanford's library resources. David Lethbridge, Norman Bethune's biographer, shared his excellent biography *Norman Bethune in Spain* with me before publication. Peter Sapienza reviewed my discussion of surgery and blood transfusion. A. J. Bauer skillfully researched documents for me at NYU's Tamiment Library.

I thank them all.

Ginger Rhodes facilitated our travel, advised on the psychology of trauma, and read every fresh chapter. If ever two were one, then surely we.

NOTES

xiv "The ambition of every": Madariaga (1958), p. 342.

xv vacuum-assisted wound therapy: L. C. Argenta and M. J. Morykwas, "Vacuum-Assisted Closure: A New Method for Wound Control and Treatment: Clinical Experience," *Annals of Plastic Surgery* 38:563–77 (1997).

CHAPTER ONE: NEWS ARRIVES OF THE DEATH OF OTHERS

3 "News Arrives": Rukeyser (2005), "Correspondences," p. 168.

3 "At the end of July, exile": Ibid., "Mediterranean," p. 144.

4 "first of the faces": Ibid., p. 145.

4 assassinated . . . a spate of bombings: Hills (1967), p. 227.

4 "hot, beautiful summer": Rukeyser (2013), p. 277.

4 "little world war": *Time,* 18 January 1937 (online).

4 "posters and notices": Rukeyser (2013), p. 8.

5 "The train stops": Rukeyser (1936), p. 26.

6 "continuous volleys of rifle fire": Fernsworth (1936).

6 "riderless horses": Fernsworth (1957), p. 194.

6 "splotches of blood": Hanighen (1939), p. 30.

7 "Glory to the heroic army": Quoted in Martin I. McGregor, "The History and the Persecutions of Spanish Freemasonry" (online).

8 "You cannot begin a war": Quoted in Proctor (1983), p. 18.

9 "to give support": Testimony of Hermann Goering, *Nuremberg Trial Proceedings,* Vol. 9, p. 280.

9 "counsels of prudence": Quoted in Alpert (2004), p. 21.

9 "We hate Fascism": Quoted in Cate (1995), p. 233.

10 "Madrid has been completely cleared": Quoted ibid., p. 232.

10 a monthly 25,000 francs: Ibid., p. 235.

10 *"When I left you":* Rukeyser (2011), "For O. B.," p. 25.

10 "the beautiful and great victory": Ibid., p. 22.

11 "If we had not seen fighting": Rukeyser (2005), p. 148.
11 thirteen thousand men . . . four hundred tons of equipment: Hills (1967), p. 247.
11 Another thousand men would follow in October: Larios (1966), p. 39.
11 "Barcelona's black July 19": Fernsworth (1957), p. 200.
12 "Frankie-boy": Hills (1967), p. 61.
13 Violent socialization: see Rhodes (1999).
13 "A political free-thinker": Hodges (2000), p. 11.
13 "It is necessary to spread": Quoted in Preston (2012), p. 179.
13 not just mercenaries: Hanighen (1939), pp. 68–69.
14 "This was the upshot": Acier (1937), pp. 4–5.
14 "on the eve of the fight": Ibid., pp. 6–7.
15 "Certain exploits": Fussell (1991), p. 219.
15 "the Spanish Reds' war": Reproduced at libraries.ucsd.edu/speccoll/swphoto-journalist/m629-f02-19.html (online).
15 17,500 schools short . . . More than 30 percent: Vilanova (1992), p. 99.
16 A new constitution: See O'Connell (1971), p. 276, n. 3.
16 "became the . . . centre": Thomas (2011b), p. 60.
16 religious would be murdered: Sánchez (1987), p. 9.
16 "the explosion of an immense store": Quoted in Cueva (1998), p. 365.
17 "You don't understand": Quoted in Maddox (1995), p. 135.
17 Malraux and the twenty pilots: Whealey (1989), p. 21.
17 Foreign Legion of the Air: Madariaga (1958), p. 503.
18 British medical unit left London: Fyrth (1986), p. 44.
18 "When finish this book": Hemingway (1981), pp. 454–455.

CHAPTER TWO: TODAY THE BURNING CITY LIGHTS ITSELF

19 "Roman sea": Benito Mussolini, "Verso il riarmo [Toward Rearmament]," *Popolo d'Italia* del 18 Maggio 1934, xii; Whealey (1989), p. 13.
19 Franco seemed surprised; forty-one tanks and armored cars: Proctor (1983), p. 42.
19 "very upset": Quoted ibid., p. 43.
20 Germans shipped Franco an impressive array: Ibid., p. 46.
20 Soviet intelligence estimated: Kowalsky (2004), chapter 9 (online).
21 eight hundred dead . . . pregnant women: Preston (2012), p. 337.
21 Moroccans "killing the wounded": Whitaker (1942), p. 106.
21 "It is uncanny how both sides know": Ibid., p. 105.
21 "You can be justly proud": Quoted in Hills (1967), p. 262.
22 "We have seen Franco": Quoted in Preston (2004), p. 288.
22 six howitzers . . . fifty ten-ton T-26 tanks: Kowalsky (2004), chapter 9 (online).
22 $518 million in gold: Whealey (1989), p. 22.

23 more than $340 million of the gold: Ibid.

23 "Reserved for General Mola": Cox (1937), p. 38.

23 "The sound of gunfire": Colodny (1958), p. 25.

23 The first bombing: Ibid., p. 83.

23 Nationalist ground forces overran: Cate (1998), p. 249.

24 The Manzanares was the only serious obstacle: Smith and Hall (2011), p. 71.

24 "Although about 1,000": Haldane (1938), p. 49.

24 government's supply of artillery shells: Cox (1937), p. 61.

24 Russian fighter aircraft: Colodny (1958), p. 35.

24 anarchist militiamen: Cox (1937), p. 65.

24 Knickerbocker even invented a little dog: Ibid., Preston introduction, p. 10.

25 "The Government has gone": Colodny (1958), p. 49.

25 artillery shells enough: Ibid., p. 48.

25 "Some looked even more soldierly": Cox (1937), pp. 32–33.

26 "They knew every corner": Colodny (1958), p. 55.

26 "Up the street from the direction": Cox (1937), pp. 74–75.

27 "including advisors, instructors": Kowalsky (2004), chapter 9.

27 "In the early morning": Cox (1937), pp. 82–83.

28 "Republican soldiers put grenades": Colodny (1958), pp. 78–79.

28 "we built barricades": Sommerfield quoted ibid., p. 75.

28 "exhausted, short of ammunition": Ibid., p. 73.

28 Tom Wintringham would argue: Cited ibid., p. 189, n. 163.

28 "I will destroy Madrid": Quoted ibid., p. 82.

28 "This moment marks the peak": Quoted ibid., p. 89.

29 So far, Italy had shipped: Whealey (1989), p. 13.

29 "despite his . . . friendship": Quoted in Proctor (1983), p. 51.

29 "General Franco had not asked": Quoted ibid., p. 57.

29 Condor Legion deployed: Whealey (1989), p. 50.

29 It consisted initially: Proctor (1983), p. 60.

29 "the Government had virtually nothing": Matthews (1938), p. 234.

30 "little black monoplanes": Ibid., p. 235.

30 Moscas ambushed Franco's fighters: Ibid., p. 234.

30 controlled the air from October: "British Military Intelligence concluded that
    the Nationalists gained permanent superiority in the air by October 1936."
    Whealey (1989), p. 102.

30 had written . . . on 19 September: Chipp (1988), p. 211, n. 12.

31 would have to call him "Director": Ibid., p. 7.

31 was distinctly apolitical: Ibid., p. 6.

31 "immediately accepted": Quoted in Freedberg (1986), pp. 603–4.

31 "an army regiment": Bowers (1954), p. 314.

31 twenty-three times in November alone: Madariaga (1958), p. 527.

31 Between 15 and 20 November: Colodny (1958), p. 85.

31 Three waves of bombing: Whealey (1989), p. 102.

32 "[The bombs] explode, thunder": Delaprée (1936), p. 3.

32 "a solidly built skyscraper": Mathews (1938), pp. 199–200.

32 "The image of future war": quoted in Colodny (1958), p. 195, n. 211.

CHAPTER THREE: THE HERO'S RED RAG IS LAID ACROSS HIS EYES

34 "The Hero's Red Rag": George Barker, "Elegy on Spain," in Cunningham (1986), p. 198.

34 Socorro Rojo Internacional: Fyrth (1986), p. 45.

34 Spanish Medical Aid Committee . . . the British public responded: Fyrth (1986), pp. 45ff.

34 "It was quite common": quoted at www.spartacus.schoolnet.co.uk/PR manningL.htm.

35 departed from Victoria Station: *Lancet* 22: 447 (August 1936); Fyrth (1986), pp. 43–45.

35 Scottish Ambulance: Alpert (1984), p. 424; "A Scottish Ambulance Unit in Spain" (translated article), 14 July 1937: Archives of the Trades Union Congress, Spanish Rebellion: Medical Aid 1937–1940, document 292/946/42/136 (online).

35 Blood transfusion before the twentieth century: Keynes (1922), pp. 1–15.

36 sodium citrate: Ibid., p. 16; Greenwalt (1997), pp. 556–57.

36 "By noon, the wounded": quoted in Stansbury and Hess (2009), p. 235.

37 Mayo Clinic maintained a list: Schneider (2003), p. 197.

37 privately organized service in London: "Percy Oliver," www.pbs.org/wnet /redgold/innovators/bio_oliver.html (online).

38 "that, due to poverty": Alexi-Meskishvili and Konstantinov (2006), p. 117.

38 Yudin published a book: Serge Yudin, *La Transfusion du Sang de Cadavre à l'Homme* (Paris: Libraires de l'Academie de Medecine, 1933).

38 They set up sixty major: Starr (1998), p. 71.

38 Duran Jordà . . . heard Yudin lecture: "Frederic Duran-Jorda," *Journal of the Academy of Medicine of Catalonia* 21(2) (May 1952, online). Unless specifically noted, the details below of Duran Jordà's life come from this source.

39 El Raval: Brugman (2009), p. 240.

39 "The only solution": Duran Jordà (1939), p. 773.

40 Barcelona Blood Transfusion Service: details from Duran Jordà (1939).

41 "A very homogeneous blood": Duran Jordà (1939), p. 774.

41 "A successful transfusion": Haldane (1940), p. 189.

41 *autoinyectable rapide*: Ellis (1938), p. 685.

43 "The only rebel plane": Matthews (1938), p. 234.

43 He was aware that Malraux: Stewart and Stewart (2011), p. 157.

43 Canadian League Against War and Fascism: Zuehlke (2007), p. 36.

43 he had decided at least a month before he left Canada: Buck (1975), p. 123; Lethbridge (2013), p. 236, n. 18; p. 237, n. 30.

44 "They passed through streets": Stewart and Stewart ((2011), p. 161.

44 "Privately, [Bethune] noted": Lethbridge (2013), p. 92.

44 Bethune found "notable optimism": Allen and Gordon (2009), pp. 158–60.

45 "a little Frenchman": Ibid., p. 160.

45 "I couldn't work with the bastard": Lethbridge (2013), p. 92.

45 "unless we were able to offer": Hannant (1998), p. 131.

45 the "definite proposal" Bethune offered: Stewart and Stewart (2011), pp. 164–65.

45 Sorensen was horrified: Ibid., p. 165.

46 "The last two days": quoted in Colodny (1958), p. 195, n. 211.

46 Bethune cabled the CASD: Stewart and Stewart (2011), p. 165.

46 none was for sale in Spain: Hannant (1998), p. 132.

46 awaiting them for $3,000: Bethune confirms this amount in his 17 December 1936 report to the CASD, ibid., p. 132.

46 "a really snappy service": quoted in Stewart and Stewart (2011), p. 165.

46 a station wagon capable of carrying: Hannant (1998), p. 132.

47 "immediately started launching": Lethbridge (2013), p. 98.

47 "My gosh, I would like": quoted in Stewart and Stewart (2011), p. 167.

47 the equipment and supplies he would need: Hannant (1998), p. 132.

48 across the Channel . . . to Valencia: Stewart and Stewart (2011), pp. 167–68.

48 "Fascist, now in Berlin": Hannant (1998), p. 132.

48 "This district, with its elegant": Colodny (1958), pp. 198–199, n. 219.

49 "the walls entirely lined": Hannant (1998), p. 133. Bethune's report gives fifteen rooms; Stewart and Stewart (2011), p. 168, have "eleven."

49 "I've got to go to Spain": Hemingway (1981), p. 455.

CHAPTER FOUR: BOMBS FALLING LIKE BLACK PEARS

50 supported Franco's battalions: Colodny (1958), p. 94.

50 Varela launched a surprise attack: Ibid., pp. 95–96.

50 each counting some fifteen thousand casualties: Ibid., p. 105.

51 bused to Paracuellos: Preston (2012), pp. 281–86.

51 La Pasionaria had branded: Ibid., p. 294.

51 "in a couple of days": quoted ibid., p. 379.

51 "From the exaltation": Colodny (1958), p. 93.

51 "Russian planes laid a trap": Matthews (1938), p. 234.

52 Nationalist aircraft bombed: Ibid., p. 200.

52 The Duce was willing . . . Hitler was not: Höhne (1976), p. 238.

52 Italian troops landed at Cadiz: Matthews (1938), pp. 237–38.

52 Delaprée, who had been covering the war: Minchom (2010), p. 9.

52 "one of the finest people": Cox (1937), p. 180.

53 "You have not published half ": Quoted ibid., pp. 179–80.

53 converted Potez 54 bomber: Minchom (2012), p. 6.

53 Georges Henny: Pretus (n.d.), p. 71ff; Delmer (1961), p. 323.

54 "Some time later": Minchom (2012), p. 6.

54 "So the diplomatic courtesies": Delmer (1961), pp. 323–324.

54 crash-landed in a field: Matthews (1938), p. 200.

54 "clearly identified": Delmer (1961), p. 325.

54 "I cannot think why": Quoted ibid.

54 Georgi Zakharov: see "Georgi Zakharov" Wikipedia entry for these details, which link to Russian sources.

55 "the full treatment": Delmer (1961), p. 326.

55 The Spanish government shipped: Cox (1937), p. 174.

56 in a hospital in St. Omer: Haldane (1925), pp. 68–69.

56 "this truly enviable life": Quoted in Clark (1968), p. 40.

56 throw himself into the nearest ditch: Haldane (1938), p. 143.

57 "those who did not die": Haldane (1925), pp. 21–22.

57 Charlotte Haldane . . . reports him eager: Haldane (1949), p. 96.

57 "J. B. S. said it was not for him": Ibid., p. 94.

58 "Pollitt was a short, square": Ibid., pp. 94–95.

58 "So he got himself a most": Ibid., p. 96.

58 "lorry loads of gas masks": Cox (1937), p. 174.

58 "spending his Christmas": Monks (1985).

59 "Gas is effective": Haldane (1938), pp. 23–24.

59 "Franco's friends in England": Ibid., p. 24.

60 "A few people camped": Ibid., p. 48.

60 "God has an inordinate fondness": See discussion of sources in J.B.S. Haldane Wikipedia biography.

60 "very appropriately": *Nature* 139: 331 (20 February 1937).

61 Courage, Haldane testified: Haldane (1937).

61 "While the rest of the world": Matthews (1938), p. 200.

61 "had scraped together": Ibid., p. 201.

62 "The street cleared": Ibid., p. 202.

62 "Of all the damage": Ibid., p. 203.

62 "to occupy Europe's attention": Quoted in Whealey (1989), pp. 54–55.

62 Shortwave radio broadcast home: Text in Hannant (1998), pp. 140–42.

68 with Italian reserves: Coverdale (1974), p. 54.

68 Blackshirts were motorized: Proctor (1983), p. 80.

68 "The character of the winter": Thomas (1986), p. 482.

68 actually increased in the nationalist zone: Seidman (2010), p. 11.

68 Mules as well: Ibid., pp. 5ff.

69 sailed from New York on the *Normandie*: Landis (1967), p. 17.

69 Abraham Lincoln Battalion: Ibid., pp. 17–18; www.spartacus.schoolnet.co.uk;
    Rolfe (1939), p. 23.

69 his wife, Marion, who found: Merriman and Lerude (1986), p. 73.

70 "428 men tumbling": Rolfe (1939), p. 31.

70 "He had a little court": Quoted in Freedberg (1986), p. 606.

71 "his paints and brushes": Richardson (2007a), p. 5.

71 "the lowest moment": Quoted ibid., p. 5.

71 "it was one responsibility": Stein (1938), p. 46.

72 "of the burning of a convent": Penrose (1981), p. 296.

72 "Louis Delaprée est mort": See reproduction in Minchom (2010), p. 5.

72 as Richardson has identified: Richardson (2010), pp. 7–8, with a reproduction
    of the painting.

72 Picasso painted *Still Life with a Lamp* that day: Palau i Fabre (2011), p. 274.

72 a pamphlet, *bombs over Madrid*: Minchom (2010), p. 10.

72 Picasso also would have heard: Freedberg (1986), p. 607.

73 *Sueño y Mentira de Franco:* This composition can be viewed online at www
    .fundacionpicasso.es.

73 "Fandango of shivering": For a reproduction of the original, with an English
    translation, see www.guernica70th.com/english/poem.html (online).

73 Studies for a woman's head: Palau i Fabre (2011), p. 241, plate 766.

74 late engravings of Goya: Both series can be seen on Wikipedia.

74 "We went to see [Picasso]": Oppler (1988), p. 198.

74 But according to Sert: Freedberg (1986), p. 608.

75 "This was a moment": Sert interview, *Treasures of the World*, television docu-
    mentary, PBS (online at pbs.org).

76 "So in 1937": Stein (1938), p. 48.

76 cataloging a thousand Madrileños: Franco, Cortez, et al. (1996), p. 1077.

76 "Doubtless a few wounded": Haldane (1941), p. 155.

76 fascist sympathizer, bent on sabotage: Lethbridge (2013), pp. 118–19.

77 "Our night work is very eerie": Bethune (1998), p. 145.

77 "Well, this is a grand country": Ibid., p. 146.

77 He had learned of it earlier: Lethbridge (2013), p. 121.

77 "a patented and complicated": Bethune (1998), pp. 148–49.

78 "We propose to start": Hannant (1998), p. 149.

78 "2 electro box refrigerators": Bethune (1998), p. 149.

78 "We have succeeded in unifying": Ibid., p. 150.

79 "The first sentence": Quoted in Lethbridge (2013), p. 128.

79 finished off most of what was left: Proctor (1983), p. 103.

80 test the Renault . . . *Daily Worker* correspondent: Stewart and Stewart (2011), p. 183.

80 a blood-transfusion network: Rodriguez-Solas (2011), pp. 86–87.

80 at nine o'clock that evening: Ibid., p. 184.

80 "flooded with a stream": Koestler (1937), p. 198.

81 "They flowed past our truck": Allen and Gordon (2009), p. 178.

81 "We drove more quickly now": Ibid., p. 179.

81 "pressed together, falling": Ibid., p. 180.

82 "They were slung over": Ibid., p. 180.

82 "*Solamente niños!*": Ibid., p. 185.

82 "The woman was young": Ibid., pp. 187–88.

83 "I banged the door shut": Ibid., p. 188.

83 "the sight of parents": Ibid., p. 190.

83 "They dived toward the road": Ibid., p. 191.

83 "I scrambled to my feet": Ibid., p. 192.

84 "Here the streets were no longer": Ibid., p. 193.

84 "I caught a glimpse": Ibid., pp. 192–93.

84 filling with hate: Ibid., p. 194.

CHAPTER SIX: A VALLEY IN SPAIN CALLED JARAMA

85 Big Joe Curran's 1936 campaign: Kempton (1955), pp. 83ff.

85 American Medical Aid: I. J. R. to Frederika Martin, 31 May 1975. Martin (n.d.).

86 more than one hundred unsolicited requests: Ibid., I–i., p. 2.

86 "We set as our immediate objective": Barsky (n.d.), p. 13.

86 "Everything from a safety pin": Ibid., pp. 14–15.

86 "In the end, just these people": Ibid., p. 13.

86 inflammatory bowel disease: I. J. R. to Frederika Martin, ibid., p. 1.

86 wanted to chair that burgeoning: Shumaker (1982), p. 159.

87 "Who was to head the outfit?": Barsky (n.d.), p. 17.

87 New York's Hotel Pennsylvania: Shapiro (1982), p. 120.

87 "We were so romantic": Quoted ibid., pp. 121–22.

88 "there had been receptions": Rackley-Simon memoir (n.d.), pp. 62–62.

88 "For linguistic and logistic": Martin (n.d.), I–iii, p. 3.

88 "In my innocence": Barsky (n.d.), p. 21.

89 "They could not understand": Martin (n.d.), I–iv, pp. 3–4.

89   "considered the American request": Ibid., I–ii, p. 6.

89   "The stunned officers capitulated": Ibid., I–iv, p. 5.

89   "We interviewed all sorts": Barsky (n.d.), p. 25.

90   Martin recalls: Martin (n.d.), "Romeral," p. 1.

90   "Why in hell": Barsky (n.d.), pp. 25–26.

90   The windows were large: Martin (n.d.), "Romeral," pp. 2–3.

91   "With alacrity they bundled": Ibid., p. 3.

91   "The Spaniards packed up": Ibid., pp. 3–4.

91   "Then came a second shock": Ibid., p. 4.

91   The cases held twenty tons: Barsky (n.d.), p. 27.

92   "The loss was a catastrophe": Martin (n.d.), "Romeral," p. 4.

93   X-ray machine, water softener: Martin (n.d.), "Romeral," p. 19.

93   "On her own": Ibid., p. 5.

93   "Carrying stones and dirt": Martin (n.d.), I–iv, p. 15.

93   "only if she could not": Barsky (n.d.), p. 31.

93   "gruesomely overcrowded": Ibid., pp. 31–32.

94   "Carl was shut up": Ibid., p. 32.

94   "The stale complaints": Martin (n.d.), p. 15.

95   "blond Moors": Cox (1937), p. 191.

95   some 225 had been wounded or killed: Beevor (1982), p. 211.

96   "The object then was": Matthews (1938), p. 222.

96   "Men may die but let them": Merriman (1937), at 17 Febrero.

96   "Making observations from": Quoted in Rolfe (1939), pp. 36–37.

97   "About 20th in the evening": Merriman (1937), at 20 Febrero.

97   "Never did get old packs": Ibid., at 23 Febrero.

97   "support the 24th": Ibid.

98   "forced a place": Ibid., at 23–24 Febrero.

98   "We could have broken": Ibid., at 24 Febrero.

99   "an act of monumental stupidity": Colodny (1958), p. 127.

99   "plan good and sounded": Merriman (1937), at 28 Febrero.

99   "We waited": Ibid., at 29 Febrero.

99   "Stated several times": Ibid.

99   "and bawled me out": Ibid.

100   "After all from Čopić": Ibid.

100   slammed into Merriman's shoulder: Merriman and Lerude (1986), p. 76.

100   "rushed to Colmenar": Merriman (1937), at 29 Febrero.

100   "I cut through clothing": Quoted in Carroll (1994), p. 104.

100   "a truly murderous": Matthews (1938), p. 224.

101   "I had only gone about 700": Gurney (1974), p. 114.

101   As many as sixteen thousand men: Coverdale (1974), p. 56.

CHAPTER SEVEN: THE OLD HOMESTEAD

102 during the Great War . . . Josep Trueta: White (1943), p. 381.

103 "We had our eyes opened": Orr (1921), pp. 16–17.

103 "enforced, uninterrupted": Thomas (1878), Preface to Second Edition, p. iii.

103 at Savenay, France: Orr (1921), p. 35.

104 "within a few days": Ibid., p. 38.

104 "During a certain stage": Ibid., p. 735.

104 "almost two hundred articles": White (1943), p. 387.

105 "At first I treated only": Trueta (1939b), p. 1452.

105 "was that the plaster": Trueta (1980), p. 63.

105 "products of tissue degeneration": Trueta (1939a), p. 29.

105 "but underneath": Coni (2008), p. 55.

105 "did not get a good": Trueta (1939b), p. 1452.

105 "Towards the end of 1929": Trueta (1980), p. 63.

106 The war tested Trueta's new methods: Trueta (1939b), p. 1452.

106 "On returning to Barcelona": Trueta (1980), p. 66.

107 "paying a dollar a day": Hemingway (2003), p. 282.

107 "graced with a bottle": Matthews (1938), pp. 190–91.

107 "one gets along somehow": Ibid., p. 190.

108 "The suffering of that first": Ibid., p. 188.

108 Italians refused to launch a diversion: Coverdale (1974), p. 56.

108 200 artillery pieces: Ibid., p. 59.

108 "In three days": Matthews (1938), pp. 255–56.

109 slow and toilsome advance: Miksche (1942), p. 20.

109 republicans attacked the Italians from the air: Ibid., p. 20.

109 "an enormous amount": Matthews (1938), pp. 263–64.

109 "It wasn't getting anywhere": Quoted in Jackson (2012), p. 20.

110 "He took one glance": Quoted ibid., p. 16.

110 "wasn't in the least": Quoted ibid., p. 22.

110 "She was a lovely": Quoted ibid., p. 30.

110 "I found poor Tom": Quoted in Purcell (2004), p. 140.

111 "If you don't perforate": Quoted in Jackson (2012), p. 27.

112 was a covert project: Koch (2005), p. 61.

112 Spender's autobiography: Spender (1951).

112 Inez Pearn: Ibid., pp. 224–25.

112 "He looked fit": Ibid., p. 242.

113 "Coming into Valencia": White (1967), p. 258.

113 thirty-seven years old: Ernest Hemingway was born on 21 July 1899 in Oak Park, Illinois.

113 "a black-haired, bushy-mustached": Spender (1951), p. 251.

113 "Hemingway said that he thought": Ibid., p. 252.

114 "Why do you talk to me": Ibid.

114 "Spender is tall": Quoted in Jackson (2012), p. 31.

115 "The thing you never get": Michael Parkinson, BBC, interviewing Orson Welles, 1974, www.openculture.com (online).

115 "We were talking about books": Quoted in Jackson (2012), p. 32.

115 antiaircraft guns: Haldane (1938), p. 71.

116 "a particularly unattractive": Hemingway (2003), p. 286.

116 "Along the roads were piled": Watson (1988), p. 19.

117 "greatly admired in Spain": Cowles (1941), p. 35.

117 "There was a tall wardrobe": Herbst (1991), p. 137.

117 "There was a kind of splurging": Ibid., p. 151.

117 "the success of his love affair": Ibid.

118 "a large, dirty man": Quoted in Moorehead (2003), p. 101.

118 "young punk": Quoted ibid., p. 104.

118 "an odd bird": Moorehead (2006), p. 45.

118 "I am going to Spain": Ibid., p. 107.

118 "She had fifty dollars": Moorehead (2003), pp. 112–13.

119 "legs that begin": Quoted in Paul (2009), p. 134.

119 "I absolutely flipped": Kert (1983), p. 296.

119 fate of José Robles: Roper (2011), p. 3.

119 "Russian secret agents": Koch (2005), p. 252.

120 "After about two minutes": Tinker (1938), p. 111.

120 the writer's rooms, 112 and 113: These are the room numbers he gives in Mc-Grath (2008).

120 "It turned out": Smith and Hall (2011), p. 128.

120 "a man with a white curly": Hemingway (1987), p. 452.

121 "I don't suppose any hotel": Cowles (1941), p. 35.

121 "Studying the terrain": Watson (1988), p. 20.

121 on 21 February had called up: "A Diary of the Civil War," *Bulletin of Spanish Studies* 14 (54):90 (April 1937).

121 "If one started from": Matthews (1938), p. 280.

122 "It was marvelous": Watson (1988), p. 25.

122 "Just as we were congratulating": Ibid.

123 "I was surprised": Cowles (1941), p. 38.

123 christened their observation post: Ibid.

123 "We had a good time": Matthews (1938), p. 282.

123 "with his usual cordiality": Cowles (1941), pp. 38–39.

CHAPTER EIGHT: NOT EVERYBODY'S DAILY LIFE

126 Basques had just six: Proctor (1983), p. 118; Corum (1997), pp. 193–94.

126 reinforced the Condor Legion: Proctor (1983), p. 118.

126 "I have decided to terminate": Quoted in Steer (1938), p. 159.

126 Von Richthofen, the Legion's chief of staff: Corum (2008), p. 119.

126 "to study the airpower": Ibid., p. 96.

127 Germany had initiated: Corum (1998), p. 1.

127 "Fear, which cannot be simulated": Quoted in Patterson (2007), p. 54.

127 "Mola threatened to raze": Southworth (1977), p. 383.

127 127 dead in Durango: Steer (1938), p. 167.

128 Another 131 wounded: Preston (2007), p. 2.

128 "in the silence": Steer (1938), p. 166.

128 sometimes bombed the wrong targets: Proctor (1983), p. 119.

128 "Each Italian performance": Richthofen (1937), p. 123 (29). My translation.

128 Between January and April: See Picasso catalogue raisonné for 1937 (on-line).

129 "speak to the singularity": Clark (2013), p. 229.

129 "Picasso did not go to work": MOMA (1947), p. 7.

129 one day in April: Work began on the pavilion building in March 1937. Freedberg (1986), p. 719.

130 "I never saw any": Quoted in Clark (2013), p. 214.

130 as Clark explores: Ibid., passim.

131 "On page 3": Minchom (2011), p. 2.

132 "no apparent interest": Ibid., pp. 5–6.

132 "a nineteen-day bombardment": Watson (1988), p. 46.

132 32 shells within 200 yards: Ibid., p. 38.

132 "had over 300 shells": Ibid., p. 46.

132 "unable to . . . avoid": Ibid., p. 34.

132 "Two terrifying thuds": Herbst (1991), p. 152.

132 "The shells keep coming in": Dos Passos (1938), p. 365.

133 "But I didn't come here to die": Herbst (1991), p. 152.

133 representing *Paris-soir*: Schiff (1994), p. 282.

133 the Rolls, ripping fenders: Ibid.

133 "He had brought two": McGrath (2008).

134 "except learn a little Spanish": Gellhorn (1988), p. 16.

134 "the shells are falling so fast": Gellhorn (1937a).

135 "the martyrdom of Madrid": Watson (1988), p. 36. Watson makes the case that Hemingway must have been drunk when he wrote this dispatch.

135 "and probably in all": Minchom (2011). For the complete text of this part of *Bombs over Madrid,* see app. 1.

135 "If Picasso reacted": Minchom (2011).
135 delivering up to one hundred units a day: Lethbridge (2013), p. 172.
136 "The noise of the artillery": Gellhorn (1937b), pp. 34, 39.
136 "None of it seemed real": Ibid., p. 39.
136 responsible for 78 percent: Franco, Cortes, et al. (1996), p. 1077.
137 "an entirely false picture": Lethbridge (2014), p. 182.
137 "a clever way": Quoted in Petrou (2005), p. 5.
137 twelve new Messerschmitt Bf 109s: Musciano (2006), p. 6.
138 "[Sidney] Franklin": Moorehead (2003), p. 113.
138 "I was with Hemingway": Ehrenburg (1963), p. 384.
138 "If you had come across Hemingway": Ibid., p. 386.
139 planning a midnight radio broadcast: Merriman and Lerude (1986), p. 127.
139 "shaking badly": Ibid., p. 132.
139 "Hemingway was animated": Ibid.
140 "Pleased with Hemingway": Quoted ibid., p. 136.
140 Hemingway left with Gellhorn: Probably on 24 April, since the broadcast puts him in Madrid on the night of 23 April.
141 "a hard ten days": Watson (1988), p. 38.
141 "would serve as part": Merriman and Lerude (1986), p. 134.
141 "a big Swede": Ibid., p. 151. For these and other details of Amlie's background, see Eby (2007), pp. 205–7.
141 "a mining engineer": Matthews (1938), p. 216.

CHAPTER NINE: A SEA OF SUFFERING AND DEATH

143 "A Sea of Suffering": Picasso, quoted in O'Brian (1976), p. 321.
143 "After a short telephone": Richthofen (1937), p. 121 (27). Emphasis in original.
144 Gernika's other military assets: Iturriarte, Del Palacio, et al. (2010), pp. 8–9.
144 Francisco Lazkano: Ibid., p. 17.
144 "Guernica was busy": Monks (1955), pp. 94–95.
144 "We were about eighteen": Ibid., p. 95.
145 "sprawled in mud": Ibid.
145 "I was trembling": Ibid., pp. 95–96.
146 A Gernika eyewitness: Martin (2002), p. 40.
146 a modern Spanish source: Vidal (1997), p. 1.
146 six bombs: Southworth (1977); Steer (1938), p. 237.
146 "The bombs with a shower": Quoted in Southworth (1977), p. 15.
146 three Savoia-Marchetti 79: Vidal (1997), p. 1.
146 "to block": Ibid.

146 "This third bombardment": Ibid., p. 2.

147 *tranvias* . . . "were so clumsy": Steer (1938), p. 238.

147 forty to fifty tons of bombs: Corum (1998), p. 8.

147 "made their attacks": Vidal (1997), p. 2.

148 Steer's hotel: Hensbergen (2004), p. 40.

148 "of beans": Monks (1955), p. 96.

148 "As the people not trapped": Steer (1938), p. 240.

149 "sobbing like children": Monks (1955), p. 97.

150 "We have had notable": Quoted in Corum (1998), p. 8.

150 "In the form of its execution": Quoted in Southworth (1977), p. 14.

150 "sacred oak": Richthofen (1937), p. 129(35).

150 more than 70 percent: Vidal (1997), p. 4, gives 271 buildings destroyed, citing Gonzalo Cárdenas Rodriguez, the general architect of Devastated Regions, "which meant, therefore, 74.4% of those that existed in the town of Guernica and the neighborhood of Rentería 19."

150 "When news of the bombing": Quoted in Baldassari (2006), p. 166.

151 "A Thousand Incendiary Bombs": Ibid., p. 167, figure 58.

151 Picasso told . . . Daix: Daix (1993), p. 250.

151 pamphlet of photographs: Minchom (2012), p. 24.

152 "not the stages": Quoted in Galenson (2002), p. 59.

154 dagger-tongued estranged wife: Daix (1993), p. 250.

157 "Picasso worked fast": Penrose (1981), p. 302.

157 series of photographs of *Guernica:* online at www.museoreinasofia.es.

157 reflection on the canvas: Baldassari (2006), p. 172.

157 a number of books and articles: See Bibliography.

157 figure of the lightbearer: Daix (1993), p. 252.

157 Dora Maar used to extend: according to Juan Larrea in MOMA (1947), p. 67.

158 Juan Larrea, who made this connection: MOMA (1947), pp. 66ff.

159 used a similar marking technique: Daix (1993), p 251.

159 "One day in the café": MOMA (1947), p. 9.

159 "This morning I came to": Quoted in Palau i Fabre (2011), p. 321.

160 "The Spanish struggle": Quoted in O'Brian (1976), p. 321.

160 "The mark of the actual event": Daix (1993), p. 251.

161 "The horror and inquisitiveness": Clark (2013), p. 270.

161 "a machine for suffering," "I am a woman": Quoted ibid., p. 225.

161 bull has Picasso's eyes: Oppler (1988), p. 97.

161 "Picasso continued [painting] his picture": Quoted in Freedberg (1986), p. 661, n. 55.

CHAPTER TEN: CUCKOO IDEALISTS

162 "I wanted a hot bath": Orwell (1952), p. 107.

162 "a tall thin man": Davison (2010), pp. 68–69.

163 "I used to sit on the roof": Orwell (1952), pp. 130–31.

163 "who was fighting whom": Ibid., p. 131.

164 "I trained my rifle": Ibid., pp. 132–33. Orwell writes "Civil Guards," but explains in a footnote that he consistently mixed them up; these were assault guards, a different category of police.

164 the city had returned to normal: Ibid., p. 141.

165 "I heard the crisp sound": Quoted in Jacobs (2001), p. 1.

165 "very interesting": Orwell (1952), p. 185.

165 "My wound was not much": Davison (2010), p. 82.

166 "My first thought": Orwell (1952), p. 186.

167 "If General Franco": "Hemingway Sees Defeat of Franco," *New York Times,* 19 May 1937 (online).

167 "The Italian force here": Matthews (1938), pp. 238–39.

168 Gellhorn had lunch: Kert (1983), p. 302.

168 "the more than three hundred thousand": Quoted in Rankin (2011), p. 12.

168 formal request for aid: Pretus (n.d.), p. 344.

168 "owing to the incessant": Ellis and Russell (1937), p. 1303.

169 "It was evident that": Ibid., p. 1304.

169 "cold and Protestant England": Quoted in Legarreta (1984), p. 101.

169 "Bombardments of cities": Steer (1938), pp. 258–59.

170 "the largest evacuation": Ibid., p. 260.

170 "The Basques had no sympathy": Quoted in Legarreta (1984), p. 106.

170 "each child was issued": Steer (1938), pp. 262–63.

171 "We want the older children": Quoted in Legarreta (1984), pp. 105–6.

171 3,889 Basque children: Ibid., pp. 106–7.

171 "I went with my two sisters": Ibid., p. 107.

172 "For two dreadful": Quoted in Rankin (2011), p. 19.

172 Children slept everywhere: Legarreta (1984), p. 107.

172 "I was awakened": Quoted ibid.

172 "extraordinary spectacle": Williams (1937), p. 1209.

172 "we thought we had entered": Quoted in Legarreta (1984), pp. 107–8; and Rankin (2011), p. 19.

173 "more distinguished persons": Steer (1938), p. 263.

173 "and no one doubted": Orwell (1952), p. 195.

173 "a horrible atmosphere": Ibid., p. 147.

173 "men, loaves of bread": Ibid., p. 201.

173 "there was going on inside": Ibid., p. 202.

174 Operation without anesthesia: Jackson (2012), p. 51, quoting Patience Darton.

174 *"Get out!"*: Orwell (1952), p. 204.

174 "It was an extraordinary": Ibid., p. 226.

175 "This war, in which": Ibid., p. 230.

175 "It is quite true": Cunningham (1986), pp. 307–8.

176 "with a football bladder": Moorehead (2006), p. 52.

176 "those tragic little dark ones": Ibid., p. 54.

176 "being emotional": Ibid., pp. 54–55.

177 "We thought she was crazy": Hemingway (1981), p. 460.

177 "make it stronger": Moorehead (2006), p. 56.

177 "They both were very moved": Hemingway (1981), p. 460.

177 "that awful voice": Moorehead (2006), p. 56.

178 pitches by both men: Schoots (2000), pp. 130–32.

178 "cuckoo idealist": Quoted in Moorehead (2006), p. 132.

178 "one of the decisive": Whealey (1989), p. 139.

CHAPTER ELEVEN: HEADS DOWN AND HOPE

180 "so if you opened": Quoted in Jackson (2012), p. 33.

180 "Her crusading fervor": Quoted ibid., pp. 33–34.

181 "crates and crates": Quoted ibid., pp. 35–36.

181 "It was nice": Quoted ibid., p. 38.

181 "found that she had": Quoted ibid.

182 "We were letting them": Quoted ibid., p. 46.

182 "If we talked politics": Quoted ibid., pp. 39–40.

183 "We were in an anarchist": Quoted ibid., p. 48.

183 "Ours not to reason why": Barsky (n.d.), p. 75.

184 "Almost before we had things": Ibid., pp. 76–77.

184 "cold, wounded boys": Ibid., pp. 77–79.

185 "could somehow use their wits": Ibid., pp. 89–90.

185 "We had a chicken": Ibid., p. 90.

185 "was a very pretty": Ibid.

185 "Many children. Screaming women": Ibid., p. 91.

186 "The hospital buildings crumbled": Ibid., pp. 91–92.

186 "We lost not a single": Ibid., p. 92.

186 "I think we all loved Villa Paz": Ibid., p. 92, pp. 93–94.

187 "In the beautiful soft sunlight": Ibid., p. 95.

187 twenty-four hospitals: Palfreeman (2012), pp. 66–67.

187 "almost 18 percent of the IB doctors": Coni (2008), p. 134.

187 "to find the Americans": Matthews (1938), pp. 225–26.

188 "idyllically peaceful": Ibid., p. 227.

188 Emilio Mola died: "General Mola Killed in Crash," *New York Times,* 4 June 1937, p. 1, p. 8.

189 "at an earthy harridan": Delmer (1961), p. 333.

189 "From the very beginning of 1935": Dupin (1962), p. 265.

189 "very uprooted": Rowell (1986), p. 146.

190 "solace in the noise": Dupin (1962), p. 292.

190 "I will see what develops": Rowell (1986), p. 146.

190 sketched the basic components: See Daniel and Gale (2011), p. 100, ill. 72.

190 "Let me tell you about": Rowell (1986), pp. 293–94. Van Gogh painted several still lifes with shoes or boots, e.g., *Ein Paar Schuhe* (F333 in Jacob Baart de la Faille's 1928 catalogue raisonné *The Works of Vincent van Gogh*).

191 "To look nature in the face": Rowell (1986), pp. 146–47.

192 "The work is going": Ibid., p. 157.

192 "The Spanish government": Ibid.

192 on 7 March: Ibid., p. 148.

192 "The stamp cost one franc": Ibid., pp. 292–93, altering Rowell's translation slightly for the more colloquial language of Freedberg's version: Freedberg (1986), p. 596, n. 87.

193 The surface on which: "*The Reaper* was executed in situ, on the six sheets of Celotex already mounted on the Pavilion wall." Joan Punyet Miró, personal communication, 23 December 2013.

194 If his commemorative stamp design: According to Sert. Freedberg (1986), p. 587, n. 47.

194 "Peace had come at last": Elliott (1963), p. 541.

195 "It was curious to observe": Quoted in Freedberg (1986), p. 690, n. 154.

195 On 13 June: Eby (2007), p. 176.

195 "retired to a series of villages": Landis (1967), p. 169.

195 "drive back or cut off": Gurney (1974), p. 180.

195 the new George Washington Battalion: Landis (1967), p. 175.

196 "That was a particularly": Matthews (1938), p. 230.

196 "wondering sadly": Ibid.

196 fifty thousand men: Palfreeman (2012), p. 118.

197 "Thursday, the eighth": Matthews (1938), pp. 231–32.

197 whining down like mosquitos: Cook (1979), p. 91.

197 "The biplanes came in waves": Musciano (2006) (online).

197 "All that night they rested": Matthews (1938), p. 232.

197 "As they surged upward": Ibid.

198 only 42 survived unwounded: Palfreeman (2012), p. 118.

198 "I realized he was the best": Quoted ibid., pp. 118–19. For a variant version of this text see Fyvel (1992), pp. 28–29.

199 Supplies ran short: Ibid., p. 29.

199 "a terrible artillery barrage": Quoted in Palfreeman (2012), p. 124.

199 "roughly 16,000 casualties": Ibid., p. 129.

200 "The horrible tragedy": Quoted in Dupin (1962), p. 290.

CHAPTER TWELVE: ONLY THE DEVIL KNOWS

203 "a marvelous little town": Jackson (2012), p. 50.

203 "Patience was not diplomatic": Ibid., p. 52.

203 "One day a couple": Ibid., pp. 51–52.

204 Hemingway, back in Spain: "Americans in Spain Veteran Soldiers," *New York Times*, 14 September 1937.

205 160 operations in twelve days: Coni (2008), p. 163.

205 "We were all living loose": Quoted in Jackson (2012), p. 55.

205 "It has been raining": Ibid., pp. 55–56; Coni (2008), p. 65.

206 moved the recovering typhoid cases: Jackson (2012), p. 57.

206 Len Crome: Preston (2006), pp. 6–7.

206 "Headquarters was in an olive grove": Crome (1980), pp. 117–19.

208 "rose to a great height": Haldane (1938), p. 51.

208 "Though they were carried": Ibid., p. 53.

208 shelter some 240,000 people: Ibid., p. 164.

208 he toured one: Ibid.

209 "The danger is greatest": Ibid., pp. 30–31.

209 children known to have been killed: Ibid., pp. 56–57.

210 forty thousand republicans: Matthews (1973), pp. 14–15.

210 "Doctor, you're going to be": Barsky (n.d.), p. 118.

210 "Teruel would prove to be": Ibid., p. 124.

210 "We have the bed-truck": Neugass (2008), p. 69.

211 "The floor was crowded": Ibid., p. 78.

211 "Friday while we watched": Hemingway (1938a).

212 "Once more our motorcade": Barsky (n.d.), p. 125.

212 "With everybody's brakes": Ibid., p. 126.

213 "What are you waiting for": Ibid., p. 129.

213 "drowsy with cold": Ibid., p. 130.

213 "Average speed three miles": Neugass (2008), p. 95.

213 the Harvard ambulance: Valenstein (2005), p. 146.

214 Colder and colder: Barsky (n.d.), pp. 135–36.

215 "He listened to my story": Ibid., pp. 136–37.

216 "you began to realize": Quoted in Cook (1979), p. 103.

216 "At the American brigade's headquarters": *New York Times,* 23 January 1938, pp. 1, 32.

216 "The roads were practically": Barsky (n.d.), pp. 169–70.

217 "He was surely a welcome sight": Ibid., p. 172.

CHAPTER THIRTEEN: HISTORY TO THE DEFEATED

218 "History to the Defeated": W. H. Auden, "Spain."

218 Patience Darton fell in love: See especially Jackson (2012), my primary source for this episode.

218 "very young, only 23": Ibid., p. 59.

218 "I met Patience": Ibid., p. 58.

218 "So I rushed over": Ibid., pp. 62–63.

219 "lots of machine gun stuff": Ibid., p. 66.

220 "It was dark": Ibid., p. 67.

220 "he got leave to go": Ibid.

220 "We floated or flew back": Ibid., p. 68.

221 "We were staggered": Ibid.

221 "one of the times": Ibid., p. 71.

222 "every town along": Bessie (1939), p. 134.

222 took some 140 Lincolns prisoner: Matthews (1973), p. 210.

222 *"Rojos! Rojos!"*: Bessie and Prago (1987), pp. 242–43.

223 "The subways were crowded": Barsky (n.d.), pp. 218–19.

223 "About a quarter of the population": Haldane (1938), p. 55.

223 "All these emotions": Barsky (n.d.), pp. 218–19.

223 "to places designated": Ibid., p. 226.

224 "I could barely get up": Ibid.

224 "filthy old monastery": Ibid., pp. 227–30.

224 With an epidemic fulminating: Ibid., p. 253; Schumacker (1982), p. 181.

225 "other men had swum": Bessie (1939), p. 135.

225 "Below us there were hundreds": Ibid.

225 "permanently so": Ibid., p. 136.

226 "When it was all over": Matthews (1973), p. 210.

226 "solemnly declare[d] its war aims": *Aims of the Spanish Republic: The 13 Points of Dr. Negrin's Government.* Warwick Digital Library (online).

227 "He and all Spanish nationalists": Quoted in Beevor (1982), p. 339.

227 *la Quinta del Biberón:* Jackson (2012), p. 59.

227 "Many had never shaved": Bessie (1939), pp. 151–52.

228 "The men all knew": Quoted in Rolfe (1939), p. 255.

228 By mid-May they had married: Jackson (2012), p. 80.

228 "They were building roads": Ibid., p. 101.

228 "The roads were jammed": Bessie (1939), pp. 208–9.

229 "eighteen to twenty fully": Rolfe (1939), p. 259.

229 "bombing the bridges": Bessie (1939), pp. 215–16.

229 all the boats used in the Ebro crossing: Coni (2008), p. 167.

229 ten thousand pounds of bombs per day: Cook (1979), p. 137.

229 "with a conscious knowledge": Bessie (1939), p. 253.

230 "The planes came over us": Cook (1979), p. 139.

230 IB medical services had identified: Coni (2008), p. 90.

230 "a natural wonder": Green (2004), p. 90.

230 "One day we suddenly": Quoted in Jackson (2012), p. 103.

230 date on her orders: Ibid., p. 105, photo 9.2.

230 120 beds: Lilian Urmston, interviewed October 1938. Spartacus International website (online). Other sources have 100 or 150.

231 "In the valley below": Jackson (2012), p. 104.

231 "I suppose that in all": Fyrth (1991), p. 104.

231 "The cave was very": Ibid., p. 69.

231 "We had an awful lot": Jackson (2012), p. 107.

232 "Nobody could speak anything": Ibid., p. 110.

232 "God how he hated us": Ibid., p. 108.

233 "children": Ibid., p. 111.

233 half a million died: See various estimates at www.necometrics.com (online).

233 "I ask you above all": Jackson (2012), p. 114.

234 "The move to the front": Ibid., p. 117.

234 "these last eight months": Ibid., p. 116.

234 "the thing that is": Patience Darton, quoted ibid.

EPILOGUE: THE FALL OF THE CURTAIN

235 "The Fall of the Curtain": From "Spain 1937," in Auden (1940), p. 93.

235 "I saw La Pasionaria": Quoted in Jackson (2012), p. 120.

235 German war supplies: Thomas (1986), p. 837.

236 "Our regime is based": Matthews (1973), p. 255.

236 "Miró's mural was sent": Soby (1959), p. 91.

236 "to write on the 'end'": Rukeyser (2011), p. 5.

236 "Long Past Moncada": Rukeyser (2005), p. 233.

236 published a brief remembrance: Quoted in Rukeyser (2013), p. xvii.

237 "on the banks of": Quoted ibid., p. xxvi.

237 "When a doctor cannot save": Quoted in "Guide to the Edward K. Barsky Papers ALBA .125," Tamiment Library & Robert F. Wagner Labor Archives, Elmer Holmes Bobst Library, New York University.

237 "premature anti-Fascist": Bernard Knox, "Premature Anti-Fascist," *Modern American Poetry* (online).

238 Medical Committee for Human Rights: "Guide to the Edward K. Barsky Papers ALBA. 125."

239 "The next morning": Jackson (2012), p. 201.

239 "When we are together": Quoted ibid., pp. 201–2.

BIBLIOGRAPHY

Acier, Marcel, ed. 1937. *From Spanish Trenches: Recent Letters from Spain.* New York: Modern Age Books.

Alexi-Meskishvili, Vladimir, and Igor E. Konstantinov. 2006. "Sergei S. Yudin: An Untold Story." *Surgery* 139: 115–22.

Alfonso X. 2002. *Chronicle of Alfonso X.* Trans. Shelby Thacker and José Escobar. Lexington: University Press of Kentucky.

Allen, Ted, and Sydney Gordon. 2009. *The Scalpel, the Sword: The Story of Doctor Norman Bethune.* Toronto: Dundurn Press.

Alpert, Michael. 1984. "Humanitarianism and Politics in the British Response to the Spanish Civil War, 1936–9." *European History Quarterly* 14: 423–39.

———. 2004. *A New International History of the Spanish Civil War.* 2nd ed. New York: Palgrave Macmillan.

Alvarez del Vayo, J. 1971. *Freedom's Battle.* Trans. Eileen E. Brooke. New York: Hill & Wang.

Amsbury, Clifton. 1995. "Reflections on Anticlericalism and Power Relations in Spain." *American Ethnologist* 22 (3): 614–15.

Ashton, Dore, ed. 1972. *Picasso on Art: A Selection of Views.* New York: Da Capo Press.

Auden, W. H. 1940. *Another Time.* London: Faber & Faber.

Baker, Carlos. 1980. *Hemingway: The Writer as Artist.* Princeton: Princeton University Press.

Baker, David. 1996. *Adolf Galland: The Authorized Biography.* London: Windrow & Greene.

Baldassari, Anne. 2006. *Picasso: Life with Dora Maar: Love and War, 1935–1945.* Trans. Unity Woodman. Paris: Flammarion.

Balfour, Sebastian. 2002. *Deadly Embrace: Morocco and the Road to the Spanish Civil War.* Oxford: Oxford University Press.

Barea, Arturo. 2001. *The Forging of a Rebel*. Trans. Ilsa Barea. New York: Walker & Company.

Barsky, Edward W., with Elizabeth Waugh. (n.d.) The Surgeon Goes to War. Unpublished MS. Edward K. Barsky Papers, Series IV, Box 5, Folder 4. New York: Tamiment Library/Robert F. Wagner Labor Archives, New York University Libraries.

Bates, Ralph. 1935. *Lean Men: An Episode in a Life*. New York: Macmillan.

————. 1936. *The Olive Field*. New York: E. P. Dutton.

Bauer, Augustin Souchy. 1982. *With the Peasants of Aragon: Libertarian Communism in the Liberated Areas*. Trans. Abe Bluestein. Minneapolis: Soil of Liberty.

Baumeister, Martin, and Stefanie Schüler-Springorum, eds. 2008. *"If You Tolerate This . . .": The Spanish Civil War in the Age of Total War*. Frankfurt: Campus Verlag.

Baxell, Richard. 2004. *British Volunteers in the Spanish Civil War: The British Battalion in the International Brigades, 1936–1939*. London: Warren & Pell.

Beevor, Antony. 1982. *The Battle for Spain: The Spanish Civil War 1936–1939*. New York: Penguin.

Benson, Frederick R. 1967. *Writers in Arms: The Literary Impact of the Spanish Civil War*. New York: New York University Press.

Bessie, Alvah. 1939. *Men in Battle: A Story of Americans in Spain*. New York: Charles Scribner's Sons.

————. 1952. *The Heart of Spain: Anthology of Fiction, Nonfiction, and Poetry*. New York: Veterans of the Abraham Lincoln Brigade.

————. 1975. *Spain Again*. San Francisco: Chandler & Sharp.

Bessie, Alvah, and Albert Prago, eds. 1987. *Our Fight: Veterans of the Abraham Lincoln Brigade, Spain 1936–1939*. New York: Monthly Review Press.

Bessie, Dan, ed. 2002. *Alvah Bessie's Spanish Civil War Notebooks*. Lexington: University Press of Kentucky.

Bethune, Norman. 1998. *The Politics of Passion: Norman Bethune's Writing and Art*. Ed. Larry Hannant. Toronto: University of Toronto Press.

Bookchin, Murray. 1998. *The Spanish Anarchists: The Heroic Years 1868–1936*. Oakland: AK Press.

Bowers, Claude G. 1954. *My Mission to Spain: Watching the Rehearsal for World War II*. New York: Simon & Schuster.

Brassai, Gilberte. 1999. *Conversations with Picasso*. Trans. Jane Marie Todd. Chicago: University of Chicago Press.

Broer, Lawrence R. 1973. *Hemingway's Spanish Tragedy*. University: University of Alabama Press.

Brome, Vincent. 1966. *The International Brigades: Spain 1936–1939*. New York: William Morrow.

Brown, Jonathan, ed. 1996. *Picasso and the Spanish Tradition*. New Haven: Yale University Press.

Brugman, Jeb. 2009. *Welcome to the Urban Revolution: How Cities Are Changing the World*. New York: Bloomsbury Press.

Buck, Tim. 1975. *Thirty Years: The Story of the Communist Movement in Canada 1922–1952*. Toronto: Progress Books.

Bush, Clive. 2010. *The Century's Midnight: Dissenting European and American Writers in the Era of the Second World War*. Oxford: Peter Lang.

Caballero Jurado, Carlos. 2006. *The Condor Legion: German Troops in the Spanish Civil War*. Oxford: Osprey.

Camus, Albert. 1960. "Why Spain?" In *Resistance, Rebellion, and Death*. Trans. Justin O'Brien. New York: Vintage.

Capa, Robert. 1999. *Heart of Spain: Photographs of the Spanish Civil War*. New York: Aperture.

Capellán, Angel. 1985. *Hemingway and the Hispanic World*. Ann Arbor: UMI Research Press.

Carr, Virginia Spencer. 1984. *Dos Passos: A Life*. Evanston: Northwestern University Press.

Carroll, Peter N. 1994. *The Odyssey of the Abraham Lincoln Brigade: Americans in the Spanish Civil War*. Stanford: Stanford University Press.

Carroll, Peter N., and James D. Fernandez, ed. 2007. *Facing Fascism: New York and the Spanish Civil War*. New York: NYU Press.

Casanova, Julián. 2010. *The Spanish Republic and Civil War*. Cambridge: Cambridge University Press.

Cate, Curtis. 1995. *Andre Malraux: A Biography*. New York: Fromm International.

Caws, Mary Ann. 2000. *Picasso's Weeping Woman: The Life and Art of Dora Maar*. Boston: Little, Brown.

Chipp, Herschel B. 1988. "The First Step Towards Guernica." *Arts Magazine* 64, October, 62–67.

———. 1988. *Guernica: History, Transformations, Meanings*. With a chapter by Javier Tusell. Berkeley: University of California Press.

"The Chronicle of 754." In Kenneth Baxter Wolf, trans. 1990. *Conquerors and Chroniclers of Early Medieval Spain, Translated Texts for Historians*. 2nd ed., Vol. 9, 111–60. Liverpool: Liverpool University Press.

Churchill, Viscount. 1964. *Be All My Sins Remembered*. New York: Coward-McCann.

Churchill, Winston S. 1937. *Great Contemporaries*. New York: G. P. Putnam's Sons.

Clark, Ronald W. 1968. *JBS: The Life and Work of J. B. S. Haldane*. New York: Coward-McCann.

Clark, T. J. 2013. *Picasso and Truth*. Princeton: Princeton University Press.

Clarkson, Adrienne. 2009. *Norman Bethune*. Toronto: Penguin Canada.

Clode, George. 2011. "*The Command of the Air* by Giulio Douhet: A *Military Times* Classic." *Military History Monthly* 10, January (online).

Cochrane, Archibald L. 1989. *One Man's Medicine: An Autobiography of Professor Archie Cochrane*. With Max Blythe. Wales: Cardiff University.

Coggeshall, L. T. 1971. "Oswald Hope Robertson 1886–1966." *Biographical Memoirs of the National Academy of Sciences*. Washington: National Academy of Sciences.

Colodny, Robert G. 1958. *The Struggle for Madrid: The Central Epic of the Spanish Conflict 1936–1937*. New Brunswick: Transaction.

Coni, Nicholas. 2002. "Medicine and the Spanish Civil War." *Journal of the Royal Society of Medicine* 95 (3): 147–50.

———. 2008. *Medicine and Warfare: Spain, 1936–1939*. New York: Routledge.

Cook, Judith. 1979. *Apprentices of Freedom*. London: Quartet.

Cortada, James W. 1982. *Historical Dictionary of the Spanish Civil War, 1936–1939*. Westport: Greenwood Press.

———, ed. 2012. *Modern Warfare in Spain: American Military Observations on the Spanish Civil War, 1936–1939*. Washington: Potomac Books.

Corum, James. 1997. *The Luftwaffe: Creating the Operational Air War, 1918–1940*. Lawrence: University Press of Kansas.

———. 1998. *Inflated by Air: Common Perceptions of Civilian Casualties from Bombing*. Research Report, Air War College, Air University, Maxwell AFB, Alabama.

———. 2008. *Wolfram von Richthofen: Master of the German Air War*. Lawrence: University Press of Kansas.

Coverdale, John F. 1974. "The Battle of Guadalajara, 8–22 March 1937." *Journal of Contemporary History* 9 (1) (January): 53–75.

Cowans, Jon, ed. 2003. *Early Modern Spain: A Documentary History*. Philadelphia: University of Pennsylvania Press.

Cowles, Virginia. 1941. *Looking for Trouble*. London: Hamish Hamilton.

Cox, Geoffrey. 2006 [1937]. *Defence of Madrid: An Eyewitness Account from the Spanish Civil War*. Dunedin, New Zealand: Otago University Press.

Crome, Len. 1980. "Walter (1897–1947): A Soldier in Spain." *History Workshop* 9 (Spring): 116–28.

Crow, John A. 1985. *Spain: The Root and the Flower*. 3rd ed. Berkeley: University of California Press.

Crozier, Brian. 1967. *Franco*. Boston: Little, Brown.

Cueva, Julio de la. 1996. "The Stick and the Candle: Clericals and Anticlericals in Northern Spain, 1898–1913." *European History Quarterly* 26: 241–65.

———. 1998. "Religious Persecution, Anticlerical Tradition and Revolution: On Atrocities Against the Clergy During the Spanish Civil War." *Journal of Contemporary History* 33 (3): 355–69.

Cunningham, Valentine, ed. 1986. *Spanish Front: Writers on the Civil War*. Oxford: Oxford University Press.

Curtis, Norah, and Cyril Gilbey. 1944. *Malnutrition (Quaker Work in Austria 1919–24 and Spain 1936–39)*. London: Oxford University Press.

Daix, Pierre. 1993. *Picasso: Life and Art*. New York: HarperCollins.

Daniel, Marko, and Matthew Gale, eds. 2011. *Joan Miro: The Ladder of Escape*. London: Thames & Hudson.

Davenport, Diana. 2011. "The War Against Bacteria: How Were Sulfonamide Drugs Used by Britain During World War II?" *Medical Humanities* doi:10:1136/medhum-2011-010024.

Davies, Alan. 1999. "The First Radio War: broadcasting in the Spanish Civil War, 1936–1939." *Historical Journal of Film, Radio and Television* 19 (4): 473–513.

Davison, Peter, ed. 2010. *George Orwell: A Life in Letters*. New York: Liveright.

Dayton, Tim. 2003. *Muriel Rukeyser's* The Book of the Dead. Columbia: University of Missouri Press.

Defalque, R. J., and A. J. Wright. 2002. "Contributions of the Legion Condor to the Wehrmacht's Surgical Care During WW2." *International Congress Series* 1242: 255–60.

Delaprée, Louis. 1936. "Bombs over Madrid." Trans. Martin Minchom, rep. *The Volunteer*. http://www.albavolunteer.org.

———. 1937. *The Martyrdom of Madrid: Inedited Witnesses*. Madrid: N.p.

Delmer, Sefton. 1961. *Trail Sinister: An Autobiography*. London: Secker & Warburg.

Derby, Mark. 2009. *Kiwi Compañeros: New Zealand and the Spanish Civil War*. Christchurch: Canterbury University Press.

Devlin, John. 1966. *Spanish Anticlericalism: A Study in Modern Alienation*. New York: Las Americas.

Diz, José Carlos, Avelino Franco, et al. 2002. *The History of Anesthesia: Proceedings of the Fifth International Symposium on the History of Anesthesia, Santiago, Spain, 19–23 September 2001*. Amsterdam: Elsevier.

Dollard, John, and Donald Horton. 1944. *Fear in Battle*. Washington: Infantry Journal.

Dos Passos, John. 1938. *Journeys Between Wars*. New York: Harcourt, Brace.

———. 1967. *Adventures of a Young Man*. Boston: Houghton Mifflin.

———. 1973. *The Fourteenth Chronicle: Letters and Diaries of John Dos Passos*. Edited and with a Biographical Narrative by Townsend Ludington. Boston: Gambit.

Dupin, Jacques. 1962. *Joan Miró: Life and Work*. London: Thames & Hudson.

Duran-Jordà, Frederic. 1939. "The Barcelona Blood-Transfusion Service." *Lancet* 33 (6031): 773–75.

Ealham, Chris, and Michael Richards, eds. 2005. *The Splintering of Spain: Cultural History and the Spanish Civil War, 1936–1939*. Cambridge: Cambridge University Press.

Eaude, Michael. 2008. *Catalonia: A Cultural History*. Oxford: Oxford University Press.

Eby, Cecil D. 1969. *Between the Bullet and the Lie: American Volunteers in the Spanish Civil War*. New York: Holt, Rinehart & Winston.

———. 2007. *Comrades and Commissars: The Lincoln Battalion in the Spanish Civil War*. University Park: Pennsylvania State University Press.

Ehrenburg, Ilya. 1963. *Memoirs: 1921–1941*. Trans. Tatania Shebunina and Yvonne Kapp. New York: Grosset & Dunlap.

Elliot, J. H. 1963. *The Revolt of the Catalans: A Study in the Decline of Spain*. Cambridge: Cambridge University Press.

Ellis, R. W. B. 1938. "Blood Transfusion at the Front." *Proceedings of the Royal Society of Medicine* 31 (6): 684–86.

Ellis, R. W. B., and Audrey E. Russell. 1937. "Four Thousand Basque Children." *Lancet* 29 (May): 1303.

Escobal, Patricio P. 1968. *Death Row: Spain 1936*. Trans. Tana de Gamez. Indianapolis: Bobbs-Merrill.

Fehrenbach, Charles Wentz. 1970. "Moderados and Exaltados: The Liberal Opposition to Ferdinand VII, 1814–1823." *Hispanic American Historical Review* 50 (1) (February): 52–69.

Felsen, Milt. 1989. *The Anti-Warrior: A Memoir by Milt Felsen*. Iowa City: University of Iowa Press.

Fernsworth, Lawrence A. 1936. "Back of the Spanish Rebellion." *Foreign Affairs* 15 (1) (October): 87–101.

———. 1957. *Spain's Struggle for Freedom*. Boston: Beacon.

Fisch, Eberhard. 1988. Guernica *by Picasso: A Study of the Picture and Its Context*. Lewisburg: Bucknell University Press.

Fischer, Louis. 1941. *Men and Politics: An Autobiography*. New York: Duell, Sloan & Pearce.

Fisher, Harry. 1997. *Comrades: Tales of a Brigadista in the Spanish Civil War*. Lincoln: University of Nebraska Press.

Fletcher, Richard. 1992. *Moorish Spain*. Berkeley: University of California Press.

Ford, Hugh D. 1965. *A Poet's War: British Poets and the Spanish Civil War*. Philadelphia: University of Pennsylvania Press.

Fox, Soledad. 2011. *A Spanish Woman in Love and War: Constancia de la Mora*. Brighton: Sussex Academic Press.

Franco, A., J. Cortes, J. Alvarez, et al. 1996. "The Development of Blood Transfusion: The Contributions of Norman Bethune in the Spanish Civil War. 1936–1939." *Canadian Journal of Anesthesia* 43 (10): 1076–78.

Fraser, Ian. 1984. "Penicillin: Early Trials in War Casualties." *British Medical Journal* 289 (22–29 December): 1723.

Fraser, Ronald. 1979. *Blood of Spain: An Oral History of the Spanish Civil War*. New York: Pantheon.

Freedberg, Catherine Blanton. 1986. *The Spanish Pavilion at the Paris World's Fair*. 2 vols. New York: Garland.

Fussell, Paul, ed. 1991. *The Norton Book of Modern War*. New York: Norton.

Fyrth, Jim. 1986. *The Signal Was Spain: The Spanish Aid Movement in Britain, 1936–39*. London: Lawrence & Wishart.

Fyrth, Jim (with Sally Alexander), ed. 1991. *Women's Voices from the Spanish Civil War*. London: Lawrence & Wishart.

Fyvel, Penelope. 1992. *English Penny*. Ilfracombe, Devon: Arthur H. Stockwell.

Gajdusek, Robert E. 2002. *Hemingway in His Own Country*. Notre Dame, Ind.: University of Notre Dame Press.

Galland, Adolf. 1954. *The First and the Last: The Rise and Fall of the German Fighter Forces, 1938–1945*. Trans. Mervyn Savill. New York: Bantam.

Ganivet, Angel. 1946. *Spain: An Interpretation*. London: Eyre & Spottiswoode.

Garcia, Hugo. 2010. "Potemkin in Spain? British *Unofficial Missions of Investigation* to Spain During the Civil War." *European History Quarterly* 40 (2): 217–39.

Geiser, Carl. 1986. *Prisoners of the Good Fight: The Spanish Civil War, 1936–1939*. Westport: Lawrence Hill.

Gellhorn, Martha. 1937a. "High Explosive for Everyone." *Reporting America at War*. PBS (online).

———. 1937b. "Madrid to Morata." *New Yorker* (24 July), 31–39.

———. 1988. *The View from the Ground*. Boston: Atlantic Monthly Press.

Gerassi, John. 1986. *The Premature Antifascists: North American Volunteers in the Spanish Civil War 1936–39, an Oral History*. New York: Praeger.

Gibbons, Wes, and Teresa Moreno. 2002. *The Geology of Spain*. London: Geological Society.

Gibson, Ian. 1997. *The Shameful Life of Salvador Dalí*. New York: Norton.

Gilot, Françoise. 1964. *Life with Picasso*. New York: McGraw-Hill.

————. 1990. *Matisse and Picasso: A Friendship in Art.* New York: Anchor.

Girard, Rene. 1986. *The Scapegoat.* Baltimore: Johns Hopkins University Press.

Gironella, Jose Maria. 1963. *One Million Dead.* Trans. Joan MacLean. Garden City: Doubleday.

Gispert Cruz, Ignacio de. 1981. *Memoirs of a Neurologist: Survivor of the Spanish Civil War.* Trans. Nacha Gispert Pouring. New York: Vantage Press.

Goya, Francisco de. 1937. *The Disasters of War.* New York: Oxford University Press.

Goytisolo, Juan. 2003. *Forbidden Territory and Realms of Strife.* Trans. Peter Bush. London: Verso.

Greeley, Robin Adele. 2006. *Surrealism and the Spanish Civil War.* New Haven: Yale University Press.

Green, Nan. 2004. *A Chronicle of Small Beer: The Memoirs of Nan Green.* Ed. R. J. Ellis. Nottingham: Trent Editions.

Greenberg, Clement. 1948. *Joan Miró.* New York: Quadrangle Press.

Greenwalt, T. J. 1997. "A Short History of Transfusion Medicine." *Transfusion* 37 (May): 550–63.

Gretton, Peter. 1975. "The Nyon Conference: The Naval Aspect." *English Historical Review* 90 (354) (January): 103–12.

Guerra de la Vega, Ramon. 2005. *Madrid 1931–1939: Il Republica y Guerra Civil: Historia de la Fotografia.* Madrid: Biblioteca de Arte y Arquitectura.

Gurney, Jason. 1974. *Crusade in Spain.* London: Faber & Faber.

Guttman, Allen. 1960. "Mechanized Doom: Ernest Hemingway and the Spanish Civil War." *Massachusetts Review* 1 (3): 541–61.

————. 1962. *The Wound in the Heart: America and the Spanish Civil War.* New York: Free Press.

Haight, Mary Ellen Jordan, and James Jordan Haight. 1992. *Walks in Picasso's Barcelona.* Salt Lake City: Peregrine Smith Books.

Haldane, Charlotte. 1949. *Truth Will Out.* London: Weidenfeld & Nicolson.

Haldane, J.B.S. 1925. *Callinicus: A Defense of Chemical Warfare.* New York: E. P. Dutton.

————. 1937. "Civil War from Both Sides." *Listener* [London, England] (20 January): 126.

————. 1938. *A. R. P.* London: Victor Gollancz.

————. 1940. *Science and Everyday Life.* New York: Macmillan.

————. 1941. *Science and Everyday Life.* London: Penguin.

Hanighen, Frank, ed. 1939. *Nothing but Danger.* New York: Robert M. McBride.

Hannant, Larry. 1998. *The Politics of Passion: Norman Bethune's Writing and Art.* Toronto: University of Toronto Press.

Harrison, Mark. 2004. *Medicine and Victory: British Military Medicine in the Second World War.* Oxford: Oxford University Press.

Harvey, A. D. 1996. "The Spanish Civil War as Seen by British Officers." *RUSI Journal* 141: 4, 65–67.

Harvey, Charles E. 1978. "Politics and Pyrites During the Spanish Civil War." *Economic History Review* 31 (1): 89–104.

Heaton, Colin D., and Anne-Marie Lewis. 2011. *The German Aces Speak: World War II Through the Eyes of Four of the Luftwaffe's Most Important Commanders.* Minneapolis: Zenith Press.

Hemingway, Ernest. 1932. *Death in the Afternoon.* New York: Charles Scribner's Sons.

———. 1938a. "Hemingway Reports Spain." *New Republic*, 12 January 1938 (online).

———. 1938b. *The Fifth Column.* New York: Scribner.

———. 1940. *For Whom the Bell Tolls.* New York: Charles Scribner's Sons.

———. 1967. *By-Line: Ernest Hemingway: Selected Articles and Dispatches of Four Decades.* Ed. William White. New York: Scribner.

———. 1981. *Ernest Hemingway: Selected Letters 1917–1961.* Ed. Carlos Baker. New York: Charles Scribner's Sons.

———. 1987. *The Complete Short Stories of Ernest Hemingway.* New York: Scribner.

———. 2003. *Hemingway on War.* Ed. Sean Hemingway. New York: Scribner.

Henry, Chris. 1999. *The Ebro 1938: Death Knell of the Spanish Republic.* Oxford: Osprey.

Hensbergen, Gijs van. 2004. *Guernica: The Biography of a Twentieth-Century Icon.* New York: Bloomsbury.

Herbst, Josephine. 1991. *The Starched Blue Sky of Spain and Other Memoirs.* New York: HarperCollins.

Hernandez, Prisco R. 2001. "The German Kondor Legion: A Firepower Force Package in Combat." *Field Artillery* (July–August): 16–21.

Hervas, C., and Marie Carmen Unzueta. 2002. "Robert Macintosh and the Spanish Civil War: A New Perspective." *International Congress Series* 1242 (12): 411–20.

Hewitt, James Robert. 1978. *André Malraux.* New York: Frederick Ungar.

Hills, George. 1967. *Franco: The Man and His Nation.* New York: Macmillan.

Hodges, Gabrielle Ashford. 2000. *Franco: A Concise Biography.* New York: St. Martin's Press.

Höhne, Heinz. 1976. *Canaris: Hitler's Master Spy.* New York: Cooper Square Press.

Hogg, Ian V. 1970. *The Guns: 1939–1945.* New York: Ballantine Books.

Hooton, E. R. 2007. *Luftwaffe at War: Gathering Storm 1933–39*. Vol. 1. London: Chervron/Ian Allen.

Hopkins, James K. 1998. *Into the Heart of the Fire: The British in the Spanish Civil War*. Stanford: Stanford University Press.

Howson, Gerald. 1998. *Arms for Spain: The Untold Story of the Spanish Civil War*. New York: St. Martin's Press.

Hubbard, John R. 1953. "How Franco Financed His War." *Journal of Modern History* 25 (4) (December): 390–406.

Hughes, Ben. 2011. *They Shall Not Pass! The British Battalion at Jarama [in] The Spanish Civil War*. Oxford: Osprey.

Hughes, Robert. 2004. *Barcelona the Great Enchantress*. Washington: National Geographic.

Ibarruri, Dolores. 1938. *Speeches and Articles 1936–1938*. Moscow: Foreign Languages Publishing House.

———. 1966. *They Shall Not Pass: The Autobiography of La Pasionaria*. New York: International Publishers.

Iserson, Kenneth V., and John C. Moskop. 2007. "Triage in Medicine, Part I: Concept, History, and Types." *Annals of Emergency Medicine* 49 (3): 275-81.

Ishoven, Armand van. 1977. *The Fall of an Eagle: The Life of Fighter Ace Ernst Udet*. Trans. Chaz Bowyer. London: William Kimber.

Iturriarte Martinez, Alberto, Vicente Del Palacio Sanchez, et al. 2010. *The Bombing of Gernika*. Trans. Arantxa Basterretxea Agirre. Gernika-Lumo: Gernikazarra Historia Taldea.

Ivens, Joris, dir. 1937. *The Spanish Earth*. Written by John Dos Passos and Ernest Hemingway. Story by Lillian Hellman and Archibald MacLeish. Contemporary Historians.

Jackson, Angela. 2002. "Beyond the Battlefield: A Cave Hospital in the Spanish Civil War." Len Crome Memorial Lecture, Imperial War Museum, 2 March 2002.

———. 2005. *Beyond the Battlefield: Testimony, Memory and Remembrance of a Cave Hospital in the Spanish Civil War*. Aberschan, Wales: Warren & Pell.

———. 2007. *Warm Earth*. Cambridge: Pegasus.

———. 2008. *Prelude to the Last Battle: The International Brigades in the Priorat, 1938*. Valls, Spain: Cossetània Edicions.

———. 2012. *"For Us It Was Heaven": The Passion, Grief and Fortitude of Patience Darton from the Spanish Civil War to Mao's China*. Portland: Sussex Academic Press.

Jackson, Gabriel. 1974. *A Concise History of the Spanish Civil War*. London: Thames & Hudson.

Jacobs, David. 2001. "The Man Who Saved Orwell." *Hoover Digest* 4: 1–3 (online).

Jellinek, Frank. 1969. *The Civil War in Spain*. New York: Howard Fertig.

Jump, Jim, ed. 2010. *Looking Back at the Spanish Civil War*. London: Lawrence & Wishart.

Kaplan, Temma. 1992. *Red City, Blue Period: Social Movements in Picasso's Barcelona*. Berkeley: University of California Press.

Kempton, Murray. 1955. *Part of Our Time: Some Ruins and Monuments of the Thirties*. New York: New York Review of Books.

Kenwood, Alun, ed. 1993. *The Spanish Civil War: A Cultural and Historical Reader*. Providence: Berg.

Kert, Bernice. 1983. *The Hemingway Women*. New York: W. W. Norton.

Keynes, Geoffrey. 1922. *Blood Transfusion*. London: Henry Frowde and Hodder & Stoughton.

Knickerbocker, H. R. 1936. *The Siege of Alcazar: A Warlog of the Spanish Revolution*. Philadelphia: David McKay.

Knox, Bernard. 1980. "Remembering Madrid." *New York Review of Books*, 6 November.

Koch, Stephen. 2005. *The Breaking Point: Hemingway, Dos Passos, and the Murder of Jose Robles*. New York: Counterpoint.

Koestler, Arthur. 1937. *Spanish Testament*. London: Left Book Club.

Kowalsky, Daniel. 2004. *Stalin and the Spanish Civil War*. New York: Columbia University Press (online).

Krivitsky, W. G. 2000. *In Stalin's Secret Service*. New York: Enigma Books.

Landis, Arthur H. 1967. *The Abraham Lincoln Brigade*. New York: Citadel Press.

Langdon-Davies, John. 1938. *Air Raid: The Technique of Silent Approach High Explosive Panic*. London: George Routledge & Sons.

Larios, José. 1966. *Combat over Spain: Memoirs of a Nationalist Fighter Pilot*. New York: Macmillan.

Larrazabal, Jesus Salas. 1974. *Air War over Spain*. London: Ian Allan.

Lee, Laurie. 1969. *As I Walked Out One Midsummer Morning*. Boston: David R. Godine.

———. 1991. *A Moment of War: A Memoir of the Spanish Civil War*. New York: New Press.

Legarreta, Dorothy. 1984. *The Guernica Generation: Basque Refugee Children of the Spanish Civil War*. Reno: University of Nevada Press.

Leighten, Patricia. 1989. *Re-ordering the Universe: Picasso and Anarchism, 1897–1914*. Princeton: Princeton University Press.

Lesch, John E. 2007. *The First Miracle Drugs: How the Sulfa Drugs Transformed Medicine*. Oxford: Oxford University Press.

Lethbridge, David. 2013. *Norman Bethune in Spain: Commitment, Crisis, and Conspiracy*. Toronto: Sussex Academic Press.

Lindsley, Lorna. 1943. *War Is People*. Boston: Houghton Mifflin.

Low, Mary, and Juan Brea. 1979. *Red Spanish Notebook: The First Six Months of the Revolution and the Civil War*. San Francisco: City Lights.

Low, Robert. 1992. *La Pasionaria: The Spanish Firebrand*. London: Hutchinson.

MacDougall, Ian, ed. 1986. *Voices from the Spanish Civil War: Personal Recollections of Scottish Volunteers in Republican Spain, 1936–39*. Edinburgh: Polygon.

Machado, Antonio. 2004. *Border of a Dream: Selected Poems*. Trans. Willis Barnstone. Port Townsend: Copper Canyon Press.

Madariaga, Salvador de. 1958. *Spain: A Modern History*. New York: Frederick A. Praeger.

Maddox, Richard. 1995. "Revolutionary Anticlericalism and Hegemonic Processes in an Andalusian Town, August 1936." *American Ethnologist* 22: 125–43.

Madeline, Laurence, ed. 2005. *Pablo Picasso, Gertrude Stein: Correspondence*. Trans. Lorna Scott Fox. London: Seagull.

Malraux, André. 1938. *Man's Hope*. Trans. Stuart Gilbert and Alastair Macdonald. New York: Random House.

———. 1994. *Picasso's Mask*. Trans. June Guicharnaud with Jacques Guicharnaud. New York: Da Capo Press.

Mangini, Shirley. 1995. *Memories of Resistance: Women's Voices from the Spanish Civil War*. New Haven: Yale University Press.

Mariani, Gigliola Sacerdoti. 2004. "Those Men and Women / Brave, Setting Up Signals Across Vast Distances." In Marina Camboni, *Networking Women: Subjects, Places, Links: Europe-America, 1890–1939*. Rome: Storia e Letteratura (online).

Martin, Fredericka. n.d. *Proud Within Ourselves*. Unpublished MS. Fredericka Martin Papers, ALBA 001, Box 24, Tamiment Library/Robert F. Wagner Labor Archives, Elmer Holmes Bobst Library, New York University.

Martin, Russell. 2002. *Picasso's War: The Destruction of Guernica, and the Masterpiece That Changed the World*. New York: Dutton.

Martinez-Lopez, Ramon, ed. 1961. *Image of Spain*. Spec. issue of *Texas Quarterly* 4 (1) (Spring).

Matthews, Herbert. 1938. *Two Wars and More to Come*. New York: Carrick & Evans.

———. 1973. *Half of Spain Died: A Reappraisal of the Spanish Civil War*. New York: Charles Scribner's Sons.

McGovern, John. 1938. *Terror in Spain*. London: National Labor Press.

McGrath, Charles. 2008. "Hemingway, Your Letter Has Arrived." *New York Times,* 10 February (online).

McNeill-Moss, Geoffrey. 1937. *The Siege of Alcazar: A History of the Siege of the Toledo Alcazar, 1936.* New York: Knopf.

Meaker, Gerald H. 1974. *The Revolutionary Left in Spain, 1914–1923.* Stanford: Stanford University Press.

Mendelson, Jordana. 2009. *The Spanish Pavilion, Paris, 1937.* Madrid: Ediciones de la Central.

Merriman, Marion, and Warren Lerude. 1986. *American Commander in Spain: Robert Hale Merriman and the Abraham Lincoln Brigade.* Reno: University of Nevada Press.

Merriman, Robert. 1937. Unpublished diary. Robert Hale Merriman Papers, Box 6, Folder 19, Tamiment Library/Robert F. Wagner Labor Archives, Elmer Holmes Bobst Library, New York University.

Meyers, Jeffrey. 1985. *Hemingway: A Biography.* New York: Da Capo Press.

Mierow, Charles Christopher. 1915. *The Gothic History of Jordanes: An English Version with an Introduction and a Commentary.* Princeton: Princeton University Press.

Miksche, F. O. 1942. *Attack: A Study of Blitzkrieg Tactics.* New York: Random House.

Miller, John, ed. 1986. *Voices Against Tyranny: Writing of the Spanish Civil War.* New York: Charles Scribner's Sons.

Minchom, Martin. 2010. "From Madrid to Guernica: Picasso, Louis Delaprée and the Bombing of Civilians, 1936–1937." *Volunteer,* www.albavolunteer.org (online).

———. 2011. "Picasso and Delaprée: New Discoveries." *The Volunteer.* 20 April. Online.

———. 2012. "The Truth About Guernica: Picasso and the Lying Press." *The Volunteer.* 9 March. Online.

Mira, Emilio. 1944. *Psychiatry in War.* London: Chapman & Hall.

Miró, Joan. 1987. *Selected Writings and Interviews.* Ed. Margit Rowell. Trans. Paul Auster and Patricia Mathews. London: Thames & Hudson.

Mitchell, Timothy. 1991. *Blood Sport: A Social History of Spanish Bullfighting.* Philadelphia: University of Pennsylvania Press.

Mitchiner, Philip H., and E. M. Cowell. 1939. *Medical Organisation and Surgical Practice in Air Raids.* London: J. & A. Churchill.

Monks, Joe. 1985. "With the Reds in Andalusia." Online at http://irelandscw.com/ibvol-Monks.htm.

Monks, Noel. 1955. *Eyewitness.* London: Frederick Muller.

Montaner, Carme, and Luis Urteaga. 2012. "Italian Mapmakers in the Spanish Civil War. 1937–1939." *Imago Mundi: The International Journal for the History of Cartography* 64 (1): 78–95.

Moorehead, Caroline. 2003. *Gellhorn: A Twentieth-Century Life*. New York: Henry Holt.

———. 2006. *Selected Letters of Martha Gellhorn*. New York: Henry Holt.

Musciano, Walter A. 2006. "Spanish Civil War: German Condor Legion's Tactical Air Power." Online at www.historynet.com.

Museum of Modern Art (MOMA). 1947. *Symposium on "Guernica."* Transcript. New York: Museum of Modern Art.

Muste, John M. 1966. *Say That We Saw Spain Die: Literary Consequences of the Spanish Civil War*. Seattle: University of Washington Press.

Nash, Mary. 1995. *Defying Male Civilization: Women in the Spanish Civil War*. Denver: Arden Press.

Nelson, Cary. 1997. *The Aura of the Cause: A Photo Album for North American Volunteers in the Spanish Civil War*. Waltham, Mass.: Abraham Lincoln Brigade Archives.

Nelson, Cary, and Jefferson Hendricks, eds. 1996. *Madrid 1937: Letters of the Abraham Lincoln Brigade from the Spanish Civil War*. New York: Routledge.

Neugass, James. 2008. *War Is Beautiful: An American Ambulance Driver in the Spanish Civil War*. Ed. Peter N. Carroll and Peter Glazer. New York: New Press.

O'Brian, Patrick. 1976. *Picasso: A Biography*. New York: Norton.

O'Connell, James R. 1971. "The Spanish Republic: Further Reflections on Its Anticlerical Policies." *Catholic Historical Review* 57 (2) (July): 275–89.

Oppler, Ellen C., ed. 1988. *Picasso's Guernica*. New York: Norton.

Orr, H. Winnett. 1921. *An Orthopedic Surgeon's Story of the Great War*. Norfolk, Neb.: Muse Publishing.

———. 1927. "The Treatment of Acute Osteomyelitis by Drainage and Rest." *Journal of Bone & Joint Surgery* 9 (4): 733–39.

Orr, Lois. 2009. *Letters from Barcelona: An American Woman in Revolution and Civil War*. With some materials by Charles Orr. Ed. Gerd-Rainer Horn. Houndsmills, Basingstoke, Hampshire: Palgrave Macmillan.

Ortega y Gasset, José. 1957. *Man and People*. Trans. Willard R. Trask. New York: Norton.

———. 1960. *The Revolt of the Masses*. New York: Norton.

Orwell, George. 1952. *Homage to Catalonia*. Orlando: Mariner.

———. 1980. *Homage to Catalonia*. Orlando: Harcourt.

Palfreeman, Linda. 2012. *¡Salud! British Volunteers in the Republican Medical Service During the Spanish Civil War, 1936–1939*. Brighton: Sussex Academic Press.

Patterson, Ian. 2007. *Guernica and Total War*. Cambridge: Harvard University Press.

Paul, Bart. 2009. *Double-Edged Sword: The Many Lives of Hemingway's Friend, the American Matador Sidney Franklin.* Lincoln: University of Nebraska Press.

Paul, Elliot. 1937. *The Life and Death of a Spanish Town.* New York: Random House.

Payne, Stanley G. 2006. *The Collapse of the Spanish Republic, 1933–1936.* New Haven: Yale University Press.

———. 2012. *The Spanish Civil War.* Cambridge: Cambridge University Press.

Paz, Abel. 2007. *Durruti in the Spanish Revolution.* Trans. Chuck Morse. Edinburgh: AK Press.

Peers, E. Allison. 1936. *The Spanish Tragedy 1930–1936: Dictatorship, Republic, Chaos.* New York: Oxford University Press.

———. 1943. *Spain in Eclipse 1937–1943.* London: Methuen.

Penrose, Roland. 1981. *Picasso: His Life and Work.* 3rd ed. Berkeley: University of California Press.

Perez, J., P. Otero, M. Rey, et al. 2002. "Immediate Consequences for the Spanish Anesthesia of the Visit of Sir Robert Macintosh to Spain in 1837." *International Congress Series* 1242 (December): 421–25.

Perez Ledesma, Manuel. 2001. "Survey: Studies on Anticlericalism in Contemporary Spain." *International Review of Social History* 46: 227–55.

Perez Lopez, Francisco. 1970. *Dark and Bloody Ground: A Guerrilla Diary of the Spanish Civil War.* Ed. Victor Guerrier. Trans. Joseph D. Harris. Boston: Little, Brown.

Permuy Lopez, Rafael A. 2009. *Air War over Spain: Aviators, Aircraft and Air Units of the Nationalist and Republican Air Forces 1936–1939.* Hersham, Surrey: Ian Allan.

———. 2012. *Spanish Republican Aces.* Oxford: Osprey.

Petrou, Michael. 2005. "Sex, Spies and Bethune's Secret." *Macleans* (19 October) (online).

Phillips, John Arthur. 1884. *A Treatise on Ore Deposits.* London: Macmillan. Reprint, Forgotten Books, 2012.

Pilau i Fabre, Josep. 2011. *Picasso: From the Minotaur to Guernica, 1927–1939.* Barcelona: Ediciones Poligrafa.

Pinkerton, Peter H. 2007. "Norman Bethune, Eccentric, Man of Principle, Man of Action, Surgeon, and His Contribution to Blood Transfusion in War." *Transfusion Medicine Reviews* 21 (3): 255–64.

Pennell, Hannah. 2008. "When the Bombs Fell." *Metropolitan Barcelona.* 1 March (online).

Pitt-Rivers, Julian A. 1954. *The People of the Sierra.* 2nd ed. Chicago: University of Chicago Press.

Plenn, Abel. 1946. *Wind in the Olive Trees: Spain from the Inside*. New York: Boni & Gaer.

Pottle, Frederick A. 1929. *Stretchers: The Story of a Hospital Unit on the Western Front*. New Haven: Yale University Press.

Preston, Paul. 2002. *Doves of War: Four Women of Spain*. Boston: Northeastern University Press.

———. 2004. "The Answer Lies in the Sewers: Captain Aguilera and the Mentality of the Francoist Officer Corps." *Science & Society* 68 (3) (Fall): 277–312.

———. 2006. "Two Doctors and One Cause: Len Crome and Reginald Saxton in the International Brigades." *International Journal of Iberian Studies* 19 (1): 5–24.

———. 2007. "The Bombing of Guernica." *History Today* 57 (5) (online).

———. 2009. *We Saw Spain Die: Foreign Correspondents in the Spanish Civil War*. New York: Skyhorse.

———. 2012. *The Spanish Holocaust: Inquisition and Extermination in Twentieth-Century Spain*. New York: Norton.

Pretus, Gabriel. n.d. "Humanitarian Relief in the Spanish Civil War (1936–39): The Independent and Non-partisan Agencies." M.Phil. thesis, Department of History, Royal Holloway University of London.

Prieto, Carlos. 1936. *Spanish Front*. London: Thomas Nelson & Sons.

Prime, L. Margueriete, ed. 1960. *A Catalogue of the H. Winnett Orr Historical Collection and Other Rare Books in the Library of the American College of Surgeons*. Chicago: American College of Surgeons.

Primo de Rivera, Jose Antonio. 1972. *Selected Writings*. Ed. Hugh Thomas. Trans. Gudie Lawaetz. London: Jonathan Cape.

Pritchett, V. S. 1954. *The Spanish Temper*. New York: Ecco Press.

Proctor, Raymond L. 1983. *Hitler's Luftwaffe in the Spanish Civil War*. Westport, Conn.: Greenwood Press.

Puente, Joaquin de la. 2002. *Guernica: The Making of a Painting*. Madrid: Silex.

Purcell, Hugh. 2004. *The Last English Revolutionary: Tom Wintringham 1898–1949*. Phoenix Mill, UK: Sutton.

Quiroga, Alejandro, and Miguel Angel del Arco, eds. 2012. *Right-Wing Spain in the Civil War Era: Soldiers of God and Apostles of the Fatherland, 1914–45*. New York: Continuum.

Rackley-Simon, Mildred. n.d. Unpublished Spanish Civil War Memoir. New York: Fredericka Martin Papers, ALBA 001, Box 11, Folder 14, Tamiment Library/Robert F. Wagner Labor Archives, Elmer Holmes Bobst Library, New York University.

Radosh, Ronald, Mary R. Habeck, et al., eds. 2001. *Spain Betrayed: The Soviet Union in the Spanish Civil War*. New Haven: Yale University Press.

Rankin, Nicholas. 2011. "G. L. Steer and the Basque Children in 1937." Basque Children of '37 Association Third Annual Lecture (online).

Rees, Richard. 1963. *A Theory of My Time: An Essay in Didactic Reminiscence*. London: Secker & Warburg.

Regler, Gustav. 1959. *The Owl of Minerva: The Autobiography of Gustav Regler*. Trans. Norman Denny. New York: Farrar, Straus & Cudahy.

Reid, John T. 1937. "Spain as Seen by Some Contemporary American Writers." *Hispania* 20 (May): 139–50.

Rhodes, Richard. 1999. *Why They Kill: The Discoveries of a Maverick Criminologist*. New York: Knopf.

Richardson, John. 1985. "Picasso and l'amour fou." *New York Review of Books,* 19 December (online).

———. 2007a. "Portraits of a Marriage." *Vanity Fair* (December) (online).

———. 2007b. *A Life of Picasso: The Triumphant Years 1917–1932*. New York: Knopf.

———. 2010. "How Political Was Picasso?" *New York Review of Books*, 25 November (online).

———. 2011. "Picasso's Erotic Code." *Vanity Fair* (May) (online).

Richthofen, Wolfram von. 1937. "Der Angriff auf Guernica." *Das Bundesarchiv, Historische Bilder und Dokumente* (online).

Robertson, L. Bruce. 1917. "Further Observations on the Results of Blood Transfusion in War Surgery, with Special Reference to the Results in Primary Hemorrhage." *British Medical Journal* 2: 679–83.

Robertson, Oswald H. 1918. "A Method of Citrated Blood Transfusion." *British Medical Journal* 1: 477–79.

Rodriguez-Solas, David. 2011. "Remembered and Recovered: Bethune and the Canadian Blood Transfusion Unit in Málaga, 1937." *Revista Canadiense de Estudios Hispánicos* 36.1.

Rolfe, Edwin. 1939. *The Lincoln Battalion: The Story of the Americans Who Fought in Spain in the International Brigades*. New York: Veterans of the Abraham Lincoln Brigade (Kessinger Rare Reprints.)

———. 1993. *Collected Poems*. Ed. Cary Nelson and Jefferson Hendricks. Urbana: University of Illinois Press.

Romilly, Esmond. 1937. *Boadilla*. London: Macdonald.

Roper, Robert. 2011. "A Hopkins Professor in the Spanish Civil War." *Johns Hopkins University Arts & Sciences Magazine* (Spring) (online)

Rous, Peyton, and J. R. Turner. 1916. "The Preservation of Living Red Blood Cells in Vitro." *Journal of Experimental Medicine* 23: 219–37.

Rowell, Margit. 1986. *Joan Miro: Selected Writings & Interviews*. New York: MacMillan.

Rubin, Hank. 1997. *Spain's Cause Was Mine: A Memoir of an American Medic in the Spanish Civil War.* Carbondale: Southern Illinois University Press.

Rubin, William. 1972. *Picasso in the Collection of the Museum of Modern Art.* New York: Museum of Modern Art.

Rukeyser, Muriel. 1936. "Barcelona, 1936." *Life and Letters Today* 15:5 (Autumn), 26–33.

―――. 1937a. "Death in Spain: Barcelona on the Barricades." *New Masses,* 14 (November): 9–11.

―――. 1937b. "Mediterranean." *New Masses,* 14 (November): 18–20.

―――. 1974. "We Came for the Games." *Esquire* 82 (October): 192–94, 368–70.

―――. 1996. *The Life of Poetry.* Ashfield, Mass.: Paris Press.

―――. 2005. *The Collected Poems of Muriel Rukeyser.* Pittsburgh: University of Pittsburgh Press.

―――. 2011. *"Barcelona, 1936" & Selections from the Spanish Civil War Archive.* Ed. Rowena Kennedy-Epstein. New York: Lost and Found, The CUNY Poetics Document Initiative, Series 3, No. 6, Spring.

―――. 2013. *Savage Coast.* Ed. Rowena Kennedy-Epstein. New York: Feminist Press.

Sabartes, Jaime. 1948. *Picasso: An Intimate Portrait.* New York: Prentice-Hall.

S. A. H. 1937. "Spain: The British Compromise Plan." *Bulletin of International News* 14 (3) (7 August): 3–13.

Saint-Exupéry, Antoine de. 1967. *Wind, Sand and Stars.* Trans. Lewis Galantière. New York: Harbrace.

Sánchez, José M. 1987. *The Spanish Civil War as a Religious Tragedy.* Notre Dame, Ind.: University of Notre Dame Press.

Sánchez Cervello, Josep, and Pere Clua Micola. 2008. *La Batalla del Ebro: Un rio de sangre.* Gandesa: Consorcio Memorial de los Espacios de la Batalla del Ebro.

Saxton, R. S. 1937. "The Madrid Blood Transfusion Institute." *Lancet* 230 (5949): 606–8.

―――. 1938. "Medicine in Republican Spain." *Lancet* 232 (6004): 751–53.

―――. 1939. "Barcelona Blood-Transfusion Service." *Lancet* 233 (6033): 905.

Schiff, Stacy. 1994. *Saint-Exupéry: A Biography.* New York: Henry Holt.

Schneider, William H. 2003. "Blood Transfusion Between the Wars." *Journal of the History of Medicine* 58 (April): 187–224.

Schoots, Hans. 2000. *Living Dangerously: A Biography of Joris Ivens.* Trans. David Colmer. Amsterdam: Amsterdam University Press.

Schumacker, Harris B., Jr. 1982. *Leo Eloesser, M.D.: Eulogy for a Free Spirit.* New York: Philosophical Library.

Seidman, Michael. 2010. "Animals in the Nationalist Zone During the Spanish Civil War." *Seminario de Historia* 20 (May session) (online).

Sender, Ramón J. 1935. *Pro Patria. Imán.* Trans. James Cleugh. Boston: Houghton Mifflin.

———. 1937. *The War in Spain: A Personal Narrative.* London: Faber and Faber.

———. 1937. *Counter-Attack in Spain.* Trans. Peter Chalmers Mitchell. Boston: Houghton Mifflin.

Shapiro, Martin F. 1982. "Medical Aid to the Spanish Republic During the Civil War." *Annals of Internal Medicine* 97: 119.124.

Silverstein Blanc, Esther. 1992. *Wars I Have Seen: The Play, in Three Acts, with Selected Short Stories.* Volcano, Calif.: Volcano Press.

Simpson, Lesley B. 1937. "Spanish Utopia." *Hispania* 20 (December): 353–68.

Smith, Angel. 2007. *Anarchism, Revolution and Reaction: Catalan Labour and the Crisis of the Spanish State, 1898–1923.* New York: Berghahn Books.

Smith, Richard K., and R. Cargill Hall. 2011. *Five Down, No Glory: Frank G. Tinker, Mercenary Ace in the Spanish Civil War.* Annapolis: Naval Institute Press.

Soby, James Thrall. 1959. *Joan Miró.* New York: Museum of Modern Art.

Sommer, Robin Langley. 1994. *Picasso.* Wigston, Leicester: Magna Books.

Sontag, Susan. 2002. "Looking at War: Photography's View of Devastation and Death." *New Yorker* 78 (38): 82–98.

Southworth, Herbert Rutledge. 1977. *Guernica! Guernica! A Study of Journalism, Diplomacy, Propaganda, and History.* Berkeley: University of California Press.

———. 2002. *Conspiracy and the Spanish Civil War: The Brainwashing of Francisco Franco.* London: Routledge.

Spender, Stephen. 1951. *World Within World: The Autobiography of Stephen Spender.* New York: Modern Library.

———. 1978. *The Thirties and After: Poetry, Politics, People 1933–1970.* New York: Random House.

Sperber, Murray A., ed. 1974. *And I Remember Spain: A Spanish Civil War Anthology.* New York: Collier.

Stansky, Peter, and William Abrahams. 1966. *Journey to the Frontier: Two Roads to the Spanish Civil War.* Boston: Little, Brown.

———. 2012. *Julian Bell: From Bloomsbury to the Spanish Civil War.* Stanford: Stanford University Press.

Stansbury, Lynn G., and John R. Hess. 2009. "Blood Transfusion in World War I: The Roles of Lawrence Bruce Robertson and Oswald Hope Robertson in the 'Most Important Medical Advance of the War.'" *Transfusion Medicine Reviews* 23 (3): 232–36.

Starr, Douglas. 1998. *Blood: An Epic History of Medicine and Commerce.* New York: Knopf.

Steer, G. L. 1938. *The Tree of Gernika: A Field Study of Modern War.* London: Faber & Faber.

Stein, Gertrude. 1938. *Picasso.* New York: Dover.

Stewart, Roderick. 1977. *The Mind of Norman Bethune.* Toronto: Fitzhenry & Whiteside.

Stewart, Roderick, and Sharon Stewart. 2011. *Phoenix: The Life of Norman Bethune.* Montreal & Kingston: McGill–Queen's University Press.

Stoltzfus, Ben. 1999. "Hemingway, Malraux and Spain: *For Whom the Bell Tolls* and *L'espoir.*" *Comparative Literature Studies* 36 (3): 179–94.

Stone, Glyn. n.d. "Italo-German Collaboration and the Spanish Civil War, 1936–1939." eprints.uwe.ac.uk.

Sugarman, Martin. n.d. "Against Fascism—Jews Who Served in the International Brigade in the Spanish Civil War." Jewish Virtual Library (online).

Sullivan, Brian R. 1995. "Fascist Italy's Military Involvement in the Spanish Civil War." *Journal of Military History* 59 (4): 697–727.

Thomas, Fred. 1996. *To Tilt at Windmills: A Memoir of the Spanish Civil War.* East Lansing: Michigan State University Press.

Thomas, Hugh. 1986. *The Spanish Civil War: Revised Edition.* New York: Modern Library.

Thomas, Hugh Owen. 1878. *Diseases of the Hip, Knee, and Ankle Joints, with Their Deformities, Treated by a New and Efficient Method.* 3rd ed. London: H. K. Lewis.

Thomas, Maria. 2011a. "'We Have Come to Place You at Liberty and to Burn the Convent': Masculinity, Sexuality and Anticlerical Violence During the Spanish Civil War." Thesis extract, www.albavolunteer.org (online).

———. 2011b. "Disputing the Public Sphere: Anticlerical Violence, Conflict and the Sacred Heart of Jesus, April 1931–July 1936." *Cuadernos de Historia Contemporánea* 33: 49–69.

Tierney, Dominic. 2007. *FDR and the Spanish Civil War: Neutrality and Commitment in the Struggle That Divided America.* Durham: Duke University Press.

Tinker, F. G., Jr. 1938. *Some Still Live.* New York: Funk & Wagnalls.

Tisa, John. 1985. *Recalling the Good Fight: An Autobiography of the Spanish Civil War.* South Hadley, Mass.: Bergin & Garvey.

Toibin, Colm. 1990. *Homage to Barcelona.* London: Picador.

Tolliver, Raymond F., and Trevor J. Constable. 1999. *Fighter General: The Life of Adolf Galland.* Atglen, Pa.: Schiffer Military History.

Tremlett, Giles. 2006. *Ghosts of Spain: Travels Through Spain and Its Silent Past.* New York: Bloomsbury.

Trester, Delmer J. 1957. "Over-the-Shoulder Bombing." *Popular Mechanics* (October): 106.

Trueta, Josep. 1939a. *Treatment of War Wounds and Fractures with Special Reference to the Closed Method as Used in the War in Spain.* London: Hamish Hamilton Medical Books.

————. 1939b. "Treatment of War Fractures by the Closed Method." *British Medical Journal* 2 (4117) (December): 1073–77.

————. 1946. *The Spirit of Catalonia.* London: Oxford University Press.

————. 1980. *Trueta: Surgeon in War and Peace: The Memoirs of Josep Trueta.* Trans. Amelia Strubell and Michael Strubell. London: Victor Gollancz.

Udet, Ernst. 1970. *Ace of the Iron Cross.* Trans. Richard K. Riehn. Garden City: Doubleday.

Ullman, Joan Connelly. 1968. *The Tragic Week: A Study of Anticlericalism in Spain, 1875–1912.* Cambridge: Harvard University Press.

Valenstein, Elliot S. 2005. *The War of the Soups and the Sparks: The Discovery of Neurotransmitters and the Dispute Over How Nerves Communicate.* New York: Columbia University Press.

Vernon, Alex. 2011. *Hemingway's Second War: Bearing Witness to the Spanish Civil War.* Iowa City: University of Iowa Press.

Vicente Ortuño, José. 1978. *Bitter Roots.* Trans. Richard Pevear. New York: Pomerica Press.

Vidal, César. 1997. "Guernica, Demolished." Chapter 9 of *La Destrucción de Guernica.* Trans. Peter Miller (online)

Vilanova, Mercedes. 1992. "Anarchism, Political Participation, and Illiteracy in Barcelona Between 1934 and 1936." *American Historical Review* 97 (1): 97–120.

Voros, Sandor. 1961. *American Commissar.* Philadelphia: Chilton.

Vries, Lini de. 1979. *Up from the Cellar.* Minneapolis: Vanilla Press.

Warner, Sylvia Townsend. 2012. *With the Hunted: Selected Writings.* Ed. Peter Tolhurst. Norwich: Black Dog Books.

Watson, Keith Scott. 1937. *Single to Spain.* London: Arthur Barker.

Watson, William Braasch. 1988. "Hemingway's Spanish Civil War Dispatches." *Hemingway Review* 88 (7), 2: 4–92.

Weal, John. 2003. *Luftwaffe Schlachtgruppen.* Osceola, Wis.: Osprey.

Webster, Jason. 2006. *¡Guerra! Living in the Shadows of the Spanish Civil War.* London: Black Swan.

Weigel, Christy. 2004. "Picasso's *Guernica:* A Sum of Destructions." Christy L. Weigel website (online at free-doc-lib.com).

Whealey, Robert H. 1989. *Hitler and Spain: The Nazi Role in the Spanish Civil War 1936–1939.* Lexington: University Press of Kentucky.

Whitaker, John T. 1942. "Prelude to World War: A Witness from Spain." *Foreign Affairs* (October): 103–19.

White, Leigh. 1943. "Dr. Orr Packs Them in Plaster." *Harper's Magazine* (March) 186: 380–387.

White, William, ed. 1967. *By-Line: Ernest Hemingway: Selected Articles and Dispatches of Four Decades*. New York: Scribner.

Williams, H. C. Maurice. 1937. "The Arrival of the Basque Children at the Port of Southampton." *British Medical Journal* (12 June): 1209–10.

Willis, Elizabeth A. 2008. "Medical Responses to Civil War and Revolution in Spain, 1936–1939: International Aid and Local Self-Organization." *Medicine, Conflict and Survival* 24 (3) (July–September): 159–73.

Wilson, Ann, ed. 1986. *The Spanish Civil War: A History in Pictures*. New York: Norton.

Wilson, Francesca M. 1945. *In the Margins of Chaos: Recollections of Relief Work in and Between Three Wars*. New York: Macmillan.

Wolff, Milton. 2005. *Member of the Working Class*. New York: iUniverse.

Wolin, Richard. 2004. *The Seduction of Unreason: The Intellectual Romance with Fascism from Nietzsche to Postmodernism*. Princeton: Princeton University Press.

Woolf, Virginia. 1938, 1966. *Three Guineas*. Orlando: Harvest Harcourt.

———. 2001. *The Three Guineas Scrapbooks: A Digital Archive*. Ed. Vara Neverow and Merry M. Pawlowski. California State University (online at http://www.csub.edu/woolf).

Woolsey, Gamel. 1988. *Death's Other Kingdom: A Memoir*. London: Virago.

Worsley, T. C. 1971. *Fellow Travelers*. London: GMP.

Yates, James. 1989. *Mississippi to Madrid: Memoir of a Black American in the Abraham Lincoln Brigade*. Greensboro, N.C.: Open Hand.

Zaloga, Steven J. 1999. "Soviet Tank Operations in the Spanish Civil War." New York Military Affairs Symposium (online).

———. 2010. *Spanish Civil War Tanks: The Proving Ground for Blitzkrieg*. Oxford: Osprey.

Zuehlke, Mark. 2007. *The Gallant Cause: Canadians in the Spanish Civil War 1936–1939*. Mississauga, Ont.: John Wiley & Sons Canada.

INDEX

CREDITS

14. Marka / Superstock
15. © 2014 Artists Rights Society (ARS), New York / ADAGP, Paris / Private Collection / Archives Charmet / Bridgeman Images
16. © Successió Miró / Artists Rights Society (ARS), New York / ADAGP, Paris 2014
17. SSPL/National Media Museum / Art Resource, NY
18. © Bettmann/CORBIS
19. Photographer unknown; courtesy Angela Jackson
20. Redux/Camera Press
21. Courtesy of the Tamiment Library, New York University
22. Photographer unknown; courtesy Angela Jackson
23. IWM
24. Richard Rhodes
25. Photographer unknown; courtesy Almudena Cros
26. © 2014 Richard Rhodes